Y0-EIW-656

THE NOVELS AND PLAYS OF
Eduardo Manet

PENN STATE STUDIES *in* ROMANCE LITERATURES

Editors
Frederick A. de Armas
Alan E. Knight

Refiguring the Hero:
From Peasant to Noble in Lope de Vega and Calderón
by Dian Fox

Don Juan and the Point of Honor:
Seduction, Patriarchal Society, and Literary Tradition
by James Mandrell

Narratives of Desire: Nineteenth-Century Spanish Fiction by Women
by Lou Charnon-Deutsch

Garcilaso de la Vega and the Italian Renaissance
by Daniel L. Heiple

Allegories of Kingship: Calderón and the Anti-Machiavellian Tradition
by Stephen Rupp

Acts of Fiction: Resistance and Resolution from Sade to Baudelaire
by Scott Carpenter

Grotesque Purgatory: A Study of Cervantes's *Don Quixote*, Part II
by Henry W. Sullivan

Spanish Comedies and Historical Contexts in the 1620s
by William R. Blue

The Cultural Politics of *Tel Quel*:
Literature and the Left in the Wake of Engagement
by Danielle Marx-Scouras

Madrid 1900: The Capital as Cradle of Literature and Culture
by Michael Ugarte

Ideologies of History in the Spanish Golden Age
by Anthony J. Cascardi

Medieval Spanish Epic: Mythic Roots and Ritual Language
by Thomas Montgomery

Unfinished Revolutions:
Legacies of Upheaval in Modern French Culture
edited by Robert T. Denommé and Roland H. Simon

Fictions of the Feminine in the Nineteenth-Century Spanish Press
by Lou Charnon-Deutsch

Stages of Desire:
The Mythological Tradition in Classical and Contemporary Spanish Theater
by Michael Kidd

Phyllis Zatlin

THE NOVELS AND PLAYS OF
Eduardo Manet

**AN
ADVENTURE
IN
MULTICULTURALISM**

The Pennsylvania State University Press
University Park, Pennsylvania

This book has been published with the aid of subventions from ESTRENO Traducciones, Ollantay Art Heritage Center, and the Department of Spanish and Portuguese of Rutgers University.

Library of Congress Cataloging-in-Publication Data

Zatlin, Phyllis, 1938–
    The novels and plays of Eduardo Manet: an adventure in multiculturalism / Phyllis Zatlin.
        p.   cm.—(Penn State studies in Romance literatures)
    Includes bibliographical references (p.   –   ) and index.
    ISBN 0-271-01949-2 (alk. paper)
    1. Manet, Eduardo—Criticism and interpretation.   I. Title.   II. Series.
PQ2673.A46Z97   2000
848'.91409—dc21   98-54792
                                                                                  CIP

Copyright © 2000 The Pennsylvania State University
All rights reserved
Printed in the United States of America
Published by The Pennsylvania State University Press,
University Park, PA 16802-1003

It is the policy of The Pennsylvania State University Press to use acid-free paper for the first printing of all clothbound books. Publications on uncoated stock satisfy the minimum requirements of American National Standard for Information

Contents

	List of Illustrations	vii
	Preface	ix
1	The Cuban Years	1
2	Novels or Movie Scripts?	33
3	The Major Novels: French Words with a Cuban Beat	43
4	Theater in Exile: Plays of Entrapment and Enclosure	75
5	A Postmodern Breaking Out: Experiments in Historiographic Metatheater	115
6	Variations on Multicultural Metatheatricalism	147
7	Continued Experimentation	197
	Conclusion	219
	Selected Bibliography	223
	Index	235

List of Illustrations

Opposite the Preface: Eduardo Manet, directing *L'Autre Don Juan* at Rideau Vert Theater, Montreal, where it premiered in 1974 (photo courtesy of Eduardo Manet)

1. *Les Nonnes*. Théâtre du Rideau Vert, Montreal. Directed by Eduardo Manet (photo by Guy Dubois, courtesy of Eduardo Manet)

2. *Les Nonnes*. Directed by Tony Willems with all-female cast (photo by M. F. Sagaert, courtesy of Eduardo Manet)

3. Etienne Bierry, the original Mother Superior, and Eduardo Manet. At the Poche-Montparnasse Theater, 1996. In the background, a poster and photos from the 1969 staging (photo by P. Zatlin)

4. *Les Nonnes*. Amsterdam (photo courtesy of Eduardo Manet)

5. *Eux ou La prise du pouvoir*. Beirut (photo courtesy of Eduardo Manet)

6. *Eux ou La prise du pouvoir*. Finland (photo courtesy of Eduardo Manet)

7. *Le Borgne*. Mexico (photo courtesy of Eduardo Manet)

8. *Le Borgne*. Poland (photo courtesy of Eduardo Manet)

9. *Madras, la nuit où . . .* Théâtre de l'Epée du Bois, Paris (photo courtesy of Eduardo Manet)

10. Susanne Wasson in *Lady Strass*. Ubu Repertory Theater, New York, October 1996 (photo by Jonathan Slaff)

11. *Lady Strass*. Théâtre du Parc, Brussels (photo courtesy of Eduardo Manet)

12. *The Day Mary Shelley Met Charlotte Brontë*. Philadelphia, 1992 (photo courtesy of Society Hill Playhouse)

13. Fatima Soualhia Manet, actor Jean-Claude Fernandez, and Eduardo Manet, at Manet's apartment in Paris, 1996 (photo by P. Zatlin)

14. Eduardo Manet with Jean-Claude Fernandez and Alain Trétout, actors from original cast of *Mr. Lovestar et son voisin de palier*. Paris, 1996 (photo by P. Zatlin)

Eduardo Manet, directing *L'Autre Don Juan* at Rideau Vert Theater, Montreal, where it premiered in 1974 (photo courtesy of Eduardo Manet).

Preface

"A lot of people will be surprised by your study," internationally acclaimed playwright José Triana (b. 1931) told me in 1991 when we first talked about the book I was planning on his fellow Cuban exile Eduardo Manet. Triana, who like Manet lives in Paris, has long been considered by American Hispanists to be his country's most famous contemporary playwright, and certainly there is no question about his stature if the discussion is limited to Spanish-language theater. Manet, on the other hand, writes in French and had been overlooked both by scholars specializing in Latin American theater and even by many exiled Cubans. Since the successful 1969 production of *Les Nonnes (The Nuns)*, under the direction of acclaimed avant-garde director Roger Blin, Manet has become the Latin American author most fully integrated into French theater—with all the advantages that the Parisian stage may offer for international recognition. In spite of Triana's considerable fame and the far greater critical attention paid to his works, Manet's plays have, in fact, been more frequently performed around the world. Moreover, whereas Triana is, as he notes, "more Cuban," he also observes that the "extraordinary, talented" Manet has never abandoned his Hispanic roots. Manet's Cuban identity and importance to the national theater of his native land has only recently been acknowledged when *Las monjas*, the original Spanish-language script of *Les Nonnes*, was chosen by Havana-based theater critic Rine Leal for publication in the anthology *Teatro: 5 autores cubanos*. His ethnic identity has also been recognized recently through his selection for a leadership role within the French branch of CELCIT, the Latin American center for theater and theater research.

I first became aware of Manet's theater in early 1987, when I was beginning my sabbatical research on intercultural relations between the theaters of Spain and France. As I glanced through years of the influential French magazine *L'Avant-Scène Théâtre*, I discovered a number of references to Manet, along with the texts of *Les Nonnes* (1969), *Lady Strass* (1977), and *Le Jour où Mary Shelley rencontra Charlotte Brontë* (*The Day Mary Shelley Met Charlotte Brontë*, 1979). I learned that *Les Nonnes* had been translated into twenty-one languages and that other Manet texts were also widely staged. My curiosity led to a bibliographic search of criticism; the only scholarly article I uncovered was Judith D. Suther's "*Godot* Surpassed—Eduardo Manet's *Holocaustum ou le Borgne*" (1975). Speaking from the perspective of a French professor, Suther suggested that Manet's 1972 play was the "most significant progeny to date" of Samuel Beckett's modern classic, *Waiting for Godot*; indeed, she affirmed that the pupil had surpassed his master (45). Such extraordinary praise for a playwright who, more than a decade later, remained virtually invisible to specialists in the field! I began reading Manet's plays for myself, met him for the first time in Paris in October 1987, and determined to fill this remarkable critical void. The dozen articles I have published since then provide the foundation for the present book-length study.

My initial research on Manet was prompted by his long and successful career as a playwright and man of theater, but he is also well known in France as a novelist. To date he has published eight novels and a ninth is nearing completion. Four of these, dealing with Cuba before the Revolution and with Cuban exile, have been nominees for the prestigious Prix Goncourt: *La Mauresque* (The Moorish woman, 1982), *L'Ile du lézard vert* (Green Lizard Island, 1992), *Habanera* (1994), and *Rhapsodie cubaine* (Cuban rhapsody, 1996). In 1989, thanks to *glasnost* with its concomitant elimination of opposition from Cuban embassies, *La Mauresque* was translated and published almost simultaneously in Poland and the former East Germany and Czechoslovakia. The success of *L'Ile du lézard vert*, which was awarded a special Goncourt youth prize, was great enough to justify three separate French editions in the space of two years: the original Flammarion hardcover; France Loisirs, for mail order sales; and the paperback Collection Points. The 1992 prize also led Manet to numerous public relations appearances throughout France to meet with groups of his enthusiastic, high-school-age readers. Although he doubtless wrote the novel without thought of a potential audience of young people, he has enjoyed his unexpected celebrity status. *Habanera*, in turn, received an enthusiastic critical response and led quickly to television interviews throughout French-speaking Europe: in France, Switzerland, and Belgium. *Rhapsodie cubaine*, runner-up for the Goncourt, was awarded another distinguished prize, the Interallié.[1] This latest novel became a best-seller, was released almost immediately in book-of-the-month and large-print editions, and was quickly translated for publication in Spain.

The present book focuses on Manet's work as playwright and creative author and therefore does not contain a detailed biography of his life and multifaceted career. In that there is a certain autobiographical underpinning to some of his writing, especially the novels *La Mauresque* and *L'Ile du lézard vert*, and because his stage plays reflect knowledge gained through years of theatrical experience as director and instructor, some background information may nevertheless be helpful to the interested reader.

By his own account, Eduardo Manet was born 19 June 1930 in Santiago de Cuba.[2] Until recently, however, most biographical notes have given his birth date as 19 March 1927 and the place as Havana. Manet attributes the confusion to the "theater of the absurd" side of his family: "My father had 'forgotten' to register my birth in Santiago de Cuba; things like that happened in Cuba. When I had to enroll in secondary school, as I was ahead for my age—I was 12—to register me, he was supposed to have me born a year early. My father, who never paid attention to dates or places, got it all mixed up. I was born in Santiago de Cuba, on 19 June 1930 (the year of the earthquake described in *La Mauresque*), but he registered me as born on 19 March 1927" (personal letter, 25 January 1991). The failure to register the baby's birth may also be attributed to the fact that Eduardo was born out of wedlock. His mother, a native of Spain, met his father when he was visiting her country and ran away with him to Cuba. Not only was the senior Manet already married, but his

---

1. The Interallié is the last major French literary prize to be awarded each season. Created in 1930 by journalists who were covering deliberations on the Femina Prize, it was first given to André Malraux. Manet's receipt of the Interallié was mentioned in numerous newspapers, often with the suggestion that it was a consolation prize for his having come so close to winning the 1996 Goncourt—which was perhaps given to someone else because of maneuvering among publishers. Manet, who has been nominated for the Goncourt four times and been a runner-up three times, expressed joy at winning the Interallié but quipped that if someday they create a Goncourt to recognize tenacity, "I have a good chance of winning it" (interview, Goulet).

2. In an October 1996 interview with Jason Weiss, Manet clarifies that his paternal surname was González-Manet and his maternal surname Lozano-Llul. As a youthful writer, he called himself Eduardo G. Manet to distinguish himself from his father; later, as an exile in France, he dropped the Hispanic surname González entirely.

young mistress was destined to be only one of several *queridas* whom he kept in his various homes around the island. The title character of Manet's first fictional autobiography is his mother, who denied her Sephardic heritage to proclaim herself to be Moorish or gypsy. The sequel novel is based on the author's adolescence.

Manet's quasi-autobiographical novels reveal the difficult side of his parents' relationship, but there is no doubt that the son benefited from his father's contacts with cultural figures of different heritages in the Cuban melting pot. "My father was what today we'd call a liberal bourgeois. He was minister of education in the administration of Zayas (who preceded Machado), ex-senator of the republic, a journalist and well known in intellectual circles as a lawyer. He was the friend of writers, poets and artists" (interview, Mambrino 360–61).

Manet began writing movie reviews for a Havana newspaper at fifteen; by 1948 his collaboration in *Pueblo* encompassed interviews, as well as reviews of theater, music, and ballet. Branching into creative writing, he published a book of poems in 1947. As a student at the University of Havana, he became actively involved in theater in various capacities, including direction. His first original play was staged in 1948.

In 1951 Manet left Cuba and, after stopovers in Miami and New York, went on to Paris with the intention of studying film at the Institut des Hautes Etudes Cinématographiques. Arriving too late to register in cinema classes, he enrolled instead in the Ecole Pédagogique pour le Jeu Dramatique, the acting school founded by Jean-Louis Barrault; there, for the next three years, he took courses in singing, dance, and pantomime. He also wrote articles on French theater and movies for a Havana newspaper. Alerted that it would be unwise for him to return home during the repressive Batista regime, he next moved to Italy, where he received a degree in teaching Italian language and literature at the University of Perugia and wrote a short novel in French, *Spirale*, which was subsequently published by Julliard.

Back in France in 1956, he studied with Jacques Lecoq and later became a member of Lecoq's famed mime troupe, which toured throughout France and Italy. Via pantomime, Manet was able to exploit his performance skills without concern about a Cuban accent that would have deterred him from acting on the French stage. During this period he also wrote three plays in Spanish and a novel in French, *Les Etrangers dans la ville* (Strangers in the city); the latter was also published by Julliard.

In 1960, at the invitation of Fidel and Raúl Castro, whom he knew from his university days, Manet returned to Havana to serve as a judge in the first Casa de Las Américas contest. He stayed on to direct the prize-winning play from Argentina, Andrés Lizarraga's *Santa Juana de América*, and to become general director of the Conjunto Dramático Nacional (National Drama Group of the National Theater of Cuba). He established cultural communication between Havana and the international stage, first promoting Brechtian theater and then, after meeting Eugenio Barba and Jerzy Grotowski at a festival in Warsaw, the Polish director's concept of "poor theater," which seemed a more appropriate model for revolutionary Cuba than the elaborate productions of the Berliner Ensemble. At the same time, Manet began directing films and, in early 1964, left the drama group to become more involved with the national cinema institute, the Instituto Cubano del Arte e Industria Cinematográficos (ICAIC).

During his eight years in Havana—despite a heavy load of directing activities, administrative responsibilities, and, for a time, the co-editing of ICAIC's official magazine, *Cine Cubano*—Manet continued his own creative writing. *Un Cri sur le rivage* (A cry from the shore), written directly in French, is considered the first novel of the Cuban Revolution. Several years later *Las monjas*, which the author himself translated into French, proved to be his passport out of Cuba.

In 1968, when Castro sided with the Soviets against Czechoslovakia, a disillusioned Manet left for Paris and the promise of a Roger Blin production of his text: "I arrived in Paris (a second exile) with one suitcase, my teenaged son, and ten dollars in my pocket" (interview, Mambrino 365). In 1979 Manet became a French citizen. Although his political leanings, as shown in his creative works, remain leftist, he has been involved with activist intellectuals who oppose Castro's rule of Cuba. In 1991 he became founding president of Cuba Démocratique, a group that comprises Triana and noted cineast Nestor Almendros. In the fall of that year, the organization quickly staged a "Contre-Congrès" at the French National Assembly; the countermeeting attracted international media attention.[3] In 1996, he

---

3. The response to the counterdemonstration is indeed impressive if one realizes how few Cubans there are in France. According to Véronique Petit, in a note on the Cuban presence in France that accompanies her review of Manet's *Rhapsodie cubaine*, there are fewer than one thousand Cubans in the country, including UNESCO officials and embassy personnel. Most of them are there "not for political reasons but in search of wider horizons and a propitious creative climate."

also became associated with a Cuban exile magazine. Manet states that the time has passed for him personally to return to Cuba and that his involvement in these organizations is therefore not political. It is this distancing that allows him to serve as a bridge between one side and the other. The important thing is that an end come to the suffering of the Cuban people (qtd. in Beltrán 6).

In the more than quarter century of his second exile, Manet's life has been a flurry of activity on a variety of cultural fronts. With the success of Blin's production of *Les Nonnes*, the French stage became receptive to the Cuban-born playwright. As of 1995, seventeen of his plays had premiered in French theaters, three of these in collaboration with the highly visible, government-subsidized Comédie-Française or Théâtre National de l'Odéon in Paris. Several other French-language texts were initially produced in Geneva or Montreal, and Manet's Spanish translation of a co-authored anti-Castro satire had its first professional reading in Madrid. On occasion he has written radio plays for France-Culture, which has also aired some of his stage plays prior to their first full-scale productions.

Many playwrights in France complain that it is difficult to get theatrical texts in print; Manet has had nine works published by Gallimard, a major press. These editions, along with the three texts selected by *L'Avant-Scène Théâtre* and four in Actes Sud-Papier, are readily available to theater groups and represent the nucleus of the author's most frequently staged works. It is indicative of the continuing interest in Manet's theater that three of his plays—*Eux ou La prise du pouvoir* (Them, or Taking power, 1972), *Madras, la nuit où* . . . (That night in Madras . . . , 1974), and *Lady Strass*, 1977—were chosen for revivals at the 1991 Avignon Festival, thus making Manet one of the most represented playwrights at that major theater event. His plays rank with those of Eugène Ionesco (1909–94) in terms of number of productions by young companies in France (Beltrán 4).

Manet is the author of essays and opinion pieces in addition to novels and theater, but even so he has not limited himself to writing. He has directed his own texts and those of other playwrights in France and abroad, most notably in New York, Montreal, and Beirut. He has also taught, sometimes running his own schools and sometimes conducting special clinics for young actors. Immediately upon his return to France in 1968, he established a workshop for film and theater research. From 1973 to 1979, during the period of his marriage to Véronique Petit, he and his wife directed the Groupe d'Expression Libre, an improvisational group that ultimately toured in Switzerland. Although Manet and Petit later divorced, they still collaborate professionally and he credits her with maintaining more organized records than he of their joint projects (letter, 20 July 1998). His training sessions for actors on body movement and vocal technique have been sponsored in Montreal and Beirut, as well as in France.

Nor has Manet totally abandoned acting himself. For some months in 1990, he and his actress wife, Fatima, performed in the Centre Dramatique des Landes at Mont-de-Marsan's production of *Les Précieuses ridicules* (*The Affected Ladies*); in 1991, in a production of several Molière texts co-directed by Manet, the company toured southern France, following "La route de Molière." At times he has also been involved in movie and television ventures. In 1995, for example, he co-authored the script of *Vroum vroum* for the Belgian director Frédéric Sojcher; the short film premiered at the Centre Wallonie-Bruxelles in Paris.

In the course of my research on Manet, I have been fortunate in having the author's full cooperation, including access to his personal files in Paris and frequent correspondence. A review of his letters over this period reveals a whirlwind of activity, always with multiple projects under way. To be sure, projects in the theater and related worlds have a way of disappearing, sometimes resurfacing a few years later with a revised title or transformation into a different medium, sometimes falling through entirely. In the case of Manet, a list of published or staged works only partially reflects the man's dynamic involvement with creative writing and projected performance. Nor could such a list even hint at extensive travel abroad, either for productions of his plays or for other cultural events, such as the speaking tour of Paris, Martinique, Guadeloupe, and Santo Domingo in which he participated in October 1993 along with a group of distinguished Franco-Hispano and Anglophone authors, including Nobel Prize–winner Derek Walcott. In 1995 he added the new commitment of serving on the executive council of the Sociéte des Auteurs et Compositeurs Dramatiques as a playwright representative.

For examples of Manet's intense and hectic life, let us consider two letters. On 20 February 1988, he reports that he is at work on or thinking about no fewer than four new plays and a novel: the just finished *Les Chiennes* (The female dogs); a text on Santa Teresa, requested by INTAR in New York City; *Le Primerissimo* (The superstar), to be written for actor Michel Galabru and staged the following summer at Malaucène; the idea for an English-language tragicomedy about the exile experience, *Born = Cubano*; and a proposed novelistic saga about an Italian family in the first half of the twentieth century. Moreover, Manet expresses a desire to go to the annual book fair in Miami, where *L'Autre Don Juan* (The other Don Juan) was to be revived by the Prometeo Company. A brief letter of 20 June 1992 refers to a pending Israeli production of the radio play *Les Poupées en noir* (*The Black Dolls*); the receipt of a Beaumarchais Foundation grant for writing the ambitious spectacle *Pour l'amour de Verdi* (For the love of Verdi); the initial reaction at Flammarion to the finished novel, *L'Ile du lézard vert*; work in progress on a co-authored satire, *Poupée Fidel, Papa Marx, Buffalo Bill et la femme à barbe* (Puppet Fidel, Papa Marx, Buffalo Bill, and the Bearded Lady); the request from a young company for a forthcoming script, *Deux siècles d'amour* (Two centuries of love); and an impending trip to Belgium to discuss a film project. No wonder that Manet plaintively wishes on occasion that there were forty-eight hours in a day, so that he could do all that he wants to (19 September 1991, 25 February 1992). "Life," he says, "is never easy but it's always fascinating" (9 November 1994). "Comme tu vois, je ne cesse de travailler. [As you can see, I never stop working] Am I a workcoholic?" (8 September 1997).

Manet's incessant activity has been rewarded by growing international recognition. In October 1997, he was prominently featured in Alan Riding's *New York Times* article about prizewinning, foreign-born authors who write in French, "Neocolonialists Seize French Language." In December 1997, he was named Chevalier dans l'Ordre des Arts et de Lettres, one of France's highest honors, and in Canada became an honorary member of the Académie des Lettres du Québec. In November 1998, the French Ministry of Foreign Affairs sponsored a whirlwind American tour for him, with public appearances in New York, Chicago, Milwaukee, and Miami.

In my discussion of Manet's works, I rely frequently on his letters and our personal interviews, which began in 1987. Unless attributed to other sources, any references to the author's plans or opinions come from this ongoing communication. I have identified the exact letter or interview only when the date has a particular relevancy.

For their support of my initial research on Manet, I am grateful to the American Philosophical Society and the Rutgers University Research Council. I should also like to express my appreciation to the journals that have published my articles on Manet and have allowed me to reprint some of that material here. Sections of chapters appeared in earlier versions as indicated:

Chapter 1:
"Nuns in Drag?: Eduardo Manet's Cross-Gender Casting of *Les Nonnes.*" *TDR The Drama Review* 36, no. 4 (1992): 106–20.

Chapters 2 and 3:
"The Cuban-French Novels of Eduardo Manet." *Revista/Review Interamericana* 23, no. 3–4 (1993; released 1996): 75–91.

Chapter 4:
"Eduardo Manet, Hispanic Playwright in French Clothing?" *Modern Language Studies* 22, no. 1 (1992): 80–87.
"Metatheatrical Games as Political Metaphor: A Triptych by Eduardo Manet." *Symposium* 48, no. 3 (1994): 239–46.

Chapter 5:
"Politics as Metatheatre: A Cuban-French View of Latin America." *Latin American Theatre Review* 23, no. 2 (1990): 13–19.
"Play or Movie Script? Eduardo Manet's Latin American Theatre." *Gestos* 16 (November 1993): 25–34.
"A Postmodern Subversion of Chivalry: Manet's Cartoon Approach to the Medieval Battlefield." *Ollantay* 3, no. 1 (1995): 92–102.

Chapter 6:
"Interlingual Metatheatricalism: Manet's *L'Autre Don Juan.*" *Symposium* 45, no. 4 (1992): 303–15. (Reprinted, with some modification, in my *Cross-Cultural Approaches to Theatre: The Spanish-French Connection.* Metuchen, N.J.: The Scarecrow Press, 1994. 163–78.)
"The Day Eduardo Manet Introduced Us to Mary Shelley and Charlotte Brontë." *Anales Literarios/Dramaturgos* 1, no. 1 (1995): 63–73.

With the exception of an occasional passage where I judged the original wording in Spanish or French to be particularly relevant, I have incorporated in the text only the English translation of quotations. Unless otherwise indicated, all translations are my own. My primary sources of printed reviews of Manet's works are his personal files and the Arsénal theater library in Paris; page numbers are generally omitted in both collections and therefore are absent from some of my citations.

The present book would not have been possible without the generous collaboration of Eduardo Manet. I would like to extend my sincere gratitude to him and to his wife, Fatima Soualhia Manet. My thanks also to Janet Burroway, André Camp, Sandra Cypess, Ileana Fuentes, Martha T. Halsey, Françoise Kourilsky, Matías Montes Huidobro, Pedro R.

Monge Rafuls, Thomas Stephens, Carlos Miguel Suárez Radillo, José Triana, and Jason Weiss, as well as to numerous other colleagues in the United States, France, and Spain for their help and encouragement. I am especially grateful to Frederick de Armas, co-editor of the Studies in Romance Languages, and to Philip Winsor, Senior Editor of Penn State Press, for their early interest and their continuing support of this project, and to Cherene Holland, for her guidance in the final stages.

1

The Cuban Years

Eduardo Manet's creative work in his native country is divided into two, widely separated periods: his student days of the 1940s, prior to his first extended trip to Europe, and his return in the 1960s to revolutionary Cuba. In the intervening years in France, he drafted three plays in Spanish as improvisational exercises but then, dissatisfied, discarded two of the scripts.[1] The third text, *La santa*, was staged by fellow students from the Ecole Pédagogique du Jeu Dramatique, first at the school and then at the Cité Universitaire Theater in Paris; later, in Cuba, it was turned into a musical. Although Manet's creative emphasis in the 1960s shifted from theater to film, *Las monjas* also dates from his second Cuban period. The play that established his international reputation as a result of its triumphant premiere in France was written in Havana; ironically, it

---

1. The titles of the discarded plays were *Los conquistadores* and *Las babosas*. Manet has only vague memories of abandoned projects from years ago and there are no other sources of information available on them. I include such titles only for the purpose of having a more complete record of his creative activities.

could have become part of Cuban theater history if the political history that inspired it had not intervened.

In Pre-Batista Cuba: The Young Poet

Manet's earliest published creative works were stories and poems that appeared in Havana newspapers, starting in 1946. His first book, *Pequeños poemas y nocturnos* (Little poems and nocturnes), was published the following year (Havana: Valcayo, 1947).[2] In the prologue to this collection of poems, Manet described his youthful work as "spontaneous and sincere." To that description the reviewer for *El Sol*, Conchita Alzola, added "enthusiastic and sensitive." Although Manet has not continued his career as a poet, the youthful volume of poetry has become an intertextual reference in his later novels, autobiographical and otherwise, and his plays and novels at times include passages in verse. The "Diálogos" at the end of *Scherzo*, his first book of plays, might also be classified as poetry. Among the sampling of Manet's early works found in his personal papers are a single story, "La clase," and newspaper clippings of eight of his "little poems."

Ricardo, the daydreaming protagonist of "La clase" (The class), is an adolescent poet who would rather be free to think about the beauty of the girls he knows or to sit in the shade of a tree and read the works of Whitman, Chocano, Darío, or Neruda than to listen to his mathematics teacher. Presented indirectly from the point of view of a third-person narrator, the young man's wandering thoughts are skillfully juxtaposed with lines from the boring geometry lecture. When the bell finally rings, the protagonist realizes that his longed-for freedom is meaningless: with a knowledge of mathematics, one can eat; but poetry "lacks vitamins." Published in *Carteles* on 20 November 1946, the story no doubt reflects the anguish of the teenaged author himself. Thirty-five years later, a Miami publication quoted the exiled Manet as saying that he had chosen to write in French because in Cuba no one, except Nicolás Guillén, had ever managed to earn a living as a poet (Villaverde 1981: 79). "La clase" is a well-written story that convincingly captures a moment in the life of

---

2. Manet no longer has a copy of this volume of poetry, which I have not been able to locate through libraries in the United States. My discussion therefore is limited to the selected poems found in the newspaper clippings he was able to take with him to Paris.

an aspiring young writer. In that respect it anticipates Manet's mature autobiographical novels, though the latter sparkle with an ironic humor totally lacking in this early narrative text.

In her brief review of Manet's collected poems, Alzola discovers in them a general tendency toward short lines of verse and toward assonance or free rhyme. She describes the "Pequeños poemas" as songs of love; the "Nocturnos" deal with the theme of nature. As might be expected in such a young poet, there is a mixture of his life experiences with what he has read or dreamed. Although she considers Manet's poetry to display originality and the poet to excel in the use of metaphor and image, she notes that there are obvious influences on his work. She cites the specific example of Federico García Lorca (1898–1936) as inspiration for "Noche maja" (Nice night). That poem's references to guitar music, gypsies, and a knife fight—along with its preponderance of eight-syllable lines—readily recall the Andalusian's *Romancero gitano* (*Gypsy Ballads*).

The writer of the anonymous commentary in *Pueblo* (14 August 1947), which accompanies a selection of the poems, ignores literary influences to stress the promising young poet's sense of reality and life. The commentator affirms that the collection gives colorful, harmonious, and emotional expression to happiness and tragedy, dreams and disappointments. In the selection of poems available from Manet's newspaper clippings, however, there is little to suggest happiness; the dominant tone is pessimistic.

In the lullaby "Duerme, pequeña" (Sleep, my little one), the little girl is urged to enjoy her innocent sleep and is warned against the future when she will have to confront the tragic mask of life: "Máscara trágica; mala mujer." Life is a "bad woman," a prostitute who deceives and humiliates us. The same message is repeated in "Un día" (One day), a poem also directed to a little girl who is warned against the future and the experience of life. Life is equated with upset dreams; youth will pass and be replaced by tears; even the memory of love will fade; and laughter may come again only in death, symbolized by the traditional cemetery trees: "Y acaso reirás entre cipreses, / mecida por la lluvia y por el tiempo" (And perhaps you will laugh among the cypress trees, while rocked by the rain and by time).

The adolescent poet, ever serious, focuses on memory and the past. A poem suggesting a passionate, secret love is titled "Aquello que fue" (What once was). Significantly, the romance is recounted in the preterit: "Todo pasó, en silencio de almohada. / Sólo quedó, un lirio sin consuelo"

(Everything happened in pillow silence. Only a disconsolate lily remains.) Memory in "Poema del recuerdo" is equated with a muted ballad, chromatic pain, and clear water forever stagnated; nevertheless it resists forgetfulness: "Es el grito de la ausencia que se ata, / a un miedo tenaz de ser olvido." (The scream of absence is tied to the unyielding fear of being forgotten.)

Like the story "La clase," these little poems invite thematic comparison with Manet's fictionalized autobiography. *L'Ile du lézard vert* begins with episodes in which the young protagonist unburdens his soul to the little daughter of his mother's friends. One can imagine that "Duerme, pequeña" and "Un día" are also directed at such a small, innocent listener. That same novel includes two idealized love affairs that end in separation. While the teenaged lover's sentiments may be the same in the poems as in the novel, the later work is tempered by the perspective of an invisible, adult narrator who sees the comic side to adolescent angst.

As the best poem in the collection, Alzola selects the atypical "Poema de una idea perdida." What is lost here is not love but rather an idea that was not expressed. The potential diamond has been left as coal, and the speaker is not sure he will be able to retrieve from the depths of his mind "una frase temblorosa y solitaria / que murió entre las redes del espacio / sin sentir el calor de la garganta" (a trembling and solitary phrase that died in the nets of space without ever feeling a throat's warmth).

In theme, "Laberinto," the "Diálogos" that conclude the 1949 play collection, continues in the pessimistic vein of the little poems. All but one of these nine brief dialogues (varying in length from ten to twenty-six lines) are written for two voices, but they more closely resemble dramatic poems than theatrical sketches. The labyrinth they evoke is once again life, viewed in an anguished, tragic sense.

Dialogues V and IX are male-female conversations related to carnal love. In the first, an experienced and disillusioned woman attempts to reject the lover who claims to offer her his soul; in the end, she resigns herself to another meaningless sex act: "Te doy lo que andas buscando. . . . Echate en mí. Calla . . ." (I'll give you what you're after. . . . Come to me. Don't talk . . . ; 65). In Dialogue IX, the ardent male overcomes the reluctance of an inexperienced woman. She worries what the priest would say but finally succumbs: "Aparta . . . no debemos . . . abrázame . . ." (Let go . . . we shouldn't . . . hold me . . . ; 69). Related to these is Dialogue II, where the source of the woman's fear ("Efraín . . . tengo miedo" [Efraín . . . I'm afraid; 60]) is not made explicit. She compares her fear to a child she carries within her. The man's response is that fear does not exist, that she created it herself ("Lo has hecho tú misma.") Four of his six responses to her litany of anguish is the repeated refrain "Mátalo" (Kill it).

Efraín's rigid, unfeeling response is mirrored by speakers in other kinds of situations. In Dialogue III one man pleads for more time to get the money that the other demands now; he is finally forced to make payment with some jewelry, the only memory he has of his mother. In Dialogue VII, the servant of a wealthy woman denies food and shelter to a friend who asks to come in from the cold. The speaker rationalizes his lack of charity thus: "El camino es la tumba de los hombres sin dinero" (The road is the penniless man's tomb; 67). The scene recalls a moment in the first act of Lorca's *La casa de Bernarda Alba* (*The House of Bernarda Alba*) when a servant similarly turns away the beggar at the door. Man's inhumanity to man is reflected as well in the cruelty of children to one another. In Dialogue VIII, one child is taunted by the others: "Tu madre trabaja en una casa donde se desnudan los hombres" (Your mother works in a house where men take off their clothes; 68). The child fiercely contends that the charge about his mother is a lie, that she is a laundress who washes clothes in the river: "Mentira... lava las ropas en el río... lava las ropas en el río..."

As might be expected, the profound cynicism that underscores "Laberinto" presents death as the only escape. In Dialogue I, two speakers journey onward, with no fixed destination and with the potential danger of falling into the abyss. To the question "¿No te importa morir?" the other replies, "No me importa ya nada" (Don't you care about dying? I care about nothing anymore; 59). The theme of existential nothingness is expressed lyrically in Dialogue IV, a monologue written as a prose poem. The passage begins and ends with the thought that a human's life will leave a memory no stronger than a blank stare: "Quedar sólo en el recuerdo como una mirada blanca" (63). The speaker's anguish is voiced without the use of a personal subject pronoun: verbs appear in the infinitive form, are omitted, or are given as an impersonal reflexive ("Escapar en silencio" [To escape in silence], "Suspendido entre dos auroras" [Suspended between two dawns], "... ya se es nada" [... now one is nothing]). Life is described as having no beginning and no destination, but the inevitable return to ashes is somewhat tempered by the possibility that one has a soul: "Quizás... alma." The speaker rejects burial at sea or in the earth in favor of the purity of fire: "Hacia el fuego, pues, ceniza, hierro, fosfato" (Then to fire, ashes, iron, phosphate).

Perhaps a belief in God would alleviate this tragic sense of life, so reminiscent of Miguel de Unamuno's philosophical stance. In Dialogue VI, a child asks his mother, "Mamá, ¿es cierto que existe Dios?" (Mama, is it true that there's a God?) She responds in the negative: "Sólo existen los hombres, las montañas y el caballo." (There are only people, mountains, and the horse; 66). She then warns the child against people and their cruelty, which will destroy his dreams, and alerts him that in attempting to climb the mountain he will take many falls. (This same metaphor of life was elaborated in Albert Camus's 1942 essay *The Myth of Sisyphus*.) Only the horse—symbol of sexuality, death, or both—will allow him to fly, to escape, to seek the light. The child's second question, in the final line of the dialogue, foregrounds the malaise that underscores Manet's youthful "Laberinto": "Mamá, ¿por qué no existe Dios?" (Mama, why is there no God?)

The cynical exploration of the labyrinth of life is not absent from the one-act plays included in the same volume, but *Scherzo*, *Presagio* (Premonition), and *La Infanta que no quiso tener ojos verdes* (The princess who did not want to have green eyes) transcend pessimism to become charming, even lighthearted. Their poetic fantasy and playful theatricality resulted in productions that form part of Cuba's stage history. Manet's youthful poems, including the dialogues, are all but forgotten. On the other hand, his early plays represent an important first step in his long writing career.

The Young Playwright

Manet's direct involvement with theater, in various capacities, also dates from the late 1940s. By 1948 his reviews for *Pueblo* included not only film but also theater, music, and ballet. That year he likewise served as sound technician for the Grupo Teatral Carreta, tried his hand at directing, and achieved the first staging of an original play—his one-act *Scherzo*. That premiere gained him prestige among young playwrights and established him as one of the most promising authors of his generation (Leal 1995: xxii).

In his brief overview of Cuban history, written for *Les Lettres Nouvelles* in 1967, Manet defines the years 1939–50 as ones of intense and enthusiastic activity. He attributes this fervor in part to exiles who sought refuge in the island because of the Spanish Civil War and World War II: the Spaniards José Rubia Barcia and Mario Martínez Allende, who founded the Academy of Dramatic Arts (ADAD), and the Austrian Ludwig Schajowicz, who directed the University Theater. He cites as well the creation of the Popular Theater, which sponsored an ambitious program of Cuban and foreign authors. Various groups opened their own little theaters in order to promote their respective approaches, and contests were held to encourage young authors. Manet notes an enormous drawback: most plays were given only one performance (288).

Another manifestation of this fervor was the monthly theater journal *Prometeo*. Established in 1947 by the first class to emerge from ADAD (1944), it nonetheless welcomed the contributions of the younger generation (González Freire 83). Thus it was Ediciones Promoteo that published Manet's early plays.

Writing from Spain in 1958, Carlos Miguel Suárez Radillo recalls the activities of foreign companies in the late thirties that preceded the flourishing of Cuban theater in the following decade. As a teenager, he was stunned by the magic of García Lorca, as staged by Margarita Xirgu. Another major Spanish playwright of the period, Alejandro Casona, visited Havana and directed plays there (Suárez Radillo 3). Not surprisingly, critical reactions to Manet's one-act plays tend to suggest relationships to Lorca and Casona. Manet declares himself an admirer of Lorca and of Ramón del Valle-Inclán (1866–1936); he says he felt no great enthusiasm for Casona (Alejandro Rodríguez Álvarez, 1903–65), whose works were not only frequently staged but also broadcast on the radio.[3]

Manet's *Scherzo* was first performed on 31 October 1948 by the ATA group at the ADAD Theater as part of a trilogy of short plays, staged with minimal resources. The other works that evening were Rolando Ferrer's *Cita en el espejo* (Date in the mirror) and René Buch's *Nosotros los muertos* (We dead). These three authors are precisely those identified by noted playwright José Triana as a decisive influence on his own early work. He

---

3. Manet made this statement to me in our interview of 5 May 1991. Unless otherwise indicated, subsequent references to Manet's personal opinions or other information attributed to him are drawn from our series of interviews, starting 19 October 1987, and the series of his personal letters to me, dating from 3 November 1987. I indicate the date of a particular interview or letter only when I believe that the chronology of the information is important. I saw Manet in Paris annually in the late spring from 1988 through 1998, with three exceptions: 1990, 1994, and 1997. Our most extensive dialogues took place in 1991, the year that I reviewed his file of press clippings.

associates their plays with the beginning of an important theater movement that guided those who followed (telephone interview).

Scherzo was not doomed to the one-performance syndrome that Manet later lamented; there are references to other stagings even among his incomplete collection of programs and clippings from this youthful period. He directed it again himself on 5 December 1948 as part of a program that included Schnitzler's *Interrogando al misterio* (*Die Frage nach dem Schicksal*) and Synge's *Jinetes hacia el mar* (*Riders to the Sea*), and it was chosen for production at the official opening ceremonies of the 1951–52 school year by the Consejo de Educación Primaria y Normal.

Manet's one-acter reached Spanish audiences in March 1958 when Suárez Radillo directed it during his Semana de Teatro Cubano. The Cuban theater festival, held at the Colegio Mayor Hispanoamericano Nuestra Señora de Guadalupe, also featured María Alvarez Rios's *Funeral*, Raúl González de Cascorro's *Parque Bar*, Nora Badia's *Mañana es una palabra* (Tomorrow is a word), and Fermín Borges's *Una vieja postal descolorida* (An old, faded postcard). Each play was given two performances.

Although original plays produced by student groups are expected to be ephemeral, the publication of *Scherzo* in 1949 no doubt facilitated subsequent stagings, like Suárez Radillo's. Two other plays included in the same volume of Manet's early theater had not yet been performed. *Presagio* and *La Infanta que no quiso tener ojos verdes* were both first staged in 1950, the former in May, in a program of experimental dance and drama, and the latter in January.[4] *La Infanta . . .* was also revived in 1954 at Havana's Academia Municipal de Arte Dramático.

Do these short plays of poetic fantasy bear any resemblance to the mature theater that was to follow so many years later? In the playwright's opinion, very little: perhaps only their "black sense of humor." In my opinion, perhaps a bit more, that is, if one probes beneath the surface. Certainly, at the time of their writing, they evoked critical descriptions that place them at a far remove from Manet's more characteristic macabre tragicomedies. In her history of Cuban theater, 1927–61, Natividad González Freire characterizes them as charming short plays, "tres piecesitas encantadoras" (126–27). In his introduction to the published texts, Luis A. Baralt describes them as playful little works—"comedietas hechas como jugando"—presented in dancing rhythms to the beat of a youthful

---

4. I have found a reference to an unpublished play, *La primera noche* (The first night), which was aired on *Teatro de Unión Radio Televisión* in April 1951.

heart (7). In spite of Baralt's desire to promote a nationalistic theater more reflective of Cuban reality, at its premiere he found himself applauding the dreamlike *Scherzo* enthusiastically (9)

The setting for *Scherzo* is a woods with a stylized Greek temple at its center. The characters are likewise stylized archetypes, and the language, while often poetic, is also parodic, intending to subvert its own exaggerated lyricism. The central character, Ivelina, represents the eternal feminine. She is a fickle young woman who cannot choose between two rival suitors: young Tristán, who offers her his passionate—and perhaps fleeting—devotion, and old Marbac, who offers her his wealth.

Unable to decide between romance and security, Ivelina toys with both suitors, assuming roles within her role to bend them to her will. Eager to win her love, first one and then the other leaves in order to bring her precious gifts. Tristán seeks the beauties of nature: a drop of blue water from the fountain, a nightingale, a bouquet of golden oleander. Marbac promises an emerald, a black pearl, a box of jewels.

In the absence of these two would-be lovers, the devil himself appears to Ivelina. He is not the traditional horned figure but rather a sad, tired, but handsome young man, dressed in a conservative black suit. In Ivelina he recognizes the thirst for life of the young, but he finds in her no purity or sincerity. It is his function to tempt, to sow evil, but he cannot do so in a world already prostituted; the woman he seeks, but cannot find, is one with an innocent, childlike heart. Ivelina is deeply attracted to him, but the devil rejects her and leaves. When Tristán and Marbac return with their gifts, Ivelina, ignoring them, pronounces her love for Satan.

The presence of the supernatural figure reminded Baralt of Casona's *Otra vez el diablo* (The Devil once more), but the playfully cynical tone of Manet's work differs considerably from that of the Spanish playwright. There is an underlying optimism in Casona's works, a faith in at least some people's ability to resist temptation or to reform if they have succumbed; his protagonists are often capable of sacrificing themselves for the happiness of others. Even Death and the Devil are at times sympathetic figures, and the introduction of such fantastic elements does not detract from a certain psychological development of the other characters. Manet's little play remains more consistently in the realm of fantasy: accordingly, Baralt describes the characters as puppets rather than flesh-and-blood figures (8). None of them reflects the essential goodness associated with Casona's view of humanity. Tristán's lyric outbursts are so exaggerated that we may find them comic, and there is no evidence of future constancy in his love. The materialistic Marbac believes that he can buy Ivelina's affection. If Satan does not seduce Ivelina, that is only because he is saving himself for corrupting virgin spirits. Ivelina initially incarnates the most perverse elements of the coquette; hence the surprise ending, in which she is the victim of unrequited love, can only delight the audience. As the title indicates, this is a light interlude, not to be taken too seriously.

The style of *Scherzo* differs considerably from all of Manet's French-language plays except, to some extent, his 1992 *Deux siècles d'amour* (Two centuries of love). The poetic fantasy's appeal in performance, however, foreshadows some of Manet's later theater in spite of its radically different style. It calls for a kind of choreography; indeed Baralt affirms that the young author smilingly converts his tragedies into "ballet pirouettes" (8). As is also true in some of Manet's mature plays, notably *Lady Strass*, the action is structured on a series of pas de deux. Ivelina's role-playing within the role as she maneuvers Tristán and Marbac is a strategy repeated and expanded in Manet's overtly metatheatrical oeuvre, including *Las monjas*. Also in *Scherzo*, as in the later works, there is a stress on linguistic games. Language is often opaque, calling attention to itself.

Scherzo is essentially lighthearted throughout; in contrast, the opening moments of *Presagio* vaguely recall Synge's fatalistic *Riders to the Sea* or Lorca's related *Bodas de sangre* (*Blood Wedding*). The setting is a cemetery. A small white mound suggests a tomb; there are stylized crosses, and stairs leading upward to some unspecified place. The characters are a priest and three women, of different generations, who are dressed in mourning. The priest preaches resignation; the women lament the loss of their respective son, lover, and father in poetic language but increasingly rebellious tones. The wife's lament borders on the erotic, and the priest is scandalized. As the priest continues his message of resignation and death, the women question the existence of an afterlife and ask what lies beyond death.

"Nothing," responds the Espíritu Loco, who has just made his unexpected entrance. Dressed in a ballet costume of varying shades of green and topped by a Harlequin collar, the Mad Spirit counters the priest with his own message of happiness and life. Dancing and laughter, not mourning, will help the women overcome their sorrow. As the priest becomes frantic, the carefree spirit wins the women over to his point of view. The women depart with the Espíritu Loco. The priest, after fighting off the temptation of the flesh posed by the spirit's words, chases after them, vainly calling upon them to return to sorrow, to memory, to their dead ones.

As in *Scherzo*, in *Presagio* Manet deliberately debunks religious traditions; in a 1986 interview, he recalls that in Cuba, priests, almost all of whom were Spaniards, were seen in a negative light (interview, Temkine 38). The priest's repression of the pleasures of life is based on fiction: heaven, hell, and the eternal soul are all unscientific inventions, says the comically nearsighted Espíritu Loco, who finally recognizes the priest and identifies him as the real source of temptation (36–37). In the earlier play, Satan informs Ivelina that the devil has had many forms, all of them fictitious: "Priests, philosophers, witches and poets created for me my dress and my way of speaking in accord with how they saw me in their imagination" (22–23). Heaven and hell are no more real than the Devil's image.

The stage action of *Presagio*, centered on the commedia dell'arte figure of the Espíritu Loco, also maintains an overt relationship to ballet, and the poetic quality of the dialogue is again foregrounded. In comparison with *Scherzo*, *Presagio* places greater emphasis on lighting and sound. The opening scene calls for an intense, violet light, symbolic of death; at the conclusion, the empty stage is bathed in bright light. The sound of bells, which frames the action, also changes from faint to strong.

La Infanta que quiso tener ojos verdes, written expressly as children's theater, has a number of conventional fairytale elements and comic moments but suggests a political message that will be foregrounded in Manet's later work. The "romantic interlude," as it is subtitled, calls for a cast of seven, and the single-act is divided into five scenes. The place is the kingdom of Matanas and the time, "several centuries before Garbo" (44).

The exposition establishes clearly the relationship between the place-name, which evokes killing, and the terrible dilemma facing the kingdom. The storybook princess—blond, sweet, and timid—has solemnly wished for green eyes and has thus inadvertently subjected the realm to attack by a monstrous dragon, who comes to claim her and who cannot be defeated by any warrior. The country's finest young nobles have sacrificed their lives in battle against the dragon. The stereotypically comic monarchs—the paunchy king, whose tender feelings for his daughter place him in conflict with the domineering queen and stepmother—determine that they will send out plebeians to fight instead. They offer the princess's hand to the victor but with the intention of killing him after the dangerous dragon is slain. The princess, however, falls in love with the poetic and handsome young commoner who succeeds in killing the dragon. At the end, he eludes the monarchs' treachery by taking the princess away from the kingdom. Together the young lovers set off for the wide world and the future. Despite an entertaining surface level, it is not difficult to read into the text a criticism of class prejudice and the exploitative old order. *La Infanta que quiso tener ojos verdes* debunks social myths in the same way that the other two plays subvert religious conventions.

In Revolutionary Cuba: Manet as Film Director

In 1960, Manet assumed the position of general director of the Conjunto Dramático Nacional in Havana. As a playwright, his most notable contribution to the Conjunto's activities was a production of *La santa*, a play that is thematically linked to *Scherzo* and *Presagio* in its rejection of certain religious beliefs. When Manet wrote *La santa* in Paris, he placed the action in southern Italy; he also prepared a Cuban version at that time for friends back home, but a rural comedy satirizing religious superstition was not acceptable during the Batista era. In revolutionary Cuba, on the other hand, it was greeted with enthusiasm. A speech by Castro had convinced Manet that his text was timely: religion was still being used to exploit the people (*La santa* playbill). To Raymonde Temkine, Manet described the title character as a woman who fell into trances and said that he wrote the play to satirize a popular Cuban radio program on which a religious "guru" invited people to send him money (interview, Temkine 38). In her favorable review of the production, Ana Oramas draws a thematic parallel with Arthur Miller's *The Crucible* but describes Gilda Hernández's staging as quite different in tone from that of the American play. *La santa* was a fast-moving, funny satire of fanaticism; the text was enhanced by the incorporation of singing narrators and typically Cuban musical numbers, performed by the actors.

Despite his involvement with the Conjunto Dramático, Manet's lifelong interest in film surfaced immediately; two of his movies date from his first year back in Cuba. Early in 1964, he left the theater position to devote more of his attention to cinema, as director and scriptwriter for the Instituto Cubano del Arte e Industria Cinematográficos (ICAIC). His film credits from Cuba include six short documentaries and four feature-length films, one of them co-directed.[5] With Alfredo Guevara, he also co-edited ICAIC's official magazine, *Cine Cubano*.

Manet describes his first documentary, *El negro* (The black man, 1960), as an "editorial against racism." It soon attracted international attention when it was chosen as among the ten best films at the 1961 London Film Festival. *En el Club* (At the Club, 1962) was intended to capture the feeling of heat on the beach and the passage of time; the later *Show* (1967), featuring Varadero's cabaret show with Sonia Calero and Alberto Alonso, similarly has a beach setting. *Salinas* (1967) is a ten-minute short dealing with finding and producing salt. *Napoleón gratis* (1961) and *Portocarrero* (1965) are somewhat related "exercises in style." The former is a visit to a museum with its collection of bric-a-brac, while the latter deals with the paintings of the great Cuban artist René Portocarrero.

In *Portocarrero*, utilizing a technique he would repeat later in *Alicia*, Manet combined the use of black and white—to relate the artist's life—and color sequences—to portray his work. He prepared the script as well as directed the ten-minute 35 mm film. Most of Manet's Cuban cinematography is now inaccessible to him, but *Portocarrero* is available in France. Included among fourteen films in a festival of Cuban short subjects, it was aired on Canal + on 2 May 1989.

At an international art exhibition in Brazil, Portocarrero was awarded an important prize at about the time Manet finished his documentary for ICAIC. Invited to participate in a tribute to the painter, Manet then printed his speech in *Cine Cubano*. In his homage Manet expresses great admiration for Portocarrero's magic paintbrush and its capacity for synthesizing both Havana's beauty and the essence of Cuba's cultural heritage. He also speaks of his respect for the Marxist ideology underpinning the Cuban Revolution. The artist, he says, like the new Communist, can transform nature (9). Portocarrero is a "popular" artist in the best sense of the word, for he treats Cuban reality with authenticity and respect while raising the aesthetic level of the "man in the street" so that he will be fully prepared for a universal "art that serves the people" (10). The documentary *Portocarrero* apparently carries an implicit message that transcends art for art's sake.

---

5. I have not been able to view any of these films. Information on them comes from interviews with Manet, programs for selected films, and the cited reviews.

The feature-length films, like *El negro*, are overtly political. *Realengo 18* (1960), begun by Oscar Torres and completed by Manet, relates a peasant uprising in the 1930s. A movie program, prepared by ICAIC in three languages (Spanish, English, and French), clarifies that the Cuban cinema institute preferred to emphasize the warm, human aspects of that brave struggle through an intense family drama rather than make a historical film. The central figure, Dominga, is married to one of resistance leader Lino Alvarez's most loyal followers; yet her son, who sides with the Rural Guard and their Yankee capitalist interests, eventually betrays the peasants' just cause and precipitates his father's death. When the rural guards kill her husband, Dominga stands firm against the forces of repression. Rather than leave Cuba, she elects to remain and fight to the end for the peasants' common ideal.

Manet's first solo feature, *Tránsito* (1964), is an action movie set in Cuba. In its treatment of individuals' efforts to flee from the island, it anticipates the play *Las monjas*, in which Manet will deal with the same theme in a far more imaginative way. On the surface level, *Tránsito* is a return to the atmosphere and characterization introduced the previous year in the novel *Un Cri sur le rivage*.

The Doctor, a militant counterrevolutionary who fears for his safety, seeks the help of José, representative of the underclass. While José makes arrangements for an escape boat, he dupes his friend René into hiding the Doctor by making up the story of a botched abortion. René's wife is chair of the local Committee for the Defense of the Revolution; René is also a revolutionary but unfortunately lacks a firm ideological base. When José wants René to steal a missing piece for the boat engine, he successfully persuades the seductive Lupe to assist him in getting René to help. In the meantime, the women members of the wife's committee realize what is happening. They denounce the escape plot, the boat is stopped, the Doctor is arrested, and José is killed. T. G. Alea affirms that *Tránsito* reveals the struggle between the old and the new but avoids labels of "good" and "bad"; it realistically shows how all of the characters are beset by contradictions (67).

The accompanying interview of Manet and photographer Ramón F. Suárez by Alea provides further insights both into this film and into the economic problems facing Cuban cinematographers at the time. Manet had initially proposed a Technicolor documentary in Cinemascope on ballerina Alicia Alonso. When that was rejected because it would be too expensive, he responded within ten days with an action script that could be done cheaply with a technical crew of only six. It called for a contemporary setting, exterior scenes, and a reliance on available light. Shot in Casablanca across the bay from Havana, the movie made use of local extras but had the advantage of experienced principal actors chosen by Manet from the national drama center.

Despite economic constraints and clichéd plot, *Tránsito* is a film remembered by Cuban exiles in the film industry. A group of seven, headed by Oscar-winning cinematographer Nestor Almendros, protested to *Variety* in 1986 that the influential newspaper had recently published a censored list of feature films produced by ICAIC. To that list they added seven titles by several different directors from the 1963–68 period, including Manet's action movie (509). Manet's own memories of the film help to explain the absence of his title from the *Variety* list. In a 1980 interview with Ezzedine Mestiri, he states that freedom of expression in revolutionary Cuba gradually disappeared. Starting in 1965, Castro adopted a Stalinist approach to power; after the Soviet invasion of Prague, censorship worsened (interview, Mestiri 155–56). Manet considered *Tránsito* to be an innocuous detective story in which the bad guys were punished, but the authorities saw it as subversive "because I showed long lines in front of stores and some of the difficulties of daily life" (156). The movie was not banned outright but its distribution was sabotaged.

Un día en el solar (A day at the tenement house, 1965), touted in the ICAIC trilingual program as "Cuba's first musical comedy filmed in color and for wide screen," also involved the collaboration of Manet and Suárez. With music by Tony Taño and the choreography of Alberto Alonso, *Un día en el solar* was a *sainete* (popular comedy) depicting a joyous slice of life: lots of things can happen when so many people are crowded into such a small space. The program notes suggest that most of those things are romantic: Tomás loves Sonia, Regla loves Tomás, El Chevere is courting Sonia, La Chismosa pursues El Chevere. . . . The day is filled with quarrels and reconciliations, singing and shouting. The stills in the program depict group dance sequences and a popular neighborhood as setting.

In *El huésped* (The guest, 1967), Manet returns to strategies previously used in *Tránsito*: close contact with the people, as reflected by reliance on local volunteer extras; a cast headed by experienced actors, preponderance of exterior scenes, revelation of conflicts internal to the Cuban Revolution, a plot that combines historical reality (the exchange of mercenaries captured at Girón after the Bay of Pigs invasion) with a love story. In this case, the romance involves a revolutionary and an anti-Castroist *gusano* (counterrevolutionary). Co-authored with Julio García Espinosa, the script is based on a story by several young writers from eastern Cuba, where the action takes place. In an interview with Pedro Ortiz, Manet talks of choosing to film in Gibara because of the beauty of that location. A particularly effective interior scene—the guest of the title being guided through a magnificent eighteenth-century house—was done spontaneously when the owner, a former actor, invited the crew into his home. Other interior scenes were shot in a spinning mill.

The Ortiz interview reveals Manet's assessment of Cuban cinema in transition. With few exceptions, commercial films made in Cuba prior to the revolution were of low quality. Initial attempts to produce movies of international stature were based on a false understanding of the Cuban situation. The next phase, which boomeranged, was an intellectual one, an attempt to copy foreign filmmakers. The new approach, to which Manet subscribed, was an effort to make films that would reach a popular Cuban audience. Manet additionally expressed his gratitude to the Party, to local authorities, and to the people of Gibara for their support and cooperation.

The following year, Manet himself was to leave Cuba. Thus the film he finally completed in 1968 on Alicia Alonso was to be lost for years to the viewing public, at least outside his native land, and was, to some extent, to be disassociated from his name. The 1986 letter written to *Variety* by Almendros and his colleagues asserted that "artistic freedom for anyone dissenting with the Cuban government became increasingly difficult," starting in 1961 when certain films were banned and confiscated. The expurgated list published in the United States led them to believe that artists had not only been "harassed, persecuted, censored, isolated [and] expatriated," but were now also being "eradicated from all historical record" (8). Carlos Miguel Suárez Radillo, a Cuban-born theater specialist who has lived in Madrid since the mid-1950s, confirms their statement: "With Cuban cinema, under Castro, it has been common to cut out the name of a director who left and give credit to some assistant" (interview, April 1991).

By July 1967, Manet was already at work on *Alicia*. In an interview with Omar Vázquez, he credited García Espinosa with the idea of combining "free-cinema" and "natural filming" to create the filmic homage to the famous ballerina. The work in progress, based on a loose structure rather than a script, included rehearsals and performances, sometimes photographed with Alonso's knowledge and sometimes without, along with a re-creation of her life taking advantage of existing stock shots, such as those from the Alonso *This Is Your Life* program. While "free-cinema" suggested the use of black and white, they would also include some color footage. Manet announced that they had already done principal scenes from several ballets (*Giselle, Don Quijote, Coppelia, La Fille mal gardée, Carmen*) and that filming would be complete by October.

When Manet left Cuba in 1968, the film had not yet been released by ICAIC. The version in Cinemascope, distributed in the United States a decade later, was dated 1976. John Mueller's 1978 review in *Dance Magazine* identifies the director as Victor Casaus, but Vincent Canby's earlier critique in the *New York Times* credits the film to Eduardo Manet. In both commentaries, the writers point out that most of the dance sequences were made in 1967 but that the half-hour segment in color at the end of Alberto Alonso's *Carmen* had been filmed only recently. The hybrid film drew mixed responses from Mueller and Canby and an acerbic opinion from the *New Yorker*'s Arlene Croce.

In exile, Manet has become involved from time to time in film projects, but the most significant impact of his years with ICAIC may be found in the cinematographic devices that underscore much of his innovative theater.

Las monjas/Les Nonnes:
The Unpredictable Results of Cross-Gender Casting

At first glance, *Las monjas* (or, *Las monjitas*, as the play was initially titled) seems far removed from Manet's youthful plays of poetic fantasy. There are, however, certain points of contact with the early works. From one perspective, the manipulative, role-playing nuns are not essentially very different from the comic monarchs of *La Infanta que quiso tener ojos verdes*, the priest of *Presagio*, or Ivelina and her would-be lovers in *Scherzo*. The nuns merely represent another stage along the continuum of a cynical but, alas, all too true view of humankind: of games we play in power struggles at personal and collective levels. Although the author contends that he had no intention of attacking religion per se, one can also find in *Las monjas* the same satire of superstition and religious manipulation that underlies *La santa*.

Whatever Manet's intentions, once a play is out of the author's hands, he or she loses control. Directors, actors, and audiences will bend the text as they see fit. *Las monjas* in Havana in the late 1960s might well have been read metaphorically as a counterrevolutionary text and caused its author the kind of political retaliation from which Triana suffered for *La noche de los asesinos* (*The Night of the Assassins*). In stagings outside Cuba, it has variously been seen as a defense of the revolution, as an attack on Catholic nuns, and as a portrayal of gay males. The production history of *Les Nonnes* provides ample evidence that theater is polysemous. The meaning of the theatrical text is not only subject to individual interpretation but also will change with the historical context of its staging. Because of Manet's flight from Cuba, *Las monjas* has never been performed there and we can only hypothesize the meaning that Cuban audiences would have given to the work at the time of its writing. *Les Nonnes*, on the other hand, has become part of French theater history.

In the spring of 1991, a historical exposition on the theaters of Paris, held in the Fifteenth Arrondissement, highlighted memorable productions from the city's most important playhouses. Among the seven items representing the experimental Poche-Montparnasse was a photo from Eduardo Manet's *Les Nonnes*, which received its world premiere there in May 1969, under the direction of the late Roger Blin.

The selection of Manet's play is not surprising, for it was a winner of the prestigious Lugné-Poë prize. Blin, a foremost avant-garde director who achieved international recognition for his creation of works by Samuel Beckett (1906–89) and Jean Genet (1910–86), always recalled his production of *Les Nonnes* as one of his favorites (Souvenirs et propos 295). Since its initial, triumphant run at the Poche-Montparnasse, *Les Nonnes* has been done throughout France, revived in Paris periodically, and entered international repertoire.

The first staging in English took place within a year of the French premiere. The March 1970 production of *The Nuns* at the Gardner Center for the Arts, University of Sussex, Brighton, England, proved to be one of the most successful of the professional years of that playhouse. The British translation by Robert Baldick was subsequently staged in New York City, where it also was revived for a three-week showcase in January 1990. Manet's macabre, metatheatrical farce has even been given a fictional staging at an imaginary small college in Georgia: it is the play-within-the-novel of Janet Burroway's 1985 *Opening Nights*. This enduring international interest notwithstanding, productions of *Les Nonnes* have at times been accompanied by controversy and confusion. It is a phenomenon that Blin already noted with respect to his 1969 staging.

The photo featured at the 1991 exhibit of Parisian theaters was the same one that graced the cover of *L'Avant-Scène Théâtre* 431, the issue in which the play was first published. It shows two people in nuns' habits listening to a third, who is playing a guitar. All three, with benevolent—or vacuous—expressions on their faces and cigars in their mouths, are men. The incongruous image of the cigar-smoking male nuns is unquestionably funny. The picture is not altogether misleading: Manet has repeatedly said that he wanted his play to be comic, not realistic; Blin stated that he was originally attracted to the unusual text by its humor (Blin 239).

Nevertheless, Manet's play is not consistent throughout with the tone of the familiar publicity shot. Were it, in fact, a light comedy, it

Fig. 1. *Les Nonnes*. Théâtre du Rideau Vert, Montreal. Directed by Eduardo Manet (photo by Guy Dubois, courtesy of Eduardo Manet).

would probably have evoked no more controversy than Jonathan Lynn's 1989 British film *Nuns on the Run*, in which robbers take refuge in a convent and disguise themselves as nuns to hide from the cops. Moreover, Dan Goggin's musical *Nunsense*—which, coincidentally, was playing next door to The 45th Street Theater, where *The Nuns* was revived in 1990—confirms that nuns can be the subjects of farce without offending Catholic sensibilities. Manet's sisters of charity are not such benign caricatures. His Mother Superior and Sister Angela are hypocritical, devious, exploitative, sinister, and, indeed, murderous; even the innocent deaf-mute, Sister Ines, proves capable of violence. Nor are Manet's nuns revealed within the text to be men in disguise, that is, not "real" nuns. Absent an outside witness to the sisters' speech, they refer to each other with feminine pronouns and, in Manet's Spanish and French versions, feminine adjectives.[6] Segments of dialogue—for example, prayers, in response to fear, or the Mother Superior's righteous admonitions, provoked by Sister Angela's use of coarse language—have the ring of religious discourse.

On the other hand, the actors are not to play the parts as female impersonators. The stage directions stipulate cross-gender casting but also state that the men are to use natural, masculine voices and gestures. The resulting ambiguity is reflected in Manet's own wording at the beginning of the script: the characters on stage are described in the feminine but the desired physical traits of the actors playing them are given in the masculine. Mother Superior is to be a muscular and manly specimen who shows a tendency toward future obesity. Sister Angela is described as short, thin, and determined. Sister Ines is younger, barely out of his adolescence; he reveals a nervous and unstable character.

In that Sister Ines does not speak and the role, inspired by Manet's own training in mime, requires the agility of a gymnast, the youngest nun may readily prove to be an androgynous figure. The lean and mean Sister Angela might also pass for female if he remained silent and motionless.

---

6. Romance languages are more gender specific than English; thus the dialogue in Manet's Spanish and French versions reinforces the nuns' identity as female far more frequently than does Baldick's translation. In Spanish, but not French, he is able to stress the feminine even on the pronouns "we" (*nosotras*) and "you/yourself" (*usted misma*). To underscore the changing attitudes of the nuns toward one another, Manet also plays with the formal and familiar forms of "you" (*usted/tú, vous/tu*), a distinction that disappears in the English. Unless otherwise noted, my references to the language of the play are to Manet's versions, and translations are my own.

But Sister Angela's rough language and aggressive actions, like the Mother Superior's burliness, will create a constant contrast with their religious garb, giving visual evidence of the old Spanish proverb "El traje no hace al monje" (Clothes don't make the monk), recast, of course, in the feminine: "El traje no hace a la monja" (Clothes don't make the nun).

Les Nonnes, subtitled *A Parable in Two Acts*, takes place in Haiti in 1804, at the time of a black revolt. The set represents the basement of an abandoned warehouse; a niche with a figure of the crucified Christ establishes it as a refuge for the nuns, a kind of primitive catacomb. The Mother Superior lures the aristocratic Señora to this enclosure by frightening her with made-up stories of an impending revolution. She promises that the nuns will help her escape the island to safety. Instead, Sister Angela kills the wealthy Señora so they can steal her jewels, flee from Haiti themselves, and live a life of luxury elsewhere.

The nuns' plot is foiled. Not only does the previously submissive Sister Ines rebel and attack Sister Angela with a knife—an action that eventually leads to her death at the hands of the Mother Superior—but the ominous sound of voodoo drums alerts the two conspirators that the imaginary black revolt is, in fact, real, and that they are trapped. The Mother Superior and Sister Angela, ever in conflict with each other, frenetically begin digging escape tunnels. Manipulating Sister Angela by fear, as she had previously done with the Señora, the Mother Superior pretends to hear threatening sounds at the door. Thus the sisters also decide to disinter the Señora's rotting corpse. Decking the cadaver out in a Spanish mantilla, as if she were a statue of the Madonna in a Holy Week processional, they prepare variant stories of the Señora's death, depending upon whether the revolutionaries or the counterrevolutionaries win the battle without. As the play ends, the barricade they have placed against the outside door is about to give way, and the spectators are left to guess the final outcome.

Manet finished writing *Las monjas* in Havana in November 1967 and then translated his Spanish text into French. Blin's expressed interest in staging the macabre comedy provided the author with a valid reason for going to France and hence, ironically, facilitated his own escape from the island. Conceived within the historical context of revolutionary Cuba, the "parable" of the subtitle was originally intended to be primarily political. In various interviews, Manet has clarified the inspiration for his play. To Raymonde Temkine in 1986, he explained that the idea first came to him in 1960 when arms and explosives were discovered in a convent (38);

after the break between Castro and the Vatican, priests and nuns allied themselves with the counterrevolutionaries. A true episode served as a more concrete source. In 1969, in response to an interview question from Simone Benmussa, Manet recalled reading in a newspaper that three women, disguised as nuns, had offered their help to a woman from Cuba's prerevolution upper class who wanted to leave the island; instead of arranging for the promised boat, they stole all her valuables (10).[7] In a 1985 interview with Jean Mambrino, Manet added that he had discussed the story with two actor friends in Cuba who encouraged him to adopt the cross-gender casting tradition of the Japanese theater so that they could play the roles of the nuns (366). The historical anecdote of the false sisters of charity, coupled with the influence of No and Kabuki, led ultimately to the creation of Manet's male nuns.

Manet has also clarified the political reading invited by the historical context in which he created *Las monjas*. He agreed with Benmussa that Cubans have long had an "island complex." In terms of revolutionary Cuba, those siding with Castro suffered a constant fear of invasion from the United States; Cuban exiles, on the other hand, shared the anguish of his nuns who wished to escape (10). Certainly it is possible to interpret the characters and situations in terms of revolution and counterrevolution. To some extent, the Cuban subtext would have been apparent to the first audiences of *Les Nonnes*. Manet attributes part of the early success of his comedy in France to support from the leftist press. If it is not overtly prorevolution, at the least Manet's comedy can be seen as a satire of the counterrevolution. That conservative critics would specifically label the work sacrilegious and anticlerical came as a greater surprise to the author. By 1976, when Manet was in Montreal to direct *Les Nonnes* at the Rideau Vert Theater, he was no longer surprised. He reported in an interview with Lawrence Sabbath that, while his play had never been banned in France for its political content, a 1973 production in Antwerp, Belgium, had not only been banned but the playhouse director had been fired for portraying "lesbians as nuns."

The greater the remove from the historical context of revolutionary Cuba, the more likely it is that audiences will bypass the original, political allegory and find other, more universal interpretations for Manet's

---

7. Several years after the production of Manet's *Les Nonnes*, interviewer Benmussa made her own playwriting debut. As Sue-Ellen Case points out, Benmussa's *The Singular Life of Albert Nobbs* also uses cross-gender casting (Case 1984). The play is based on the life of a nineteenth-century woman who lived her life as a man.

nuns. For her staging in Dublin, director Rebecca Schull described the comedy as a metaphor in which the hypocritical and evil title characters incarnate all the faults of the church, including a lack of concern for the poor and a desire to ally themselves with the rich and powerful. Symbolized by Sister Ines, the church has become "deaf to the real purpose of God, mute in the face of murder." In 1974, when a production of *Les Nonnes* from the Maison de Culture in Reims toured some forty theaters in the region, the municipal council publicly deplored the choice of text and the damage it would do to the city's reputation (Roussel).

The ill-fated staging in Antwerp complicated the potential charge of anticlericalism by its not having men play the nuns. The production elected to avoid the "problem" of the sexually ambiguous, transvestite sisters by casting women in the roles, but that decision creates new problems of its own. A reviewer of a 1970 staging at Brussels's Théâtre de Quat'Sous, also with women in the nuns' roles, asserted that there was a

Fig. 2. *Les Nonnes*. Directed by Tony Willems with all-female cast (photo by M. F. Sagaert, courtesy of Eduardo Manet).

significantly different response to Blin's original production than to the all-female version: even if women actors were funnier, the male nuns, in contrast, had given the story a greater intensity and had raised anguish, laughter, magic, and cruelty to the symbolic level (J. S.). Other critics in Brussels were simply left cold by women smoking cigars, brandishing knives, and engaging in violent wrestling matches.

Manet has not hesitated to create unexpected female characters. His *Lady Strass* (1977), also directed by Blin at the Poche-Montparnasse, is the portrait of an aristocratic Englishwoman as a cigar-smoking, whiskey-drinking, gun-toting Annie Oakley figure. The contrast between her proper British manners and her eccentric—that is, stereotypically unfeminine—actions is certainly comic, but within the text there is no ambiguity about her sexuality. When women actors play Manet's nuns, the audience may not only see incongruities between their actions and the anticipated behavior both of nuns and of women in general, but they may also tend to give the play a more "realistic" and hence subversive reading than that invited by the male nuns.

Whether one interprets Manet's cross-gender casting as male actors playing "real" nuns, or as male actors playing male characters disguised as nuns, or, less likely, as male actors playing female characters disguised as nuns, there is nothing intentionally realistic about their portrayal of women. In deconstructing "classic drag"—the male creation of female parts in Greek theater—Sue-Ellen Case concludes, from a feminist perspective, that "these roles contain no information about the experience of real women in the classical world" (*Feminism and Theater* 15). Her observation is even more applicable to Manet's grotesque farce: with men in the roles of the nuns, as indicated in the stage directions, there is no pretense at mimesis and hence no information about the experience of real nuns in nineteenth-century Haiti, or twentieth-century Cuba, or anywhere else.

With female actors in the roles that Manet intended for men, the comic incongruity at the verbal level all but disappears: the distancing effect from the use of feminine pronouns and adjectives is gone. Perhaps, for some spectators, like the critic at the Théâtre de Quat'Sous production, the total result is funnier: the unexpected participation of women in physical fights may be played as farce, causing audiences to laugh from discomfiture if not because of the incongruity. The danger lies in the audience's reading the play as realistic. How will spectators interpret the sometimes tender relationship of the aggressive Mother Superior and the passive Sister Ines, particularly in view of the stereotypically masculine language and actions of Sister Angela? The conservative reaction in Antwerp is not unpredictable: whether they are "real" nuns or women gangsters disguised as nuns, the cigar-smoking, violence-prone female characters are likely to be seen as lesbians and therefore offensive to many Catholics—more offensive than men in drag, who can more easily be dismissed as comic or symbolic figures.

The other resolution of the sexually ambiguous male nuns, at the opposite pole from female actors being cast in the roles, is the overt recognition that male actors are playing male characters in disguise. Manet's dramatic text, of course, never provides this explanation.

Janet Burroway, author of *Opening Nights*, was the costume designer for the English-language premiere of *The Nuns*, directed by Walter Eysselinck at the Gardner Centre. Her intimate knowledge of the play, from script to performance, informs her novelistic re-creation of Manet's macabre farce. Her fictional director's reading of the text is quite consistent with the intent of the stage directions:

> The unexplained thing about the script was that the nuns were to be played by men, with no attempt at passing for women, but no acknowledgment even among themselves that they were anything but nuns. It wasn't clear, ever, whether they were men characters disguised as nuns or male actors playing nuns, so it worked in a lot of directions at once. Boyd wanted to work them all: the sexual ambiguity, the comedy, the dazzle and the rot; the voodoo drums in the background, the suspense in the first act and the horror in the second. He had a dark amorphous vision of the way the whole thing ought to be. (12)

Roger Blin, of course, had worked directly with Manet and understood the play's ambiguity in these same terms. To avoid potential confusion, he communicated the stage directions to the spectators. Some critics ignored the program note and told their readers that the "nuns" were three male gangsters disguised as sisters of charity (Blin 242). Seventeen years later, when the Théâtre de Feu brought its production from Mont-de-Marsan to Paris, Pierre Marcabru's favorable review found that Manet's "baroque ritual" had not aged; it also still identified the characters as three men in disguise.

The 1990 revival in New York City went two steps farther. The program and publicity from Merry Enterprises Theater featured a cartoon image of cigar-smoking male nuns—reminiscent of the 1969 publicity shot—with this brief caption: "Three men pose as Sisters of Mercy to escape retribution for their misdeeds." To reinforce this unambiguous interpretation, except for the dialogue with the Señora, the male nuns reverted to masculine pronouns in referring to each other. With such a change, the script no longer "worked in a lot of directions at once."

As various scholars have noted, cross-gender casting has been a source of controversy over the centuries. The Puritans not only adhered to the division of the sexes and the biblical injunction against men in women's clothing but also found all theater to be essentially evil: the players for assuming a self other than the one given them by God, and the plays for being "notorious lying fables" (Barish 89–93). Cross-dressing raises questions of sexual identity and, because bisexuality is traditionally viewed as a threat, is one reason for a continuing antitheatrical prejudice (Hornby 68–70). (One might add that bisexuality poses a threat to homosexuals as well as to heterosexuals.) While "breeches parts"— women dressed as men—are typically eroticized, male-to-female cross-dressing on the contemporary stage has generally been treated on the comic level, as a way of allaying "social anxieties associated with male transvestism" (Macintyre and Buchbinder 28–29).

If Manet had not considered these ramifications before, the experience of his nuns in performance certainly raised his awareness. In his *L'Autre Don Juan*, a complex metatheatrical farce written in 1972, he introduces examples of both kinds of cross-dressing in the play-within-the-play as well as a running debate on the issue in the frame play. At one point, a constable plans to shut the performance down for being "subversive and porno." He is persuaded to accept a shapely woman in a male role but remains outraged at the reverse situation: "Une femme peut jouer à l'homme, c'est mignon, c'est sain . . . mais un mâle ne doit jamais faire la femelle" (A woman can play a man, that's cute, that's wholesome . . . but a man should never play a woman; 21). He proceeds to hurl insults at the actor in skirts, questioning the cross-dresser's sexual orientation.

The historical prejudice, verbalized by Manet's constable, surfaced in the recent New York staging of *The Nuns*. In first casting the play, director William E. Hunt thought he had found the right Mother Superior, but the actor's wife was so upset to learn that her husband would be dressed as a nun that he turned down the part (personal interview). Neither Hunt nor his two leads understood how the male nuns could use natural, masculine voices and gestures and yet address each other in the feminine, so they revised the dialogue. In essence, they opted not to play the roles of women and not to run the risk of being taken for gay males in drag.

The total rejection of sexual ambiguity in the roles of the Mother Superior and Sister Angela also poses problems. When the "nuns" and the spectators are always conscious that they are men, why does the Señora—portrayed as reasonably intelligent and sensitive—not notice their manly voices and physiques? In the second act, when the unkempt men are trapped in their convent-basement and are running out of food and drink, why are they still clean-shaven? By suppressing the key element of the farcical fantasy, the production moved dangerously close to realism, thus raising such questions.

But, as Blin was to discover, playing the nuns as Manet intended likewise led to surprises. In his memoirs, the director recalled that Etienne Bierry (Mother Superior) and André Julien (Sister Angela) had used no makeup, gestures, or tones of voice that could be construed as anything but "masculine." Regardless, some spectators interpreted the subject of *Les Nonnes* to be homosexuality and the play "met with great success in the Parisian gay community" (242). Blin conjectured that the interpretation came from the scenes of physical contact—the knife fights and wrestling—between men in sisters' habits, juxtaposed with the appearance of little Sister Ines, as portrayed by the dancer and mime Pierre Byland. The killing of Sister Ines was seen as ritual by some and as the assuagement of a homosexual desire by others. Blin finally decided that "what the audience saw was probably latent within the text" (242). In that respect, the effect of the male nuns is not unrelated to the (homo)eroticism implicit in the use of drag on the Elizabethan stage.

Marjorie Garber, in her 1992 book on cross-dressing, affirms that the male nun and the female monk "are recurrent figures of fantasy as well as of history and propaganda" (213). There are many transvestite female saints; male transvestites are not similarly revered: "to wish to be a man is regarded as somehow 'natural' or of higher status, whereas to wish to be a woman is perverse" (215).

Whether audiences today—in Paris or New York—would see the same homosexual subtext in *Les Nonnes* that playgoers at the Poche-Montparnasse did in 1969 is debatable. Twenty-five years ago, male-to-female cross-gender dressing in Western theater was relatively uncommon, outside of popular comic-burlesque, pantomime, and farce (Macintyre and Buchbinder 29). Today "drag performers have emerged

Fig. 3.   Etienne Bierry, the original Mother Superior, and Eduardo Manet. At the Poche-Montparnasse Theater, 1996. In the background, a poster and photos from the 1969 staging (photo by P. Zatlin).

from back-street bars to pop up in TV commercials, movies and plays" (Stearns D1). They are no longer, as Jill Dolan once observed, male performers mirroring woman-as-myth, primarily for male spectators (8). Coming after *La Cage aux Folles* and *Torch Song Trilogy*, Manet's male nuns may still shock, but they are not likely to be seen as "gender benders."

If Manet's nuns are not interpreted as masculine women, feminine men, or manly men hiding under habits, how is his cross-gender casting to be read? What are the possible audience responses to his metatheatrical game?

At the most obvious level, particularly in the first scenes, the male nuns are as funny as the Poche-Montparnasse photo would indicate. The audience should react in amused—or disconcerted—surprise at finding men in nuns' habits. Each of the early speeches and actions—the Mother Superior's pious clichés as well as Sister Angela lighting her cigar—creates comic contrasts, either with the physical traits of the male actors or with the religious garb. Gradually, as the nuns fail to identify themselves as not-women, or even as not-nuns, the spectators should begin to accept the costumes as opaque, rather than continuously seeing through to male actors playing female roles. At that point, not every speech will automatically evoke laughter.

Burroway captures this potential effect in her description of her fictional director in the opening scene of the dress rehearsal: "When the lights faded up again the Mother Superior was seated at a laden table, delicately mopping her chin. She motioned to Sister Ines to pour more wine, and Sister Angela stalked in from stage right, leering under brows and wimple. Boyd was so used, by now, to the notion of male nuns, that the titter from the guests in the front row took him by surprise" (257). To be sure, spectators cannot be expected to accept the male nuns as thoroughly as may a cast and crew involved in weeks of rehearsals, but some transition will occur. Guy Dumur, reviewing the original production of this "crazy, baroque play," observed that at first people could not stop laughing, in part from discomfiture, but that they were soon won over "by a tragic truth that recalls the best moments of Arrabal and of Jean Genet (who also wanted male actors cast in the female roles in his plays)."[8]

The early scenes establish a critical, satiric tone. Dumur suggests that the spectators quickly understand that the basement is a "bad place" and that they can expect the worst from the sisters precisely because the roles are played by men. There is an obvious process of defamiliarization or distancing: religious robes thereby lose their conventional, symbolic value, and spectators are invited to question their previous assumptions about nuns, or whatever they represent. David Bradby, agreeing that the dramatic interest of *Les Nonnes* stems from the fact that men play the roles, finds a Marxist underpinning to Manet's grotesque farce. The title characters are men in their actions but think like nuns, conditioned by their convent life; the two levels of reality never merge. The revolution has shown the nuns in a new light, revealing the egotism previously hidden by a repressive, Catholic ideology (Bradby 237).

Like the homosexual reading of *Les Nonnes*, mentioned by Blin, or the political allegory of revolutionary Cuba, the anticlerical interpretation is undoubtedly in the text, but is narrow and limiting. When Burroway placed Manet's farce within *Opening Nights*, she interwove the themes of her fiction with those of the play-within-the-novel without the subject of religion—or Fidel Castro—ever surfacing. When she wrote to the playwright in 1984, seeking permission to use his work in her novel, she

---

8. Genet wanted the title characters of *Les Bonnes* (*The Maids*) to be played by male actors, but in practice the roles have generally been done by women.

recalled the "spectacularly good production" at the Gardner Centre and its impact on her. "The play impressed, and stayed with me, profoundly—partly no doubt because in those days in England (as well as France) we were hearing a lot of easy rhetoric about revolution from both right and left, and the play seemed to reach beneath the rhetoric to the human condition" (letter to Manet). The endurance of Manet's nuns is attributable no doubt to that deeper meaning.

The Spanish-French playwright and novelist Fernando Arrabal (b. 1932), with whom Manet has been compared, often writes overtly sacrilegious works that emphasize sexual taboos hidden under the imposed, surface morality. They are doubtless his way of confronting the ghosts of his repressive education under the "National Catholicism" of Franco's Spain. Manet, on the other hand, states that his own childhood in Cuba was free of such religious intolerance. We may anticipate, then, that the intended target of Manet's satire was not the church, or not only the church. Manet told Benmussa in their interview that he conceived his work as an investigation of "simulation," a term he defined as going beyond mere hypocrisy to include complex theatrical games (10–11).

One of the compelling aspects of metatheater is its function as a mirror of role-playing and pretense in the external reality of the spectators. The more aware we are of the games being played by the characters on stage, the more likely we are to analyze the games played by people in the real world. For a Cuban audience in the late 1960s, had the play been staged there, *Las monjas* would have been an ambiguous reflection of the revolution, not unlike José Triana's controversial *La noche de los asesinos* (1965). As Diana Taylor has lucidly explained, the Cuban Revolution itself was theatrical, and the Genetian metatheatrical games of Triana's play were misread by Castro's supporters as antirevolutionary. It is quite possible that Manet's farce would have met the same fate: does the Mother Superior not mirror the histrionic skills of Fidel himself? Manet is surely not the only person to note that Castro "is a great actor who has an extraordinary sense of staging" (interview, Mestiri 157). In a more universal frame of reference, does she not mirror anyone who assumes a mask in order to achieve greater power or wealth—or to save his or her own skin?

In *Les Nonnes*, the Mother Superior has cast herself as a dramatist/director-within-the-text. She suggests appropriate dialogue for Sister Angela, invents a tense drama of impending black revolution to instill fear in the Señora, and attempts to direct Sister Angela's actions through a continuation of that fictional drama. She instructs Sister Ines to play the guitar so that the music will set the desired, idyllic mood. The Señora's cadaver becomes the central prop in a grotesque play-within-the-play (a parody of Catholic ritual inspired, no doubt, by Valle-Inclán and Spanish-born film director Luis Buñuel). The Mother Superior even owns a trunk of disguises from which she can select costumes for the next scene of her creation. She sees life theatrically, and hence regrets Sister Angela's lack of artistic sensibility. "What," she asks, "would the world be like if human beings did not have a theatrical sense?" (*Les Nonnes*, Gallimard: 19). Prone to lengthy monologues filled with religious platitudes, even to herself she continues to play a role.

The Mother Superior's metatheatrical games fail both because two of her cast members refuse to follow her direction and because her fictions have a peculiar way of turning into "reality." Sister Angela is not a good actor: she improvises inappropriate dialogue, cannot find the right tone for her part, and when she tries to smile, she grimaces instead. The previously submissive Sister Ines rebels after the Señora offers her an alternative script. Unable to hear the words, the little nun is able to decode other signs: the Señora's beauty, her tender gestures, and the cross she puts around Sister Ines's neck in a burst of sentimental generosity. The Mother Superior loses control of her production and of herself. Someone else is in charge of the sound track (voodoo drums, battle noises, pounding at the door). When she kills Sister Ines, she is out of her self-imposed character.

Cross-gender casting adds another layer of meaning to these metatheatrical games, for it visualizes the conflict between an authentic self and the mask. Sister Angela is never comfortable with her role as nun. In her case, we always tend to see double: the wimple (female role) cannot hide the coarseness and cruelty beneath (male actor). Therefore, there is a jolting effect near the end of the play when she remembers a painting in the church she attended as a "little girl" (*Las monjas* 101).[9] Without the direct-

---

9. The Spanish phrase is "cuando yo era niña" (when I was a little girl). The French ("quand j'étais fille," 68) loses the sentimental connotation of "little" girl but remains an overtly feminine self-reference. Baldick's translation ("when I was a kid," 80) is not only gender neutral but also lowers the register.

It should be noted that "when I was a little girl," or the Spanish equivalent, could be construed as comic speech that gays would use among themselves in referring to their childhood. Manet was aware of that and deliberately left open more than one possible level for the actors to work with; he notes that the Mother Superior and Sister Angela are "actors" within the text, and as crooks pretending to be nuns, they would also have begun to use the feminine forms automatically (letter, 2 October 1991).

ing skills of the Mother Superior, Sister Angela would be less dangerous, for one could readily see through her conventional cloak.

Sister Ines is mute and simpleminded. Until she reacts to the Señora's murder, she appears to lack any will of her own. Even though she has internalized her stereotypically female role as submissive sister of mercy, the aggressivity that surfaces with her rebellion has always been present in her dualistic nature as a male nun.

The Mother Superior is more complex, for she attempts to deceive herself as well as others. She appears unaware of the surface contradictions in her behavior: her gluttony and greed in juxtaposition with her litany of pious promises to the saints. As a "muscular and manly specimen," she always projects contrasting verbal and physical signs. If it is Sister Ines's authentic self that makes her rise up in vengeful anger, it is likewise the Mother Superior's suppressed nature that reveals itself in the killing of Sister Ines. In a *mise-en-abîme* of roles within roles, the Mother Superior has concealed her violent (masculine) self underneath the exploitative and manipulative inventor of pious images and frightening tales.

The cross-gender casting, with its associated sexual ambiguity, gives visual force to this layering of masks. On the surface, within the tradition of farce, Manet has toyed with exaggerated sex-role stereotypes, but the continuing impact of *Les Nonnes* has less to do with contrastive masculine/feminine traits than, as Burroway notes, with the human condition. Not only may outward appearance be a deliberate disguise, but no one can be sure what latent forces are hidden under the cloak of meekness or respectability. Manet's male nuns reveal metaphorically how we all attempt to fool others and ourselves. As Judith Suther tellingly points out with respect to *Holocaustum ou le Borgne*, Manet's tragicomic vision of the contemporary world goes beyond an existentialist, absurdist view of the human condition to plumb the depths of human nature.[10]

---

10. Manet recalls that the Paris premiere of *Le Borgne* preceded the Belgian production and that the latter added *Holocaustum* to his original play title. He is doubtless correct about the inconsistency in the play's title: French reviews identify the play as *Le Borgne*; the published text is called *Holocaustum ou le Borgne*. However, based on the dates of reviews in the Arsénal collection, I believe that the Belgian staging took place in 1972 and the French premiere the following year. I have generally used Manet's preferred title.

2

Novels or Movie Scripts?

Until recently, with the considerable success in the 1990s of a series of novels related to the Cuban experience, Manet's fame as author rested primarily on his theater. Although his narrative works are not so numerous as his plays, Manet's career as a novelist, writing in French, actually antedates his first success on the Parisian stage.

Manet wrote a novella, *Spirale*, in 1956 while studying in Italy. It was subsequently published in France, in a softcover collection of short novels, but the edition has long been out of print and the author himself no longer has a copy.[1] Manet recalls that the action takes place in postwar Italy. A Jewish woman unwittingly marries a Nazi; when she discovers his political background, she kills him. This Holocaust-related theme would not surface again in Manet's works until his 1990 radio play, *Les Poupées en noir*.

The publication of Manet's first full-length novel, *Les Etrangers dans la ville* (Strangers in the city, 1960), coincides with the year of his return

---

1. I have not been able to locate this early work through library catalogs either in France or the United States.

to Cuba. The city referred to in the title is Paris, and the strangers are international students housed at the Cité Universitaire. Among them are Cubans who debate joining the revolution back home. Manet's native island is the setting for his 1963 novel *Un Cri sur le rivage* (A cry from the shore), touted by the publisher as "the first novel of the Cuban Revolution."

Almost twenty years separate this novel of revolutionary Cuba and Manet's third long fictional work, the quasi-autobiographical *La Mauresque*, which was to introduce the series of Cuban novels examined in Chapter 3. A fourth full-length novel, *Zone interdite* (Forbidden zone), followed shortly thereafter, in 1984; it is, appropriately enough, an Orwellian view of life under a repressive regime.

In the past decade, Manet has not slowed his pace as a writer. He often has several projects simultaneously vying for his attention. Most of these are dramatic works, but they also include a diversified group of unfinished novels. By the late 1980s he had begun *Nunzietta*, the saga of a family in Italy over the years 1905–45, and two short novels, *Eloïse, 2C27* and *La Nuit de la Terreur* (The night of terror). The former is "The story of a little, ten-year-old girl who no longer 'communicates' except through computers. Her father, one of the last 'humanists,' tries to awaken in her a love for the 'old traditions'; the reading of a printed book, for example" (letter, 9 October 1989). The latter, dealing with the French Revolution, in 1991 was being reshaped as a film script. Another projected novel, tentatively titled *Zarah* and responding to neo-Nazi anti-Semitism, would be divided into five parts with action taking place in Paris, Bucharest, a Romanian village, Beirut, and Rome—all places far removed from Cuba (letter, 22 April 1993). These works in progress will not concern us here, but they are evidence of Manet's increasing commitment to narrative writing.

Typically, Manet's fiction reflects his interest in film through the incorporation of cinematic devices and frequent references to movies. In a recent interview, the author clarifies that there is a close connection for him between film and novel, that when he thinks about a novel, he visualizes "absolutely everything.... Sometimes they talk about the influence of cinema in my novels, saying that they would make good film scripts.... That's normal because that's the way I see them" (interview, Leroyer 12).

Two Works of the 1960s

Because of its fragmented structure, shifting locales, and large number of characters, *Les Etrangers dans la ville* can readily be classified as a cinematic novel. In this respect, Manet acknowledges a possible influence of John Dos Passos, as well as his admiration for Ivy Compton-Burnett, who is directly quoted in the text. The structure, emphasizing the interwoven lives of multiple characters in an urban setting, could be compared not only to Dos Passos's *Manhattan Transfer* (1925) and Aldous Huxley's *Point Counter Point* (1928), but to such later works as Erico Veríssimo's *Caminhos cruzados* (*Crossroads*, 1940) or José Camilo Cela's *La colmena* (*The Hive*, 1951).

The first section of *Les Etrangers dans la ville* is divided into forty-eight fragments, ranging from one to five pages in length. Like sequences in a film script, most of these are marked by "realistic space," fluctuating between interior and exterior scenes: at the Cité Universitaire; outdoors at specific places in Paris; in various characters' residences, labeled by the streets or suburbs where they live; at rehearsals in a Montparnasse theater; in a car along the national highway. Also reminiscent of film is a kind of musical sound track suggested within the narration.[2] As is typical of this kind of novelistic network, characters who appear in one setting will later reappear in other locales. Interspersed among the objective action scenes narrated in the third person, which readily translate to filmic images, is a series of ten diary entries from the subjective point of view of a would-be novelist within the text.

In the second section of the novel, as some of the characters seek to resolve their identity problems elsewhere, the background shifts back and forth from Paris to the Côte d'Azur, Madrid, and Rome. The subdivisions of this section are fewer in number (fourteen) and more extensive in length (three to sixteen pages). As might be expected, they tend to develop more fully some individual stories as the group of international students begins to disperse. The final segment, which takes place at the same restaurant in the Cité Universitaire where the action began, provides an accounting of where some of the old companions have gone in the intervening time.

---

2. Music of different varieties serves an important function in Manet's theater and novels. In his 1996 interview with Jason Weiss, Manet asserts that he cannot live without music and listens to it constantly; he attributes this tendency to his mother, who always had the radio on when he was a child.

With the sense of immediacy associated with film, in *Les Etrangers dans la ville* Manet portrays the various young people caught in their quest for personal, professional, sexual, or political identities. The decisions they make at this critical point in their lives inevitably lead to separations: after his father dies, Joe goes home to Arkansas, leaving the young actress Ana-María with a farewell letter; Carlos, who has overcome his sexual identity crisis and his temporary desire to enter a monastery, goes back to Havana, where the revolution is under way; Ada, an eighteen-year old pianist, breaks up with Alberto, has an abortion, and goes on to give a successful concert in Brussels; the would-be Spanish novelist tears up his 250-page manuscript, gives up both his writing career and his thoughts of entering the anti-Franco movement, and takes a job in a French travel agency.

In structure and style, *Les Etrangers dans la ville* differs notably from Manet's later fictional autobiographies, but chronologically it continues the episodes recounted in *L'Ile du lézard vert*. That novel ends with the narrator's desire to follow his love, Hanna, to Paris where the young woman will pursue her piano studies. The Alberto-Ada story within this first novel is somewhat related. Indeed, of the numerous characters, Alberto is the one who might be associated most closely with the author's own experiences. The nineteen-year-old Cuban hopes to become a French writer, not a Latin American revolutionary. He has a great love for poetry and, like the polyglot Manet, for languages. In Cuba, with the financial help of his Aunt Emilia, Alberto had published a little book of his poems. (In *L'Ile du lézard vert*, the narrator pays for a similar edition with his own savings.)

There is no unifying central figure in *Les Etrangers dans la ville*, parallel to Martín Marco in Cela's *La colmena*, but Manet does develop a counterpoint among his characters to hold the fragments together. Alberto, in particular, is contrasted both with Carlos and with the would-be novelist of the diary segments. In one of the sequences at the Cité Universitaire, Carlos's words about returning to Cuba are juxtaposed with Alberto's thoughts on the same subject. The preoccupation of the Cubans with political repression under the Batista regime is played against the Spaniard's guilt at not being involved in the clandestine fight against Franco. The Spaniard's efforts to find a publisher for his novel repeats the theme of Alberto's desire to become a writer.

Although quite different from the fragmented structure of *Les Etrangers dans la ville*, Manet's novel of revolutionary Cuba, *Un Cri sur le rivage*, can also be described in cinematographic terms. The central love story, handled as an extended flashback, is played against the panoramic sweep of society in the midst of radical change. The retrospective scenes, crosscut into a drive across the island in the fictional present, include anecdotes involving numerous secondary characters of various nationalities who enter the rapidly shifting locales. A large percentage of the text is dialogue, not narrative description. Some of these secondary episodes focus on love affairs and personal lives, but they also include the frantic activities prompted by the Bay of Pigs invasion. The text could readily be transformed into a film script and invites an intertextual reading with Hollywood movies that are set against the background of civil unrest; Manet in fact suggests *Casablanca* as one such related film.

The protagonist of *Un Cri sur le rivage* is the young writer Gavilan. In spite of his ambition to write serious literature, at twenty-three he has scripted a popular soap opera and is now involved in a literacy project in rural Cuba. He is far away from Havana when he receives word that his former lover Elsa—several years older than he and married—has attempted suicide and is in critical condition. His long drive across the island is thus juxtaposed with memories of his relationship with Elsa, along with the series of filmic sequences that provide multiple perspectives on the changing situation in Cuba. At the novel's end, we do not know if Elsa has died or if Gavilan reaches her while she is still alive.

We also do not know if the third-person narrator favors revolution or counterrevolution. *Un Cri sur le rivage* is not agitation propaganda, intended to sell the reader a particular political position, but rather a balanced presentation. Manet recalls that he wrote the novel at a time when the revolution was still evolving and one could not be sure where it was going. He considers his work to be objective: "giving testimony rather than taking a position" (interview, 15 May 1991). There is a political underpinning to Gavilan's rupture with Elsa, who had once fought in the clandestine movement against Batista but who now sides with her brother Ricardo, a stereotypical *gusano* (counterrevolutionary), but the reader is left to form his or her own opinion.

Un Cri sur le rivage is written as popular fiction: a blend of soap-opera-style love stories and familiar filmic scenes (barroom brawls and undercover deals), along with political discussions. It is the least innovative of Manet's novels, but yet of interest for its inside view of Cuban society in 1960–61. Rich in local color, it even introduces fragments of Spanish-language songs within the French text, at times with translations in accompanying footnotes.[3] Thus an early scene in the novel provides the cheerfully partisan song "Fidel... Fidel... / Qué tiene Fidel? / Qué ni los americanos / Pueden con él?" (What is it about Fidel that not even the Americans can stand up to him? 13). At the same time, the background action indicates that the American presence, or absence, on the island will have an enormous impact on all Cubans. There are growing scarcities of many items, ranging from butter and cheese to American cigarettes and condoms. The forced marriage of Mathias, announced near the end of the novel (195), is a direct result of the latter shortage. In that Mathias has boasted that he plans to seduce his teenage art students and delights in buying books and records from friends who are leaving Cuba, the lack of contraceptives is presented in a more or less humorous tone: Mathias does not have our sympathy. The seriousness of Cuba's prior dependence on United States imports is underscored throughout the novel, however, by the fact that Gavilan is driving a Pontiac.

Juxtaposed with such practical matters as the growing shortage of contraceptives is a French journalist's romanticized image of the Cuban Revolution. Why are you here instead of Cambodia or Thailand, Gavilan asks her. Marie-Anne responds that Cuba has the "sexiest" revolution. She predicts that many of those in the bar will shortly have left for the United States and those who remain will be talking of productivity and five-year plans, but in the meantime: "Havana, in December 1960, is more amusing, but it rather resembles the *dolce vita* of Rome. Guys talk to you about politics while making love with their revolver by their side" (42).

Fidel Castro, the central figure of the "romantic" revolution, is the natural subject of conversation. Gavilan, Elsa, and their friends visit a statue of Christ that paradoxically still overlooks the city at a time when terrorist priests are being imprisoned. Commenting that revolutions demand myths, they note that this revolution's leader is both praised for his physical resemblance to Christ and condemned as the Antichrist. For some he is a Christ figure: not only does he welcome little children, but in his first Havana speech, a dove perched on his shoulder. For others, he is a child molester and the dove was lured by corn (123–25). Later, when Gavilan decodes Elsa and Ricardo's comments about their horse ("Horse" = Castro) and the stable catching on fire, he realizes that they are conspiring against the revolution (173).

---

3. As we shall see later, such use of bilingualism is characteristic of Manet's mature theater.

The image in the novel of counterrevolutionaries like Ricardo is basically negative, but there is corresponding criticism of the revolutionary movement. One aspect that comes under a satirical light is the growing restriction on artistic freedom. In an early bar scene, a filmmaker says that he is leaving for San Juan because the Cuban Film Institute wants to rewrite his proposed script to make it convey a political message: "The Cinema Institute is going to film only those scenarios that have positive heroes" (50). To be sure, the proposal—the love affair between a Greek sailor with syphilis and a Cuban prostitute with breast cancer—strikes his companion as a joke, but the filmmaker's comments on the requested transformation into a Soviet-style movie praising the working class hints at a possible imposition of socialist realism.[4] The theme recurs when Elsa proposes to Gavilan a continuing series based on a symbolic heroine who is the victim of rape during the Batista regime and then becomes a Communist military leader under Castro; she suggests further metamorphoses in the character should an American invasion succeed, with the heroine eventually marrying a Yankee millionaire (194). Popular culture, at least in the opinion of Elsa, is subservient to ideology under Castro and will continue to be so if the Americans take over Cuba.

Un Cri sur le rivage does not take an overt pro- or antirevolutionary stance. It does project an image of a state that is gradually supplanting individual freedoms. Whether the actions taken are necessary in a just cause is open to interpretation both by characters within the novelistic world and by the reader. Considering that Manet himself had voluntarily returned to Cuba and was to remain there for five years after the publication of this work, it is somewhat surprising that his view of the revolution is a balanced one that includes negative perspectives. The kind of unofficial censorship that was applied to his film *Tránsito* apparently did not affect a French-language novel that was published at a safe distance from Cuban readers.

Manet's Vision of 1984

Zone interdite is, to date, Manet's one full-length novel that does not refer directly to Cuba. It is set in an unspecified country at an indeterminate

---

4. Manet's first films made in Cuba, discussed in the preceding chapter, would not contradict this assertion.

time. In reviewing it for the Spanish-language edition of the *Miami Herald*, Fernando Villaverde astutely observes that Manet has avoided any simplistic allegory; the book encompasses any country and any system by creating a stylized, but possible, world. Yet it is tempting to read the novel as an extension of *Un Cri sur le rivage*: a vision of what happens when the state, embodied in a supreme leader, becomes all powerful. According to the author, his fictional world was inspired in part by events in Romania, not Cuba. Nevertheless, Manet's sensitivity to life under any repressive regime has to be flavored by his personal knowledge of the Cuban experience, not only under Castro but also during the years of dictatorship that gave impetus to the leftist revolution.

Like the fictionalized autobiographies, *La Mauresque* and *L'Ile du lézard vert*, *Zone interdite* is narrated in the first person from the limited perspective of an unnamed protagonist. The central figure does not relate his story retrospectively; rather the action occurs in the fictional present with a cinematic sense of immediacy. As Villaverde observes, the narrative unfolds in the style of a popular detective or adventure novel; but this, too, is a text whose changing locales and considerable action could readily be converted into a film script.

The country is ruled by an unseen, degenerating dictator and a coterie from the Center for Information and Surveillance, familiarly called the Maison (House). The narrator, proficient in five living and four dead languages, is initially a translator but gains entry to the House after playing poker with and losing to some of the leaders in the power structure. To each of these men he gives code names, concealing always their actual identities. In his new position, the narrator helps to ferret out traitors: he monitors calls from children denouncing their parents and then assesses the truth of their accusations in follow-up meetings. In one curious episode, reminiscent of the film *Blow-Up* and the Julio Cortázar story on which it is based, the narrator uncovers the truth in a family's relationships only by studying a still photograph. The result of his investigations is generally the imprisonment and execution of the accused.

Although appearing to believe that the accused are guilty, the narrator suffers a certain malaise in his role. In spite of being part of the omnipotent House, he remains idealistic. In spite of being aware that the House has records of all citizens' every action, he bends rules to assist the refugee Lin-Ah and her children. The tubercular Vietnamese boat-person becomes the concierge of the narrator's modest apartment building and then his lover. He is deeply moved by her illness and death, and thus more inclined to accept the challenge of becoming part of the Project.

Whereas the House symbolizes the loss of individual freedoms, the Project is a metaphor for the absurd world created by a decadent regime. The mysterious project, which will reportedly turn the country into a virtual paradise, is rumored to be a special reward for a select few. In fact it is a kind of prison work camp. In stage one, the crews are made to split a never ending pile of huge rocks. The survivors are then sent to stage two, where they manually build mile after mile of marble wall to shut the country off from the sea. The workers' periods of rest are spent at an idyllic brothel, staffed by the graduates of the elite school where the most promising girls were sent for special training. As the novel ends, the protagonist's mentor takes control and the narrator at last has authority to make changes. He orders the brothel dismantled and prepares to blow up the wall. There is a note of hope but no indication that the new government will totally discard the abuses of the past.

In *Zone interdite*, there is an interesting use of self-betraying irony in the portrayal of the narrator-protagonist. The narrative voice may be openly and even comically self-deprecatory: he describes himself losing patience with callers or finding himself in ridiculous positions. At other times, he appears unaware of the traps he will inevitably fall into, for example from his drinking or poker playing. He is not an unreliable narrator who deliberately deceives himself or his reader, but on occasion he creates an ironic distance from the narrated self. This same narrative strategy is even more prominent in *La Mauresque* and *L'Ile du lézard vert*.

3

The Major Novels

FRENCH WORDS WITH A CUBAN BEAT

Manet's most successful novels to date center on the Cuban experience, tracing the sociohistorical background of pre-Castro Cuba and then of exile in the United States. Manet considers *La Mauresque* (The Moorish woman, 1982) to be his "first real novel" (interview, Weiss). It and the next of his major works, *L'Ile du lézard vert* (Green Lizard Island, 1992), are based on the author's memories of his childhood and youth. *La Mauresque* centers on the 1930s, primarily from the perspective of a young child. *L'Ile du lézard vert*, whose action specifically occurs in the years 1948–50, is in part a sequel to the fictional autobiography of *La Mauresque*, with the same unnamed first-person narrator. The enthusiastic reader response to *L'Ile du lézard vert* inspired *Habanera* (1994), set against the background of Havana at the time of Batista's 1952 coup d'état. The reception of *Habanera* in turn led Manet to write the episodic *Rhapsodie cubaine*, revolving around a protagonist who was thirteen when he left Havana; dealing with exile life in Miami, it spans a period from 1960 to 1995.

With some variations, the four novels fall into a familiar category of exile literature: "living outside the borders of the 'homeland' and inside the borders of 'another country' often entails a border journey into the memory and imagination that negotiates between old and new, past and present, self and other, safety and danger" (Henderson 4). In the process of making that border journey, Manet has intentionally become an intermediary between Cuba and the French reading public: "I'm a sort of liaison, you see, a dangerous liaison between Cuba and France. Because I think I know French people very well, and I think I know Cuban people very well, so I try to be a bridge between them" (interview, Weiss; translated Weiss).

Fictionalized Autobiography: Childhood and Youth in Cuba

To a certain extent, *La Mauresque* and *L'Ile du lézard vert* may be placed within the genre of Childhood (equivalent to the French *souvenirs d'enfance*), as defined by Richard N. Coe: "*a conscious, deliberately executed literary artifact, usually in prose* (and thus intimately related to the novel) . . . *in which the most substantial portion of the material is directly autobiographical, and whose structure reflects step by step the development of the writer's self; beginning . . . with the first light of consciousness, and concluding, quite specifically, with the attainment of a precise degree of maturity*" (8–9).

That first light of consciousness in *La Mauresque* is humorously equated with birth; the novel ends with the eleven-year-old narrator's awareness of childhood's loss: "I know that I am no longer a child" (216). Coe places the usual termination age of Childhood works at fifteen or eighteen, and suggests that a concentration in time, particularly of adolescence, is a common literary strategy (7). Manet's sequel novel precisely follows that pattern; the narrator of *L'Ile du lézard vert* traces his experiences over a three-year period, starting at age fifteen and ending with the dramatic death of a friend and his own decision to leave Cuba: "He is dead, completely dead, along with my adolescence" (400); "I shall go away. I shall leave this prison forever" (402).

It is not my purpose here to determine how faithfully these novels reflect Eduardo Manet's life even though the author does not deny their autobiographical underpinning. Because of its relationship to his own experiences, he considers *La Mauresque* to be the key to understanding his theater. The novel was written with deliberate selectivity: for example, Manet's sisters have disappeared in order to foreground the mother; and the historical background is the product of careful research, not vague childhood memories.

The continuity between *La Mauresque* and *L'Ile du lézard vert*, as well as the resulting connection with Manet, poses a particular problem. The narrator gives the day—19 June—but not the year of his birth, in an initial chapter titled "Le jour où la terre trembla à Santiago de Cuba" (The day when the earth trembled in Santiago, Cuba). One might be able to verify when the earthquake occurred, but such research is not necessary; as the novel progresses, specific dates are provided within the text for other historical background, often in conjunction with the narrator's age. Thus we can fix his birth year as 1927, for we find the precocious three-year-old already reading magazines—or at least looking at the pictures—in 1930, and we are expressly told that he is eleven in 1938, when the novel ends. At the beginning of the sequel novel in 1948, the narrator is only fifteen—presumably having been born in 1933—but is listed in official records as being nineteen. His mother relates the episode: the father had intended to falsify the boy's age by a year to facilitate his admission to secondary school, but the chauffeur he sent to handle the errand "obviously misunderstood completely. The day, the month, the year, the place of birth, you wouldn't recognize them" (*L'Ile* 32). The registry has him born in Havana, four years earlier than his actual birth, and under the wrong sign of the zodiac. Even the narrator's falsified birth year is thus 1929, not 1927, and there is no way to reconcile the chronology of the two novels; nor is there a way to reconcile the chronology of the second one with Manet's own life.[1]

---

1. The issue of *L'Avant-Scène Théâtre* in which *Les Nonnes* was published in 1969 (no. 431) identified Manet as having been born in Havana in 1927. The issue of this same theater journal in which *Lady Strass* appeared in 1977 (no. 613) repeated the information and added 19 March as the birthday. In the personal letter of 25 January 1991, cited in the Preface, Manet clarified that in fact he had been born in Santiago de Cuba on 19 June 1930, the year of the earthquake described in *La Mauresque*.

It is tempting to ask whether this is a case of art imitating life or life imitating art, but Manet is not the only Latin American of my acquaintance who tells similar stories of erroneous birth records, including ones falsified in order for a precocious child to enter high school early. A Chilean colleague tells me that it is simply easier to maintain the false age than try to convince people that she is really two years younger than the records reveal. In the case of *La Mauresque*, the narrator's birth year is established within the novel as 1927; much of the background action of this first novel would have taken place before the birth in 1933 of the narrator of *L'Ile du lézard vert*.

In her review of *La Mauresque*, Michèle Gazier observes that the novel is a melding of three stories: Soledad, the title character; the childhood years of the author, and Cuba. She is certainly correct about the interweaving of multiple strands, but for at least some readers the dominant component is the Childhood. In fact the brief notice in *Figaro* by A. B. V., titled "Viva Eduardo!," emphasizes not only that this charming tale recounts childhood memories but that they are happy ones, without a trace of trauma or conflict: "The little boy lives at peace surrounded by his mother and loving, clever servants."

There is no doubt that the focal point is the child, known by the generic term Niño. But a careful analysis of Manet's text does not support the *Figaro* reviewer's image of an idyllic childhood. The Niño was born out of wedlock, and his mother experiences crying spells and jealous rages after she discovers that the boy's father, known only as the Docteur (courtesy title in Cuba for anyone with a college degree), maintains other *queridas* and has other such children, some of them younger than her son. The little boy, who sleeps in his mother's big bed except when the Docteur surprises them with nocturnal visits, has a full-blown Oedipus complex. He receives his own sexual initiation at the age of five, seduced by the "magic" games of the ten-year-old girl next door. Nor is he serenely oblivious to Cuba's political upheaval. During the revolution of 1933, his father is forced into exile, his mother invents ways to earn a living, and the little boy finds himself helping the Communist student Myrna smuggle explosives to her clandestine cohorts. He sees—and smells—bodies of the executed being dragged through the street in front of his house.

Moreover, the servants are perhaps too "loving and clever." The mother's final crisis comes when she discovers that Dulce María—a former servant who has become a popular singer—is among the Docteur's lovers. Resentful of his father ("Dandy-Docteur. Docteur Don Juan and very macho"), the narrator would avenge his mother if he could: "If I weren't only eleven years old, Mama, if I weren't eleven . . ." (213). An unexpected telegram from Spain causes Soledad to forget her jealousy: her estranged brothers, at last forgiving her for running off with a married man, are fleeing to Cuba to avoid Nazi persecution. (The self-proclaimed Mauresque is not Moorish at all, but Jewish; her particular identity problems will underscore the growing self-awareness of her narrator-son in the sequel novel.)

The potentially traumatic childhood of *La Mauresque* does not negate A. B. V.'s assertion that this is a "charming tale." The tone is generally humorous, and the overall effect is indeed charming. The use of various narrative strategies shifts the work from the purely autobiographical—where conflicts might have been foregrounded—to a fictional, often comic plane.

For Barrett J. Mandel, autobiography can readily be distinguished from fiction. In reading the former genre, we see the life of the person sitting behind the typewriter: "At every moment of any true autobiography (I do not speak here of autobiographical novels) the author's intention is to convey the sense that 'this happened to me'" (53). Louis A. Renza agrees that "we have little difficulty recognizing and therefore reading autobiographies as opposed to works of fiction" (272), even though autobiography "transforms empirical facts into *arti*facts" and "self-consciously borrows from the methodological procedures of imaginative fiction" (269). Coe does not exclude all autobiographical novels from the genre of Childhood, but he perceives basic differences between the novel and autobiography. In the former, the character is "determined by the plot" and is required to act; in autobiography, instead of plot there may simply be a pattern that "affects exclusively the narrator-subject, not the characters who surround him" (6). In that verbatim conversations cannot be remembered over time, significant fictionalization may also be detected from the use of dialogue (Coe 7). By these various measures, *La Mauresque* is a novel, not a true autobiography;[2] *L'Ile du lézard vert* falls even more clearly into the category of novel.

In *La Mauresque* the experiences of the narrator, his mother, and their household are marked by several moves: from a large house in Santiago to a smaller one, from Santiago to a large house in Havana, from there to a smaller house in the capital. These moves reflect changing financial situations and, at times, the changing relationship between Soledad and the Docteur. In Havana Soledad first reacts to the Great Depression by renting rooms to students, and then becomes a seamstress and fortune-teller to supplement her income. Later, when the Docteur's Mexican exile forces her to move to a smaller house, she discovers her talent as a spiritist. In terms of Coe's definition, the child-narrator is seldom required to act; there is more plot than pattern here, but it is Soledad, not he, who responds to the current of events. She and the household are most

---

2. *La Mauresque* is clearly a novel, not a pure autobiography, but Manet recalls that one of the Prix Goncourt judges told him the work did not win the fiction prize because they considered it "totally autobiographical." It was, however, the recipient of the 1982 Prix Jouvenel of the Académie Française.

affected by the Docteur's behavior and by economic crises, but also by natural disasters (the Santiago earthquake and the hurricane of 1933) and political circumstances (the Machado dictatorship, revolutionary activity among University of Havana students, the rise of Batista, and the government of Grau San Martín).

Overall, *La Mauresque* does not give us the image of the adult author sitting at his typewriter for the purpose of revealing his life. The absence of a family surname—and even of first names except for that of the mother—removes the explicit connection between author and narrator. An objective narrator provides periodic digressions about Cuba: its popular culture, cuisine, clothing, climate, geography, history, politics, and sociology. On the other hand, much of the autobiographical action is given in the present tense, sometimes with extended dialogue; as a result, there is a cinematic sense of immediacy and a deliberate fictionalization process. Even within the autobiographical passages written in the narrative past, the adult narrator's voice is not always obtrusive; at times, however, there are interventions by an older narrator. For example, this older narrator provides observations, such as this one, about his father: "In that he had a woman in almost every town (something my mother learned only later), my father generally avoided traveling with his young lover" (16–17). Or he may clarify the child's mistakes, as in the case of the invented words "*Ouami, ouami, haoualovou, haoualovou*" for a song heard on the radio: "Some years later I learned the real words: '*Swanee, How I love you / how I love you*'" (80). As the child-narrator matures, even these retrospective interventions are of decreasing frequency. In the sequel novel, with its adolescent-narrator, they have virtually disappeared; moreover, the passages on Cuban political history and culture flow more naturally from the young man's awareness in the fictional present and hence do not stand apart so obviously from the main narrative strand.

Part of *La Mauresque's* comic effect stems from episodes being narrated at the cognitive level of the developing child, thus leaving the reader to smile at the little boy's innocence or to fill in the gaps of what the narrator sees and hears but does not fully comprehend. Remembering "a word that my mother uses sometimes but whose meaning I don't fully grasp," he declares himself to be an "anarchist" (46). Inspired by the story of David and Goliath, the three-year-old imprudently yells at mounted police he sees attacking unarmed students, then runs to his mother for protection (59). In considerable detail we experience a *santería* rite from the perspective of the child. When the little boy fails to grasp the double meaning of the word *tortillera*, a footnote is provided to help the French-language reader get the Spanish joke: "A woman who makes omelets, slang word for a lesbian" (151). On the other hand, in the final chapter when the young boy believes his mother is calling her brothers "cochons" (pigs), no explicit definition of *marranos* (pigs, or Jews who have converted to Christianity) is provided. The reader is expected to guess the second meaning from context. (The mother refers to Hitler's atrocities and the brothers' justifiable fears: "Your uncles are in danger, even if our family has been integrated into the nation for generations, even if they are *marranos*" [216].) Thus the novel ends with the comic irony of the narrator's misunderstanding, even as he declares himself to be no longer a child.

Although the narrator of *La Mauresque* often avoids clarifications from the vantage point of the adult, he typically separates himself from the child protagonist in order to view him from outside. In the early pages dealing with his birth and infancy, he also puts impossible thoughts into his mind, thus providing comic images. For example, the baby, who is taking a bath with his mother, sees their figures in a mirror and agrees that they look like a Murillo painting of the Virgin Mary and the baby Jesus (27). The idyllic scene is interrupted by the baby's attack of green diarrhea (29). When the little boy, caught in a downpour while dressed in his best clothes, confronts poor people for the first time, he sees himself from their perspective: "I'm wearing on my person the equivalent of a month's salary for this peasant family" (125). He runs to his mother, repeating her kind of emotional words: "Mama, I have just seen the face of misfortune!"; but he also sees his comic image in the mirror: "the image of a little boy with his formless hat falling to one side, dripping with water. A tiny silhouette more nearly resembling a miniature scarecrow than the symbol of refined elegance that he had been before his stroll" (126).

Such images of the narrator are only part of the visual, cinematic effect of the novel. In a brief preface, the narrator informs us that his mother was blessed with the memory of an elephant and that he can relive many moments of his life, starting from his birth, because of her detailed descriptions. "But these recollections that evoke images, sounds, words that have been buried within me for so long, are they truly real? Or isn't perhaps my vision of them what brings back from the past scenes that have been etched in my memory as if by branding irons?" It is precisely this effect of "image" or "scene" that gives to much of the narration a sense of immediate reality rather than remembered past. Shifting narrative perspectives, including narrations-within-the-narration and action in the present tense, are sometimes indicated typographically through an inch-wide indentation of entire passages; at times dialogue is set apart with the characters' names, like a play or movie script.

The evocation of these scenes "etched in his memory" is done in a highly fictionalized, or theatricalized, manner. Thus, during the earthquake when Soledad is in labor, we see the midwife Ma Dominga, the servant Senta, and the lover Senta had hidden in her bedroom, all struggling to get Soledad and her heavy wooden bed out of the house. The narrator describes the scene as a comic opera, complete with quartet: the contralto, baritone, and mezzo-soprano voices of the blacks, singing to a voodoo god, are joined by that of a dramatic soprano: "the voice of my mother rends the air with an apocalyptic lament" (20). When his mother and Senta heatedly discuss the household situation, the child both eavesdrops and attempts to listen to his favorite radio program: the juxtaposed voices of the women and of the characters in the competing soap opera are set out as play dialogue (143–47). Typographical juxtaposition is used in a later episode, recounted in the present tense, when the narrator places a text from the society page of the newspaper side by side with his own satirical analysis of the accompanying photo (189–90).

The charm of *La Mauresque* for French readers in general might be attributed primarily to its portrayal of childhood coupled with the evocation of an exotic Cuban setting. For those interested in the theater of Eduardo Manet, the novel contains at least two specific elements worthy of attention: the emphasis on *santería*, evoked through the Haitian servant Senta, and the fascination with movies, shared by the child and his mother.

Chapter 6, "Un soir chez les ñañigos," presents an evening *santería* celebration in detail. The child-narrator describes it as a spectacle: "It's just like the theater" (99). In Manet's own theater, he has repeated these rituals: the sacrifice of a rooster, described here, is also represented in *Eux, ou La prise du pouvoir* (Them, or Taking power, 1971); a related section of *L'Ile du lézard vert* ("Le Toque"), in which Soledad asks Senta for voodoo protection against a rival in her love affair, has a counterpart in *Ma'Dea* (1986), Manet's reworking of Medea set in modern Haiti. The Senta figure, based on Manet's real-life Haitian nursemaid, is also repeated directly in *Madras, la nuit où . . .* (That night in Madras, 1974) and indirectly in *Les Nonnes*. As part of the *santería* ritual of *La Mauresque*,

Senta becomes Ochoun: she is taken over by a male voice and even smokes a cigar.[3] *Les Nonnes* calls for cross-gender casting: cigar-smoking male actors are to play the Sisters of Charity.

References to Hollywood films are a constant in Manet's theater. The same pattern holds true in *La Mauresque* and *L'Ile du lézard vert*. The child-narrator tells of seeing his first movie, *The Sign of the Cross*, at the age of three.[4] His mother subscribes to several movie magazines, which he avidly devours. When Myrna tells him that she is going to Moscow to study Marx, she has to clarify that she does not mean the Marx Brothers (199). Throughout the two novels, both mother and son self-consciously attempt to look like their favorite stars. In *La Mauresque*, when Soledad gets her hair cut and bleached, the boy remarks that she looks like Shirley Temple turned into an old lady (195). The eleven-year-old insists on having his hair cut like George Raft (213). The narrator consistently comments on both his own and others' appearance and actions in terms of familiar filmic codes. For example, when the bus from Santiago to Havana breaks down, his mother checks into a hotel and relaxes in a bubble bath "like the ones she had seen in the movies" (121). At Camagüey, when she finds just the right earthen jars to take to her new home, she stops short, turns pale, and places her hand on her chest "as if to control her beating heart—a gesture of actress Gloria Swanson that she particularly admired" (130).

The use of such self-conscious gestures and the tendency of the narrator and other characters to view people and actions in filmic terms are among the techniques that unify the two novels, and a complete list of movie references in *L'Ile du lézard vert* would be long indeed. Gipsie, the teenager's twenty-five-year-old lover, recalls an episode when someone tried to force her car off the road "like gangsters in grade-B American movies" (111). Even nature is described in filmic terms: "Lents fondus enchaînés de nuages" (Slow dissolves of clouds; 152). The fifteen-year-old narrator imagines that shaving with his Gillette will give him "the hardened, desperate face of Ray Milland" (19); for his seventeenth birth-

---

3. In his analysis of Cuban and Brazilian drama, Robert Lima identifies Ochún (or Oshun) as one of several powerful Orishas grouped together as the African Powers. Oshun, who represented love in African myths, was syncretized in Cuba with Our Lady of Charity of Cobre (Lima 119, 175 n. 9). Manet in his novel emphasizes a Haitian influence, but Ochún is also a popular deity in Cuban *santería*.

4. The De Mille movie was released in 1932. Although most internal evidence in the novel points to the narrator's birth in 1927, this one item suggests 1930.

day, he asks his mother for a sharkskin suit like one in a Robert Taylor movie (280). Facing her fiftieth birthday, Soledad fixes her hair like Lucille Ball's and chooses a dress like Barbara Stanwyck's in *The Strange Love of Martha Ivers*; the alternative to these changes, she says, is having long, white hair and resembling the witch in *Snow White* (218–19). The narrator's father has taught himself to manipulate his cane "like Fred Astaire in his comedies" (178). When the boy is finally invited to his father's newspaper office, he is dismayed to discover that a former correspondent from the Spanish Civil War in no way resembles the romantic figure of Gary Cooper in *For Whom the Bell Tolls* (188). The addiction of mother and son to movies includes reruns of newsreels from the 1930s; a detailed analysis of a filmed demonstration against Machado is interpolated in the novel (135–36).

To a greater extent than in *La Mauresque*, filmic strategies in *L'Ile du lézard vert* are part of the novel's basic story and structure. The narrator agrees to become involved with the Communist student movement because he sees it "as a romantic adventure worthy of the action films that he so loved" (147). Political activities become inseparably intertwined with discussions about cinema, not only because the youth's acquaintances are movie buffs, but also because representatives of rival political factions run their respective film series and movies thus have ideological implications. References to specific musical works are so prevalent that, as in *Les Etrangers dans la ville*, they form a kind of sound track. External, realistic settings are evoked through numerous street and beach scenes, sometimes presented as the backdrop to the narrator's walks, sometimes flashing by outside car windows. The adolescent's experiences during these three critical years in his development are divided between the personal (his love affairs with the nonconformist and cosmopolitan Gipsie and the young Romanian-Jewish pianist Hanna) and the political (his involvement in the exploits of Lohengrin and Manu). As the rhythm of the novel accelerates in the final chapters, action is crosscut between these two planes of reality, often through the use of flashbacks to evoke the personal sequences. The result is a cinematic-style narration comparable in some ways to that of *Un Cri sur le rivage*.

Even though movie references and filmic narrative strategies underscore the close relationship between the two fictionalized autobiographies, *L'Ile du lézard vert* is not a seamless continuation of *La Mauresque*. We have already noted the discrepancy in the birth year of the two first-person narrators, but there are other ruptures as well. The earlier novel ends with the impending arrival of the child's maternal uncles; there is no reference to them in the second work. Certain minor details also change: for example, the origin of the bed in which Soledad gives birth or the length of time she ran a boardinghouse. More significant changes may be attributed to the age of the narrator. From the perspective of the child in *La Mauresque*, his mother is generally seen to be a fascinating person with almost magical powers; her portrait for the adolescent has degenerated to that of a woman primarily given to wild emotional swings and irrational conduct. The underlying problems of the narrator's childhood, which remained partially hidden in the subtext until the final pages, are readily apparent from the beginning of the second novel. When his father does not arrive for the boy's fifteenth-birthday celebration, the narrator responds to his mother's crisis by getting drunk. He evokes all the past images of an absent father and his mother's suffering: "Other dinners, just like this one, other periods of waiting, hoping to see him arrive, other secret pleadings to evoke a smile, to be happy, calm, relaxed, then other vain waits followed by the same disappointments" (*L'Ile* 30–31). In *L'Ile du lézard vert*, there is a noticeable shift of emphasis from the objective to the subjective level and hence a more complete psychological portrayal of the narrator-protagonist.

    The narrator's adolescent angst, rooted in his extreme unhappiness with his home life and lack of a real family, permeates the surface level of the opening chapters. It leads him on the night of his failed birthday celebration to make a halfhearted attempt at suicide, no doubt inspired by some vaguely remembered movie scene. Even as he approaches seventeen, he blurts out to his mother, "I wish I were dead! I wish I'd never been born!" (274). Nor is his expressed longing for a brother in any way alleviated when he discovers that among the employees at the newspaper is another of his father's illegitimate sons.

    L'Ile du lézard vert did not receive the coveted Goncourt. It was chosen for a special youth prize, the "Goncourt des lycéens," by a panel of 230 students representing ten high schools. In his letter from Paris for a Madrid newspaper, Spanish-born playwright and novelist Carlos Semprun Maura conjectured that Eduardo Manet would be "horrified to find himself appearing on television with illiterate teen-age panelists who confess to reading, laboriously, only one or two novels a year." On the contrary, Manet found the experience exhilarating; it led to public appearances across the country, where young readers gave him a celebrity's welcome.

Because of the novel's initial success, within months it was already slated to be issued in paperback.

To what may we attribute the great popularity of *L'Ile du lézard vert*? The novel's historical background would function as a fascinating roman à clef for Cuban readers of Manet's own generation: one source of their pleasure in reading the work would come from their deciphering who might have served as model for the various student leaders, professors, and journalists. But such questions can have no special significance for general readers in France, and particularly not for high school students.[5] In his laudatory review in *Le Monde*, Jean-Noël Pancrazi makes no reference at all to the fictionalized autobiography's concomitant function as historical novel, instead characterizing it only as the "dazzling and sensual tale of growing up as an adolescent, caught in an island trap" (Pancrazi 1992). In some respects, *L'Ile du lézard vert* builds upon the winning combination of *La Mauresque*: a portrait of adolescence coupled with the evocation of an exotic setting. As the narrator's self-awareness increases, the tone here shifts from the lighter humor of the earlier work to a more complex irony.

I have previously noted that adolescent angst is an important motif from the opening pages of the novel. The narrator has multiple concerns about his family, his nationality and ethnic background, his relationships with others, his sexuality, his talents, and his future. These motifs, which link *L'Ile du lézard vert* thematically with *Les Etrangers dans la ville*, no doubt are also responses to concerns of many young readers. As in the

---

5. It is not my purpose here to determine how faithful Manet has been to Cuban history. Clearly there are numerous references to real political and cultural figures and to historical events. No doubt some other writer, equally familiar with Cuban reality of the period, might have placed more emphasis on the gangsterism of certain student leaders at the university, or on the election of 1948. Similarly it may be possible to find some discrepancies in Manet's many allusions to actual happenings. For example, the novel refers to Eddy Chibás's on-air suicide in 1948, when in fact he killed himself in 1951 (Thomas 770). But few readers of the novel, particularly in French, will note such minor errors or even be able to distinguish between real and invented names. The relative accuracy of the historical backdrop is thus irrelevant to understanding the novel's immediate success in France.

When Manet first planned the novel, he thought of blending fictional characters along with real people, including his mother, Communist leaders from the period, and a student named Fidel Castro. He later opted for a greater degree of fictionalization and decided to replace Fidel Castro with Manuel ("Manu") Mas Fortin, a fictional character based on the real-life Luis Mas Martin; similarly the character named Marcos Felipe Ramírez, an influential Communist professor, was inspired by Carlos Rafael Rodríguez. In Hugh Thomas's massive history of Cuba, Rodríguez receives numerous citations but Mas Martin rates only two passing references.

other first-person novels, there is at times a deliberate ironic distancing from the narrated self. Thus the lonely fifteen-year-old protagonist shows himself confiding his innermost thoughts to his best listener: Senta's three-year-old daughter. Although the narrator's maturation process is reflected in the subsequent substitution of older companions, he is always more guarded and self-conscious with Lohengrin, his friend from a wealthy German-Jewish family that fled from the Holocaust, and even somewhat so with his lover Gipsie, than with the little, nonjudgmental girl. To Lohengrin, for reasons that the narrator says he cannot explain, he can never confess his own Jewish ancestry. Only with Hanna does he find himself free to talk about his real feelings toward his family and even his ethnicity: "And there I was, talking to Hanna as I have never talked to anyone" (270).

Pancrazi affirms that *L'Ile du lézard vert* avoids becoming erotic pulp fiction because of its serious theme of identity, not only of the adolescent narrator's malaise but of all those who find themselves exiled within Cuba: "The text branches out into a series of fictions of self, of mini-novels about their origins to which the characters resort because Cuba is a revolving mirror, incapable of giving back to them a fixed image of themselves" (Pancrazi 1992). He refers specifically to the narrator's mother and to Gipsie, whose first-person accounts are set off from the main narration by italics. His observation could be extended as well to Lohengrin: the narrator's friend eventually admits that his suave exterior and clandestine commitment to the Communist Party conceal his anguished identity as the Jewish Jacobo. Several of the principal characters are either not native-born Cubans or are of mixed ancestry. Luis Wong, the Haitian Senta's Chinese husband, theorizes that the island would be a veritable paradise were it not at the center of the Caribbean, making it "a bridge, a stopping-off place" (28). Wong's comments introduce the important theme of Cuban geography, history, and ethnic diversity but other characters—such as the anticommunist professor Guillermo Marsac, the journalist Nelson Mendès, and Nelson's nymphomaniac girlfriend Sylvia—also have reason to ask themselves who they are. The identity questions and interpersonal conflicts that inform the various characters' psychological problems are in fact universal.

On the one hand *L'Ile du lézard vert* reflects identity problems that face many young people; on the other it plays out adolescent male fantasies with Hollywood flair. Our hero, in a kind of Clark Kent conversion, is a mild-mannered, bespectacled fifteen-year-old who worries about what to wear and feels ill at ease when he enters a class party; yet he succeeds in passing for several years older than he really is and suddenly becomes the protagonist of adventures ranging from the erotic to scenes out of spy films. The extended interlude with Gipsie begins in her red Porsche convertible and moves to her high-rise apartment with its breathtaking view of Havana, her impressive library, and her fabulous collection of records. In the later romance, Hanna's equally luxurious surroundings include her music corner with its white grand piano and her separate cottage, where the narrator joins her for their trysts. These personal exploits are crosscut with the narrator's political involvement. The Communist student conspiracy takes him on high-speed rides in convertibles, to posh ocean-view restaurants, seamy bars, and the famed Tropicana, and to the Hollywood-inspired mansion of the Tropicana's titillating star dancers. The picture we receive of Cuba at the end of the 1940s is that of a violent and sexy culture: one that gives rise to corrupt politicians and revolutionary movements, as well as to the homicide-suicide of the narrator's journalist friend and his ill-fated love.

Hollywood sensationalism is mediated by the narrator's irony. As Pancrazi suggests, "he is quick to smile internally at Manuel's obsession with secrecy, and his way of surrounding himself in mystery" (Pancrazi 1992). The narrator distances himself from the conspiracy in which he participates, mocking the action even as he recounts how he obediently takes circuitous routes and multiple rides on the Havana buses he detests in order to throw off anyone who might be following him. During the elaborate conspiracy against Manu's nemesis, the conservative professor Guillermo Marsac, the narrator suddenly converts the whole affair into a stock soap opera scenario (324). He allows the reader to laugh not only at Manu's plotting but also at himself. The ambience of Cuba is steamy not just because of its flamboyant eroticism but because of its tropical climate. The narrator's preoccupation with his appearance becomes a comic leitmotif of the novel: he frequently debates what to wear but inevitably finds himself sweaty and bedraggled while his father, Lohengrin, and Manu manage to remain cool and elegant in their impeccable white clothes. Preparing for his exciting position as cultural affairs writer for his father's newspaper, he describes in detail how he packs all the things he will need for his desk at the office: writing supplies, books to read, handkerchiefs, cologne, photographs of his mother, Gipsie, and his favorite film stars (183). By morning's end, he discovers that there is no desk; his father intends for him to freelance from home. Throughout the novel there are similar scenes in which the narrator subverts his idealized or theatricalized self-image.

The self-mocking tone prevents the narrator from becoming an exaggeratedly romantic figure far removed from the present or remembered reality of his readers. His disillusionment with Manu's conspiracy and his sensitivity toward others—including the anticommunist professor that Manu sets out to blackmail and discredit—likewise make him a more likable character. He attempts to understand others rather than accept an "us and them" mentality. He is still prone to his own kind of unrealistic romanticism: thus he calls Hanna and proposes that they go off to Israel to work unselfishly in a kibbutz even as the young woman eagerly prepares to fulfill her dream of studying piano in Paris. At seventeen the narrator may declare that his adolescence has died along with his friend, but its demise has not yet brought him to full maturity. Manet's young readers in France can no doubt identify as well with the narrator's uncertain future.

In the trajectory of his novel, from the 1960 *Les Etrangers dans la ville* to the 1992 *L'Ile du lézard vert*, Manet has retained a kind of popular, cinematographic style that emphasizes movement and setting. His fiction has evolved from an external third-person narrator who does not reveal the characters' inner worlds to a first-person narrator who provides a complete and convincing self-portrait. In *La Mauresque*, the narrator provides a relatively superficial image in a predominantly comic tone. In *L'Ile du lézard vert*, Manet has not lost either his humorous touch or his ability to capture the sociological background in detail. The salient feature of his culminating work to date, however, is its compelling and probing portrait of a Cuban author as a young man.

Habanera: Cuba in the 1950s

In some ways, *Habanera* is a continuation of *L'Ile du lézard vert*; in a 1994 interview with Jean-Rémi Barland, Manet states that he had unintentionally ended up writing a trilogy on Cuba before the revolution. The action of *Habanera* begins shortly after the second novel ends, and the cinematic treatment of sociohistorical background remains in place. The youthful, intellectual protagonist has many personal traits in common with the previous narrator and lives similar adventures. As we shall see, certain thematic elements and structural strategies from the fictional autobiographies are repeated in the more recent work.

Habanera also differs from the earlier novels in significant ways. Here Manet returns to an omniscient third-person narrator, thereby sacrificing the self-effacing irony and much of the comic tone and psychological realism found in *La Mauresque* and *L'Ile du lézard vert*. The first-person narrator, who shared Manet's experiences growing up in Cuba, is replaced by a main character who is Italian: Count Mario Versini Della Porta. The fictional Mario reverses the transatlantic crossing of the real Eduardo Manet; he arrives in the Caribbean island from Europe at the same moment in time that Manet, along with central figures in *Les Etrangers dans la ville* and *L'Ile du lézard vert*, left Cuba for France. Perhaps because the events described in *Habanera* are farther removed from the author's life, they sometimes have less of a ring of authenticity. Manet affirms that his point of departure is always reality, "and the memory of people I've known" (interview, Barland). The novel is laced with direct references to real people, ranging from cultural icons—actress Antonia Rey, ballerina Alicia Alonso, writer Alejo Carpentier—to political figures, including "a certain Fidel" (245). No doubt it likewise offers to the Cuban reader of Manet's generation some elements of the roman à clef.

Critical response to the novel in France was enthusiastic. Writing for *Le Nouvel Observateur*, Jean-François Josselin described the book as a "delightful read." In *Magazine Littéraire*, Leila Sebbar found Manet's characteristic style in his evocation of turbulent Havana with its "mixture of colors, classes and languages" and in his skillful blending of popular and political fiction. Jean-François Cerf of *Cooperation* identified Manet's warm baroque style and sensual language with the purest tradition of the Latin American novel.

La Mauresque ends with the announced arrival of the narrator's uncles, who are seeking political exile in Cuba to escape from fascist Spain; earlier in the same novel, the narrator's liberal father had fled to Mexico because of repression in Cuba. Key characters in *L'Ile du lézard vert* have taken refuge in Cuba to escape Nazi persecution; at the closing pages, the narrator is headed to voluntary exile in Europe. In the third work, the theme of exile appears at both beginning and end. Present in all three novels is a background of political turbulence, violent repression of dissent, and the resulting mass displacement of people. The disastrous impact of fascist governments in Europe and military strongmen in Latin America underscores many of Manet's narrative and dramatic works.

In *Habanera*, Mario's wealthy, aristocratic father allies himself with Mussolini; at the end of World War II, he seeks safety in Geneva. Cuba, where Mario's Uncle Arsenio lives, is another possible safe haven, but Mario's mother had lost all contact with her brother years before. Repeating Soledad's story in *La Mauresque*, Arsenio was disowned by his family in Italy because of his unorthodox romance with a Cuban. After his parents' deaths, Mario elects to go to Havana to seek his uncle but at the novel's conclusion, following the military coup and his inadvertent collaboration with the dissidents, he is forced to flee to Mexico. *Habanera*'s final image is that of a ship leaving Cuba.[6]

Habanera is narrated in Manet's usual cinematic style. The novel begins in 1951 in a Geneva cemetery, where the twenty-one-year-old Mario is saying good-bye to his parents' graves. This romantic scene cuts to flashbacks of his childhood in Mussolini's Italy and conflicts with his domineering, fascist father; the sensitive little boy and his mother had found a sympathetic friend in the boy's tutor, Danilo Millanti, but reluctantly had gone into exile with the count. A temporal ellipsis takes us to Geneva and the night of the father's suicide.[7] Returning to the fictional present, albeit with occasional flashbacks, the narration shifts to Mario's travels: by train to Paris, ocean liner to New York, and plane to Havana. Once he begins his love affair with Sonia Suez, famous Cuban nightclub singer and star of Mexican cinema, Mario also spends idyllic interludes in Florida. Using the temporal and spatial fluidity characteristic of film, Manet interpolates the sequences that recall the development of the romance into the lovers' automobile drive down the two-lane Overseas Highway to the Keys: "[Mario] closes his eyes in order to let roll the film of the evening that had so definitively changed his life" (205). A somewhat related filmic strategy is used in a dialogue between Mario and his Cuban friend Carmen; their conversation about Carmen's matrimonial problems is intertwined with a street scene and with the wiggling of

---

6. In his 1996 interview with Jason Weiss, Manet stated that, like Mario, he left Cuba in 1952, following the Batista coup. In this case, I believe that life is imitating art, that Manet's memory was temporarily blurred by interference from the recent novel.

7. The closeness of Mario to his mother and the relative absence of his father from his daily life obviously recalls the family relationships in the autobiographical novels. The now reclusive father chooses to commit suicide on the evening of his sixty-fifth birthday. His failure to appear at the celebration his wife has planned partially repeats the situation of the boy's disastrous birthday party that opens *L'Ile du lézard vert*. Another familiar factor here in the disharmony between father and mother is a wide difference in age. (Manet has observed that when he was born his own father was already "old" [interview, Weiss].)

Carmen's little girl whom Mario carries as they walk. Throughout the novel, dialogue and exposition are frequently juxtaposed with action to create the impression of moving images.

As was true in *Les Etrangers dans la ville*, the realistic space of *Habanera* fluctuates between interior and exterior scenes, and the novelistic world is peopled by numerous secondary characters. To a greater extent than in the early novel, which lacked a central character, these minor figures in *Habanera* disappear after their episode has passed. The reference to Paris is brief, but the New York sequences include a penthouse party on Fifth Avenue, a car ride through Manhattan streets, and a visit to Spanish Harlem. Havana is evoked in detail as Mario, the objective outsider, becomes familiar with streets, hotels, restaurants, nightclubs, beaches, luxurious homes, popular neighborhoods, and shantytowns. The description of a *solar* (tenement house) reminds us that Manet himself made a movie with that background in the 1960s. Free to let his memory go on location, Manet re-creates the vibrant Cuban city's many contrasts; in this respect, his verbal images are far more effective than the visual ones in the 1980 movie *Havana*, in which a similar blend of romantic and political action is played against the static background of borrowed stills of Cuban landmarks.[8] Less convincing in the novel are the story of an alcoholic Swedish painter who lives in the Florida Keys and Manet's evocation of that locale; he repeatedly refers to Tampa, which is far away from the Keys, when he apparently means the city of Key West.

A number of scenes in the novel utilize familiar filmic codes. Examples range from Mario's placing of flowers on his mother's grave, to the Dobermans that armed guards unleash under the glare of spotlights

---

8. Directed by Sidney Pollack, starring Robert Redford, and inspired by *Casablanca*, *Havana* is set in 1958, on the eve of Castro's revolution against Batista. Although Manet's *Habanera* focuses on the beginning of the decade, at the time of Batista's military coup, the sociopolitical background is comparable in its depiction of a clandestine plot against a repressive regime. Manet has seen the Hollywood film and considers it "dreadful" (interview, 5 June 1995); his assessment is one shared by many critics. It is perhaps inevitable that the stories have elements in common: an outsider comes to Cuba at a moment of impending political strife; he becomes friends with a revolutionary leader who is part of a privileged family; despite the revolutionary's influential connections, he is captured and tortured. The points in common are superficial. Mario bears no resemblance to Redford's role as a gambler and his romance with Sonia does not repeat the *Casablanca* love triangle that is central to the movie.

The subject of *Havana* continues to be of interest. Cuban American actor Andy García has recently announced plans to produce another "Cuban *Casablanca*," also set in prerevolutionary Havana. The film, in which he would star, will be titled *The Lost City* (Zaslow).

when he first tries to enter his uncle's estate in a friend's car, to Sonia's suddenly being surrounded by reporters when she arrives unannounced at the Havana airport. These sequences readily establish a young man's feelings as he embarks on his voyage of adventure, the viciousness required to defend capitalist privilege, and a movie star's celebrity status. Another brief sequence with filmic overtones takes place at the Shanghai burlesque house. As outlandish as anything invented by Spanish film director Pedro Almodóvar, the show represents a convent where, from economic necessity, flabby, middle-aged nuns perform striptease from midnight to five. This grotesque image is consistent with Manet's overall picture of a society where, according to Uncle Arsenio, "Sex is the country's major industry"; since Cuba has always been a brothel, why not turn the national activity into profit-making ventures? (133).

References to Hollywood movies and movie stars are as prevalent in *Habanera* as they were in the fictional autobiographies. A guest at the penthouse party wears makeup like Lucille Ball's (42); Mario registers at the Hotel Nacional, where Barbara Stanwyck and Robert Taylor stayed in the bridal suite (97); Uncle Arsenio bears a striking resemblance to Orson Welles, specifically in his role as Harry Lime in *The Third Man* (159); in Florida, Mario and Sonia see *Affair in Trinidad*, starring Rita Hayworth (222).[9] In *Habanera*, Manet additionally exploits the metafictional potential of having a movie star as a character. Mario sees Sonia on screen and those performances become movies-within-the-text. When he is with her later, he "sees double".[10] He has difficulty separating the real Sonia from the role he has seen her play; the memory of a character who awakens men's brutal passions paralyzes him (209). Sonia's profession leads to a discussion of cinema in terms both of product and process. Other characters comment on her movies, and she talks about the problems she confronts in the movie world of Mexico.

When Barland asked Manet to define the protagonist of *Habanera*, the author responded that he felt quite close to the epicurean Mario. The intertextual reference no doubt escapes most readers, but that closeness

---

9. *Affair in Trinidad* was released in 1952 and thus correctly coincides with Batista's coup. For movie buffs, films mentioned in the novel may have special meaning. *The Third Man* (1949) takes place in the politically volatile, morally corrupt atmosphere of postwar Vienna. In *Affair in Trinidad*, Rita Hayworth plays a singer; the character in the movie thus mirrors the character in Manet's novel.

10. For Hornby, "seeing double" is one of the requisites for fully developed metadrama. Typically, the spectator sees the character but is simultaneously reminded of the actor playing the character; here Manet has reversed the pattern.

is revealed directly in the novel when Mario writes a story called *Scherzo*; the synopsis parallels the young Manet's short play of the same title. Moreover, Mario, like Manet, has studied Italian language and literature, loves art and music, and is a polyglot. In his interview, the author also stated that his character displays candor bordering on idealism and that he easily falls in love. One might add that he also readily inspires love in the women he meets. If the narrator of *L'Ile du lézard vert* experienced adolescent male fantasies with Hollywood flair, Mario surely is the extension into early adulthood of that same tendency.

In the flashbacks of Mario's adolescence in Geneva, there is a slight hint of the self-deprecatory irony that characterized the narrator of the fictional autobiographies. During a period of mysticism, Mario receives nocturnal visits from God. Tricked by a friend, he finds himself trapped into accompanying three ridiculous, middle-aged American women tourists. But these episodes serve to lead into Mario's amorous adventures. God's nightly visits are replaced by those of an attractive twenty-year-old maid who first comes to the boy's room because she thinks she has heard him call out. An equally attractive young woman is traveling with the caricatured older tourists. She is saving her virginity for her impending marriage, but the romantic interlude is otherwise enjoyable enough that Mario goes to Havana via New York just to see her again. In Cuba, he and Carmen may resist the desire they feel for one another out of loyalty to her husband, but Mario is being provided with the full services of a passionate mulatto maid at his uncle's estate. Soon he meets the much celebrated Sonia Suez, sex symbol of the Mexican screen and the Cuban stage, who finds the younger, intellectual Mario irresistible. She has known many men but it is with Mario that she finds true love. The relationship of Mario with the older and more sophisticated Sonia recalls counterparts in *Un Cri sur le rivage* and *L'Ile du lézard vert*.

Mario, like the younger narrator of *L'Ile du lézard vert*, may sometimes be self-conscious and feel that he has chosen the wrong clothing for a social event, but he is independently wealthy, well read and well traveled. His fabulously rich uncle is primarily interested in making money and wielding power, but he readily gives Mario the opportunity to found a high-class Latin American art and culture magazine and provides him with a luxurious suite of offices for that purpose. What more could a twenty-one-year-old ask than to edit his own glossy international magazine and be the lover of a famous movie star?

Speaking of *La Mauresque*, Michèle Gazier observed that the novel is a melding of three stories. The same observation might be made of *Habanera*, which similarly interweaves multiple strands: the exotic background of Cuba, the romantic life of the protagonist, and the political intrigues of his friends.

In *Habanera*, Mario is vaguely aware of his friends' clandestine activities but is not so directly involved as is the narrator of the previous novel. Like the child in *La Mauresque* who had no idea Myrna was smuggling arms in the car in which he is riding, Mario is stunned to learn that his editorial assistant Alfonsina has her trunk filled with weapons when she picks him up at the airport. He knows that Alfonsina, a follower of the late Eddy Chibas, is playing a dangerous game, and he lets Ruben use a private area in his offices, no questions asked, but yet he remains somewhat oblivious to what is going on. Similarly he finds his uncle an ambiguous figure whose sphere of influence he enters determined "to avoid getting his hands dirty" (137). Remaining isolated from the political power plays is impossible. His departure at the end is again precipitated by a friend's death, but this time murder stems, not from amorous passion, but from the climate of repression.

Mario meets Ruben Ruiz Aldana, a young Cuban doctor, at the penthouse party in New York. Even before Batista's takeover, Ruben is a radical anarchist who rejects his family's affluence in favor of helping the poor: "I am at war with my family, my social milieu, and a good half of the island's inhabitants" (48). Through Ruben, Mario meets Arturo, a Communist lawyer. Lifelong friends, Ruben and Arturo come from opposite backgrounds; Arturo's black mother was a servant for Ruben's white family. Carmen, Arturo's seamstress wife, would prefer that he put his family ahead of his cause, but Carmen's sister Alicia, a nurse, willingly works by Ruben's side. At the time of the military takeover, Ruben and Arturo disagree on the proper response. Ruben favors violence and ultimately is tortured to death by Batista's police after he helps arrange the assassination of a black senator who is one of Arsenio's business partners.

Centering on these four characters and their acquaintances, Manet introduces a series of dialogues on political tensions in Cuba. His cinematic narrative style further visualizes the causes of unrest. The abject poverty of those whom Ruben and Arturo want to help and the struggle of the working class represented by Carmen and Alicia's family stand in vivid contrast with the luxury enjoyed by Uncle Arsenio, a man some refer to as a "tropical Machiavelli" (239). Adviser to Batista and an admitted admirer of Mussolini, Hitler, and Franco, Arsenio affirms that

"Italians, like Cubans, need authority"; they must be controlled with an iron hand (256). Mario, the romantic, would prefer to remain aloof from politics, but it is clear within the novel that exploitative capitalism and military dictatorship have allied themselves against the Cuban people.

Arsenio scoffs at the possibility that leftist radicals could ever destroy his kind of island paradise. As he asks a Party leader, "Tell me, Lázaro, do you sincerely believe that one could ever see a communist regime two steps away from Florida?" Lázaro laughs and admits that he does not think so, but he says that will not prevent him and his comrades from giving the Americans and the Cuban capitalists a hard time for a good part of the twentieth century (136). The historical irony of Arsenio's position and Lázaro's answer is one of the factors contributing to the appeal of Manet's novel. His French readers are curious to learn more about Cuba, how Castro rose to power, and how he has managed to stay there for forty years. Manet's trilogy, by presenting an overview of prerevolutionary Cuba, suggests some partial answers.

Rhapsodie cubaine: A City in Exile

A chronological gap between *Habanera* and *Rhapsodie cubaine* allows Manet largely to skip over the Batista military dictatorship of the 1950s. The action of *Habanera* ends in 1952; the fictional present at the beginning of *Rhapsodie cubaine* is January 1960, a year after Castro came into power. Despite the negative aspects Manet reveals of Cuba in the decades preceding the Batista takeover, he considers the period recounted in his autobiographical novels and *Habanera* to be one of relative hope: "Cuba was a sort of limping democracy where everything was still possible. Batista's coup d'état took us back a century" (qtd. in Larraburu). Implicitly, the extreme repression of the Batista regime created the conditions that would lead to the Cuban Revolution and its concomitant displacement of a large percentage of the Cuban people.

While the first three novels in the cycle focus only peripherally on the subject, exile becomes the central theme of *Rhapsodie cubaine*. Manet has frequently pointed out that Cuba was itself a melting pot for people from Europe, Africa, Asia, and the Americas, some of whom had arrived there as voluntary exiles from other places; in this latest work of fiction, most of his characters are Cuban residents who find themselves forced to take refuge in the United States. Some chapters are set in Havana and Boston, but the action takes place primarily in and around Miami, the city referred to in Manet's working title: *Une Ville en exile*. (The phrase appears in the novel on page 229.) The protagonist, Julian Sargats, ever conscious of his Cuban origins and his biculturalism, struggles to achieve a sense of self-identity against the background of family and national conflict. As a Harvard student in 1972, he ponders how he can explain himself to his Bostonian friend, Louis Duverne-Stone: "How can I tell him that I . . . am double, that I am divided between two languages, two minds, two ways of reasoning, that my exile is permanent, that I live up here and down there, that I belong to two cultures. Seaweed floating along the Charles River. A strange species that cannot take root anywhere" (60). In Boston, he feels out of place, but when he returns to Miami, he is "doubly exiled" (165). The review of the novel that appears in *Le Monde* is appropriately, and poetically, labeled "L'adieu aux racines" (A farewell to roots; Pancrazi 1996).

As the years pass, both Julian and Louis will come to view related questions of biculturalism from a more positive stance. Louis emigrates to Japan; when he returns briefly in 1985 on a family trip, he wants his children, Louis-Minoru and Machiko-Laureen, to understand the value of multiculturalism in the United States:

> I want them to realize that in Miami they speak more Spanish than English; that there are more red-, brown- and black-skinned people than white ones. That's what I would like them to remember from their visit to the United States. Because I'm convinced that the future of the world depends on racial mixing. The possibilities for feeling and reacting are doubled. Like your dual capacity for understanding Hispanic character and American mentality. I see racial mixing in America as the survival of our democracy and the future of the planet. (274)

The positive assessment of multiculturalism in the novel nevertheless remains subordinate to the central theme of exile. Véronique Petit correctly observes that the subject of exile in *Rhapsodie cubaine* has universal implications in our contemporary world: "The novel's broad perspective is especially impressive in a time when exile has become the lot of vast numbers of men and women all over the planet: Manet takes on the thorny question of integration and its price. What do we do with our roots, our past, our culture, in the search to be free on different soil? How do we become another without betraying who we are?" (20). Manet's work voices that universal aspect explicitly. Julian, now a professor at Florida International University in 1983, looks at a documentary film on the Cuban emigration from Mariel and prepares his lecture notes. He will point out to his students, with examples, that the previous seven decades of the twentieth century have been characterized by "a long succession of ruptures and separations" (247).

The film within the text is only one of Manet's familiar cinematic techniques repeated in this latest novel. As the reviewer for *Le Journal du Dimanche* astutely observes, the opening pages reveal the author's considerable talents as a scriptwriter: Julian sees his last images of Cuba through the window of his father's moving Cadillac (Sauvage). In the mode of Hollywood movies, there are sequences set in cabarets and elegant restaurants or at fashion shows. The action shifts from Havana to Boston, from Miami to the Florida Keys and Disney World, or to Prague, always with the accompanying background scenery. Often there is a suggested sound track: action is associated with specific characters' favorite music. Once again, various characters try to emulate movie stars: Julian's grandmother thinks she looks like Barbara Stanwyck (18), his mother dresses à la Lana Turner (19), and Julian, like the child narrator of *La Mauresque*, plasters his hair in the style of George Raft (68). In Julian's imagination, Che Guevara is a figure surrounded by women guerrillas, all of whom look like Ingrid Bergman in *For Whom the Bell Tolls* (36).

The cinematic devices remain constant, but in terms of structure, the episodic *Rhapsodie cubaine* differs from Manet's previously published novels. In its sweeping view of thirty-five years in the life of Julian, of his family and acquaintances, and of the Cuban American community, it recalls *Nunzietta*, the projected saga of an Italian family over a period including the two world wars. Moreover, *Rhapsodie cubaine* sets aside the unified narrative perspective of the preceding works: first person in *L'Ile du lézard vert* and third person in *Habanera*. In the earlier *La Mauresque*, an objective narrator from time to time interrupts the first-person account to provide digressions about Cuban culture and history. In *Rhapsodie cubaine* there is a more pervasive and sophisticated interweaving of voices: Julian's memories and personal journal, marked by italics, alternate with the dominant third-person narration. Thus the narration is both external, told in an objective third person, and internal, relayed through the subjective voice of Julian. The first-person sections often break with linear time; Julian's thoughts may return to moments in the past or he may reread his notebook entries from previous years. As a result, there is greater temporal fluidity and hence a greater emphasis on how the past influences the present.

The use of the first person here does not indicate a return to the comic tone prevalent in the fictional autobiographies; there is no self-betraying irony or self-deprecatory humor in Julian's comments about himself, and even potentially comic figures—such as the militant anti-Castro Rudi, who is simultaneously the drag queen Ruby and the doctor Rodolfo—are treated seriously.[11] The critic for *Le Figaro Littéraire* describes this "classic" novel's tone as "muted": the protagonist's life is told "with a slow, underlying sadness" (Saint Vincent). In keeping with this tone, the flamboyant eroticism of the earlier novels has also disappeared.

In discussing the alternation between "I" and "he" to interviewer Emmanuelle Leroyer, Manet confessed his admiration for the French New Novel of such writers as Nathalie Sarraute and Alain Robbe-Grillet, and his interest in the associated debate of the 1950s about whether the author could best disappear behind a first- or third-person narrator. But he affirmed that his own approach is different: "There are moments when I feel like a movie camera and others when I feel the need to use the first person" (interview, Leroyer 13). Manet's use of "I" is not so much a way of disappearing as author, as he believes was true of the New Novel, but rather of giving expression to his own anxieties. Indeed, he affirms that in writing *Rhapsodie cubaine* it was likewise not his main intent to seek his country: "It's more a need to settle accounts with myself, my past, my family. . . . In the Cuban situation, I speak of myself, my childhood, my adolescence" (interview, Leroyer 12).

On the surface level, Julian Sargats is not a continuation of the unnamed, quasi-autobiographical, first-person narrator of *La Mauresque* and *L'Ile du lézard vert*. Nor does he repeat the outward signs of identity of the Italian character at the center of *Habanera*. Certainly Julian's biog-

---

11. I have not asked Manet whether he agrees with me about the relative absence of humor in *Habanera* and *Rhapsodie cubaine* and, if so, to what he would attribute it. It is my working theory that in telling and retelling, to himself or to others, the anecdotes taken more or less directly from his own life, he has gradually shifted them to the comic mode—a strategy not uncommon among stand-up comedians or a playwright of comic bent such as Neil Simon. In explaining his reasons for writing *L'Ile du lézard vert*, he has stated: "I have so many funny memories about my adolescence in Cuba" (interview, Weiss; translated Weiss). This crystallization process has not taken place with the stories of his fictional characters, whose painful experiences are presented straight.

raphy does not coincide with that of Manet. The thirteen-year-old protagonist of *Rhapsodie cubaine* unwillingly leaves Cuba in 1960 at the time that the adult Eduardo Manet was returning to the island after a decade's absence. Julian, educated at Harvard, becomes a professor of Spanish literature and an editor who must deal with the internal conflicts of the Cuban American community on a daily basis—even if he feels estranged from that community. Eduardo Manet, educated in France and Italy, is a playwright and novelist who can witness that community only from the outside. When asked if this latest novel is autobiographical, Manet responds that he has neither lived in Miami nor wants to, but that, as Jean-Paul Sartre once said, if he could not write, he would go mad (interview, Goulet).[12] In a separate interview, he quotes Sartre in a slightly different way: "Thanks to my books, I don't need a psychoanalyst" (interview, Leroyer 12). Manet's words imply that, even if he does not share Julian's life experiences exactly, he and his character may be haunted by the same demons.

In *La Mauresque*, Manet interpolated short, factual lessons on Cuban culture. In *Rhapsodie cubaine*, there are digressions on the history of Boston and of the Everglades that reflect Julian's knowledge—and the author's research. On the other hand, at times superficial details of *Rhapsodie cubaine* seem anachronistic or may otherwise puzzle the reader. In the first line of the novel, Manet confuses models of Cadillac and Lincoln, creating a nonexistent Cadillac Continental. In 1940 Edelmiro Sargats and his future wife, Magdalena, listen to a radio program dedicated to Nat King Cole, an artist whose first important recording hits, "The Christmas Song" and "Route 66," were not released until 1946. In the late 1970s, Julian makes the transition from teacher in a private school to university professor without any reference to his obtaining either a master's or doctoral degree, normal requisites for a college position. Such points, however, are minor. What Manet does convey masterfully is the sensitive Julian's inner world: his sense of loss and solitude, his dismay at what his parents and sister have become, the breakdown of his marriage to Emma, whose intransigent, anti-Castro stance never mellows.

---

12. Manet speaks of Miami at greater length in his interview with Jason Weiss. He affirms that he has visited the city briefly on an almost yearly basis but is dismayed by the prevalent anti-Castro fervor: "I love the place, but I don't like the people. I have some good Cuban friends in Miami who are very close. But this strange feeling of Cuba before the Revolution, and Cuba after Fidel. Fidel is everywhere, every day in Miami, they are crazy!" (interview, Weiss; translated Weiss). Manet's attitude is mirrored by Julian's in the novel.

There may be a few anachronisms in the initial narration of past events, but there is no question about the depth of the unhappy teenager's feelings as he sits in the plane to Miami with his parents and remembers his beloved grandmother who has recently died or the island he leaves behind. The authentic feeling behind his words "Je n'ai rien. Ni pays, ni personne. Rien" (I have nothing. No country, nobody. Nothing; 48) overshadows the occasional narrative lapses and reveals Manet's empathy with his character.

Setting aside the question of when and where the action of the several novels takes place, the reader may well discover that a similar protagonist with a similar, dysfunctional family is repeated throughout the cycle. At the very least, Manet's central character has unresolved conflicts relating to an absent or neglectful father. Edelmiro, a self-made, politically conservative capitalist who came to Cuba from the Spanish region of Aragon, in some ways more closely resembles Mario's Uncle Arsenio of *Habanera* than the liberal, intellectual father in *La Mauresque* and *L'Ile du lézard vert*. The latter's greatest defect, the primary cause of the young protagonist's angst, is his quasi polygamy. With Edelmiro, there is no hint of multiple *queridas*; as a leader of the counterrevolutionaries in Miami, Edelmiro is more interested in making war, not love. In parallel to the fictional autobiographies and *Habanera*, Julian's alienation from his father underscores the novel nonetheless.

From the opening pages of *Rhapsodie cubaine*, Julian reveals that he long ago took sides with his grandmother Rita in her ongoing hostility toward his father. On the way to the airport, he contemplates jumping out of the Cadillac and seeking refuge with his literature teacher, Luis Armando Argüelles. Like Mario in *Habanera*, the boy feels closer kinship to the mentor who is left behind than to the father whom he accompanies into exile. Julian develops a love for the sixteenth-century Spanish mystics, Saint Teresa of Avila and Saint John of the Cross, the writers most admired by Argüelles. He never feels sympathy for his father's business or political ventures, and certainly not for his anti-Castro militia that trains in the Everglades or the armada he later funds for a prospective invasion of the island. During a sabbatical in Europe in 1985, Julian makes a trip to Aragon; upon his return, he goes to see Edelmiro in a nursing home where the mute old man now sits, motionless, in a wheelchair. Only then, when reconciliation is no longer possible, is Julian able to express the feelings he has long suppressed: "I must tell you, Father, that in Jaca, standing before the tombs of my Spanish ancestors, for the first time I realized that I cordially disliked you throughout my childhood. Because you were always distant, inaccessible, and I felt that I wasn't loved. My hatred was a sort of defense, a shield against you. Today I know that I was unjust, Father, because I never made the effort to understand you. That's what I wanted to tell you" (268).

Another basic cause of the protagonist's unhappiness in all four novels relates to the unharmonious relationship between father and mother. The child narrator in *La Mauresque* is more and more affected by his mother's screaming and crying; his teenaged counterpart in the sequel novel is deeply anguished as the mother's emotional state degenerates into irrationality. In *Habanera* and *Rhapsodie cubaine*, the underlying marital problem is incompatibility rather than infidelity, but the son is equally deprived of a normal family. Magdalena, in the culminating novel of the series, represents the extreme case. Long before they leave Cuba, she is an alcoholic; Julian recalls that his tenth birthday present from her is a nocturnal confession of why she drinks: "From that moment I am in possession of a precious secret, that only I know: Magdalena doesn't drink as a vice or out of despair but to recover joy, that joy that she must have felt in her childhood and adolescence and that she lost along the way, for reasons I don't know" (25). Edelmiro wants more children; without his knowledge, Magdalena has her tubes tied. When Julian is away at Harvard, she moves into a posh rehabilitation facility where she squanders a fortune on clothes, jewelry, and gigolos; she replaces alcohol with cocaine.[13] In a last phase of her extreme alienation from husband and community, she joins a religious sect, appropriating much of Edelmiro's remaining fortune to the cause, becomes a missionary and then disappears somewhere in the Philippines. Rita's intuition had no doubt been correct when she vigorously opposed Magdalena's marriage to Edelmiro.[14]

There is an obvious conclusion if we take literally Manet's quoted comment on writing as psychoanalysis. Over the course of the Cuban novels, whether overtly autobiographical or not, the author appears to

---

13. At the rehabilitation center, Magdalena has a German chauffeur, Fritz. She idealizes the blond young man's flight from East Germany and his future plans, while Julian characterizes him as a "rejeton de nazi" (a Nazi kid; 78). The passing reference recalls the figure of Hans in *Lady Strass*, thus linking the marital disharmony of the Cuban novels to that play. It is worth noting that *Lady Strass* has been staged in several countries in the 1990s, so the earlier text would have been fresh in Manet's mind as he worked on *Rhapsodie cubaine*.

14. The mother in *Rhapsodie cubaine* freely chose to marry Edelmiro, but her unhappy marriage, like that of the mother in *Habanera*, recalls the related story of Raquel in Manet's *Mendoza, en Argentine* . . . , a tragedy written a decade earlier than these novels.

have been working through a lingering resentment of his father. In *Rhapsodie cubaine*, for the first time, the protagonist seeks reconciliation with the father. Throughout the novels, the protagonist has also explored the impact on his childhood of his mother's unhappiness. In *Rhapsodie cubaine*, perhaps as a result of his greater effort to understand the father, he also becomes more judgmental with respect to the mother. The surface details may not always correlate with Manet's own parents, but the repeated deep structure of the story is inescapable to any reader of the cycle of Cuban novels.

Equally conspicuous are the aesthetic interests and dreams that Julian shares with Manet's other protagonists. Like his author, Julian has written poetry and loves literature and music. Manet has stated that he feels quite close to the epicurean Mario of *Habanera*. He doubtless feels equally close to Julian, in that Mario and Julian are soul mates. Both come from wealthy families and appreciate fine food and beautiful objects. Thanks to the intervention of wealthy acquaintances (Mario's Uncle Arsenio and Julian's friend Louis), both become editors of high-class literary publications that they run from elegant high-rise offices.

Although other characters and situations in *Rhapsodie cubaine* are further removed from the earlier novels, some of them do reflect familiar elements. For example, Rita is the only grandmother figure in Manet's novels, but she incorporates certain typical motifs. Like the mother in *La Mauresque*, she is Andalusian. Recalling various characters in previous novels, she has been a famous singer and dancer. Through her, little Julian becomes acquainted with many aspects of Cuban life, including *santería* rituals. And with her, he learns to admire Fidel Castro. Castro's first Havana speech, when the dove perched on his shoulder, is an historic moment previously related in *Un Cri sur le rivage*. In *Rhapsodie cubaine*, the seemingly interminable but impassioned speech is viewed by an increasingly enthusiastic Julian, Magdalena, and Rita, who sit before the television set, snacking and drinking wine. "Upon his return, when Edelmiro Sargats found his wife, his son, and the Andalusian completely drunk, chanting in chorus the name of his hated enemy, he went over to the television set, picked it up, brandished it over his head, and smashed it on the floor with all his might" (39). Rita and her young grandson have been secret supporters of the revolution. The older woman's hostility toward her son-in-law thus comes to symbolize the political divisions within Cuba.

In *Rhapsodie cubaine*, Manet emphasizes brother-sister relationships for the first time. Julian's beautiful older sister, Gisela, also sides with the grandmother, but before the move to Miami, she elopes with an Argentinean dancer. The young boy is brokenhearted by what he perceives as her betrayal; he tears up all the photos that he had taken of her. Years later, when an overweight Gisela, now widowed, shows up in Miami with her brood of noisy sons, the Harvard student is initially repulsed by her. After they become friends again, Julian realizes that his nephews may have a Cuban mother and live in Miami, but they are Argentineans; even his sister has a nostalgic feeling for tango music. Eventually Gisela joins the sect with her mother and likewise disappears.

The Julian-Gisela relationship serves to reinforce the portrait of a dysfunctional family and, in a broader sense, to suggest the breakdown of the family in contemporary society. The relationship of Emma to her brother Ricardo bears a more compelling message with respect to the Cuban tragedy. For many readers, the greatest interest of *Rhapsodie cubaine* may lie in its representation of a divided people rather than in conflicts at the individual level.

Julian first sees Emma Álvarez Sierra in 1972 when she, her brother, and her mother are speakers at an anti-Castro rally. Emma's father, who had fallen out of favor with Castro, is serving a twenty-year prison sentence in Cuba and will not be released until 1983. Laura Sierra, dressed in widow's black, arouses the listeners' compassion, but it is the seventeen-year-old Emma whose sincerity holds the audience spellbound. She asserts that her father's tragedy is not his alone but "that of an entire people" (105). Emma herself, for the intensity of her feeling and single-minded dedication to her cause, is repeatedly compared to tragic heroines. Gisela says she is like Antigone (107). Other young Cubans may become Americanized, but they admire Emma for being "our tropical Joan of Arc" (120) and, in an allusion to Brecht, "our Saint Joan of the Stockyards" (234). After she has become a lawyer, Julian describes her in his journal: "Emma the passionate, Emma who brings about justice. She who makes the most recalcitrant judges smile at her youthful enthusiasm, her zeal, and her rebellion. She who unhesitantly knows where to find the boundary between Good and Evil" (187–88). Emma's intransigence has negative consequences. As Manet points out, it leads to the couple's divorce: "Because, what is the Cuban rhapsodie? Two people who love each other, who could be the most wonderful couple in the world, but she is very against Castro, militant, and he is a writer, a poet, he loves her and wants to be with her, and not with Castro everywhere" (interview, Weiss; translated Weiss). And it precipitates Ricardo's suicide after he confesses to his sister that he has been a double agent, working for Castro.

Rhapsodie cubaine is an ironic novel, not in the sense of the comic irony that pervades the autobiographical fictions, but in a more profound way. People are more complex than Emma's binary view of Good and Evil allows. Ricardo, who has been raised to see Castro as the enemy, is seduced into the Communist conspiracy through his love for Casilda, a beautiful, sophisticated and wealthy Bolivian. Casilda Linares Flores, reminiscent of Ruben in *Habanera*, has determined to use her privileged status for the good of the poor after confronting the ravages of poverty; as a mestizo, she also becomes increasingly conscious of her Indian roots. Emma's father, upon his release from Castro's prison, where he had gained serenity through reading Saint Teresa, refuses to join the anti-Castro cause; he retreats to the Everglades, becomes a naturalist, and, upon Laura's death, marries a young Seminole. Jerry Brown, the tough Vietnam War veteran who tries to turn the ragtag Cuban exiles into a real fighting force, writes poetry and feels genuine affection for the gay Rudi, whose romantic overtures he rejects.

Julian, as the most developed character in the novel, is even more complex. After the inevitable divorce, he spends lonely hours looking at videos of Emma and reliving his lost love. From the Florida Keys, he looks across longingly at his lost island. Only when he is free to return to Cuba will he also be able to free himself from Emma. The novel ends with the following poetic lines:

> L'aile bleue de la nuit répand son ombre sur la lagune.
> Perdu entre le ciel et la mer, un homme seul attend. (329)

> Night's blue wing spreads its shadow o'er the lagoon.
> Lost between sky and sea, a man waits alone.

On the individual level, that man is the protagonist, Julian Sargats. On the symbolic level, that man is any exile who will not find peace until he or she can set aside divisiveness and go home again.

4

Theater in Exile

PLAYS OF

ENTRAPMENT

AND ENCLOSURE

Eduardo Manet recalls that he began his second exile in Paris in 1968 with one suitcase, a teenaged son, and ten dollars in his pocket (interview, Mambrino 365), but that is only a superficial evaluation of his assets. From his previous years in France, he had numerous contacts, not the least of whom was his former teacher, the influential avant-garde director Roger Blin. He knew theater people in other countries as well; indeed, prior to the opening of *Les Nonnes*, he wrote and directed a production at L'Ecole National de Théâtre, the national theater school, in Montreal: *Helen viendra nous voir de Hollywood et nous lui ferons la plus belle des parties*. Unaware of Manet's works written in Spanish, David Bradby, a noted specialist in French theater, affirms that Manet "possessed a thorough grounding in theatre practice when he wrote his first play *Les Nonnes* in 1967" (Bradby 236). With the unexpected triumph of that first theatrical work in French, doors opened for the Cuban-born author, and, as Osvaldo Obregón notes, among French-language dramatists of Latin American origin, he soon became the one who has achieved the greatest audience and critical acclaim (Obregón 1983: 37). Among Manet's other intangible assets in 1968 one must include his knowledge of cinematic strategies, his multilingualism, his Latin American cultural heritage, and, albeit more indirectly, his experience as an exile.

What Is Cuban Theater?

In writing about Cuban theater in the United States, Luis González-Cruz and Francesca Colecchia contend that exile can actually enhance creativity. Writers by nature are always set apart like exiles "who view the world from their own individual and, therefore, unique perspective"; the further distancing that comes from living in a new land causes a deeper appraisal of the authors' circumstances and "heightens their awareness of their own identity" (4). In their survey of plays by some forty-five Cuban playwrights residing in the United States, González-Cruz and Colecchia observe that all of them "have a historical awareness as if all wished, or felt obligated, to leave a written account of their unique experience" (3); the plays in their anthology are actually more thematically diversified than such generalizations about Cuban theater in exile would lead one to expect. In her discussion of the stage in Miami, Maida Watson-Espener identifies two kinds of theater: Cuban American, which deals with the experiences of Cubans in the United States, and Cuban theater in exile, which maintains the preexile culture (34–35). She points out that her definitions parallel those of González Reigosa with his "frozen culture" of those idealizing the values of a pre-1959 Cuba and his "Cubish" for a Hispanic American culture that retains Hispanic values while confronting problems in American society (qtd. in Watson-Espener 36). With reference to Cuban American narrative and poetry, Silvia Burunat and Ofelia García similarly recognize only one theme: Cuban experience in Cuba or in the United States. The theme may take two forms: realistic, dealing with local situations in the island or in adaptation to the United States, or "mythical and universal, dealing with Cuban mythology in order to search for universal roots with which to transcend the crisis of displacement" (Burunat and García 11).

Several of Manet's novels readily fall into the pattern described by Burunat and García. Were *La Mauresque*, *L'Ile du lézard vert*, *Habanera*, and *Rhapsodie cubaine* available in English or Spanish, they would undoubtedly find a large readership among Cuban Americans. In *Habanera*, Manet even creates in the Italian Mario the perspective of an outsider in order to achieve the kind of distancing to which González-Cruz and Colecchia refer. In a direct way, Manet's Cuban identity and the experience of exile have informed his narrative, but the same does not hold true for his theater. When I first interviewed Manet in Paris in October 1987, I had not yet read all of his published plays. When I asked him if I would find Cuban elements in his theater, he assured me that I would not. And he did not mislead me. Prior to 1993, when he co-authored a satire of Fidel Castro, there were no obvious Cuban settings and characters in his plays.

Had Manet followed the thematic pattern at times associated with Cuban American theater, it is unlikely that he would have achieved the same success that he has on the French stage. The Cuban American playwright of greatest international stature is Maria Irene Fornes (b. 1930), who has resided in the United States for more than fifty years; her theater, written in English, reaches out beyond Latino circles. A concentration on historical and ethnic awareness can lead to a theater that is aimed at a limited audience, particularly if the plays are written in a minority language within the new country. In the United States, Cuban American playwrights may elect to write in Spanish or bilingually and yet reach an audience, for there is an active Hispanic theater in this country. In France, no such option exists for a Cuban-French playwright who wishes to be staged in the country of residence. The Spanish-language theater of the Spanish exiles that flourished during the Franco years in southern France has now practically disappeared, and it tended to be an amateur or university-based venture rather than professional theater. Paris is simply not New York. In France, the Hispanic theater person who does not assimilate has nowhere to go. In the 1950s Manet himself discovered that his acting career was forestalled by his heavy accent; it was for that reason that he left France for further study in Italy (interview, Mambrino 363). It was also for that reason that, once back in France, he turned to mime.

In examining exile drama in Argentina in the years following the Spanish Civil War and World War II, Ward B. Lewis underscores basic differences that may arise because of the language question. German dramatists in Buenos Aires dealt repeatedly, in a realistic way, with the problem of exile; Spanish playwrights were far more varied both in theme and aesthetics. The German authors wrote, in German, for their exiled compatriots; such plays are likely to be ephemeral. Absent a language barrier, Spanish playwrights were free to write for a general Argentine public and, potentially, for an international audience as well. Accordingly, a Spanish Argentine play like Alejandro Casona's *Los árboles mueren de pie* (Trees die standing, 1949), which has only a peripheral reference to exile and return, has traveled well, becoming part of international repertoire. Sometimes the period of displacement is relatively brief, as was the case for the hundreds of Argentine theater people who fled their country during the Dirty War (1976–83); returning home remains a real possibility and reaching out only to the natural audience of compatriots is reasonable. But the Castro regime has now been in power in Cuba more than forty years, even longer than the Franco dictatorship in Spain (1939–75).

By any rigid thematic definition of Cuban theater in exile, Eduardo Manet ceases to be a Cuban playwright. His stage plays, unlike some of the more or less propagandistic films he directed in Havana in the 1960s, also do not fall within the framework that came to dominate within revolutionary Cuba: a "theatrical method that employs theatre as a means of formulating solutions to communal problems" (Versényi 167).[1] As we probe deeper into his French plays, Manet's Latin American roots become increasingly evident. Havana-based theater critic Rine Leal has done just this kind of probing in identifying the Cuban elements in the works of authors, living in France and the United States, who are included in his anthology *Teatro: 5 autores cubanos*. Plays written in languages other than Spanish—such as those of Fornes and Manet—may still be Cuban just so long as they communicate ideas, feelings, values, life experiences, and a spirit that can readily be classified as Cuban; not Cuban in a tourist sense—mulatto women under palm trees in the sun—but within a universal context (Leal 1995: x). Regardless of the fact that *Les Nonnes* became known through its French version, Leal recognizes it not only as a Cuban play but, because of its initial continuous run at the Poche-Montparnasse of 360 performances, as the longest-running Cuban work on the island or abroad (Leal 1995: xxii). From the perspective of the French stage, Osvaldo Obregón affirms that Manet's Cuban origins strongly mark his creative work, most of which has been done in France (Obregón 1991: 525).

---

1. Rine Leal refers to a period of theatrical renovation introduced by Triana's *La noche de los asesinos* and then a "dark decade" starting around 1976. By the mid-1980s, he believes that the renovation began anew. (Leal 1995: xxii). Leal places Manet's *Las monjas* and plays by others who left the island within the current of renovation. Although he does not define the "dark decade," Triana's keystone play is poles apart from socialist realism or agitation propaganda.

Manifestations of Manet's Latin American Roots

In *Persona, vida y máscara en el teatro cubano*, Matías Montes Huidobro identifies several general characteristics of Cuban theater that we can readily associate with Manet: a metatheatrical tendency revealed in the play-within-the-play and self-conscious role-playing within the role, an incorporation of Afro-Caribbean religion and magic, verbal humor (*choteo*), and, faced with the question of revolution/counterrevolution, a kind of schizophrenia. Works, bordering on existentialism and the absurd, wrestle simultaneously with the desire for and fear of freedom. "[L]ove in its normal form is disappearing. The determining words are those typical of a terrible, schizophrenic love: trap, prison, destruction" (Montes Huidobro 57). "One might say that in a revolutionary state there are concentric circles, all of them without an exit" (Montes Huidobro 63).

In a vein similar to that of Montes Huidobro, Rine Leal synthesizes traits that underscore both the selection of Cuban exile theater in his anthology and plays written in the island. He signals the presence of verbal humor and parody, and of a reality/appearance theme. He discovers a culture of otherness that either considers the gaze from the other shore or discovers the island from a distance. Another repeated pattern is that of family confrontations. "In our theater, the family, or its equivalent, is a social nucleus trapped in an extreme situation . . . ; beyond the story there lurks the dangerous specter of disintegration" (xv–xvi). There is also resistance to a reality "that becomes impossible for us to change" (Leal 1995: xviii).

The overviews of Montes Huidobro and Leal provide a basis for considering as "Cuban" Manet's theater, particularly plays from the first decade of his return to France, even though they have no direct thematic links to the kind of Miami theater described by Watson-Espener. Certainly *Les Nonnes* embraces all of the characteristics cited from both critics. Leal specifically notes that the microcosm of the nuns' basement suggests "variations on the family and the formula of a mirror that reflects its own image" (Leal 1995: xxiii).

Metatheatricalism, often with an associated reality/appearance theme, pervades Manet's theater and will be referred to repeatedly throughout this study.[2] Frequently the metatheatrical impulse takes the

---

2. In his discussion of contemporary Latin American theater and the "French connection," George Woodyard points out the persistent presence of metatheatrical games in the

form of intertexuality with Hollywood film images and cinematic strategies. While at first glance such techniques would seem far removed from Cuban origins, in fact they reflect that experience. Manet affirms that the Latin American youth of his generation was raised on American movies; as a child, he skipped school to watch Mae West, Greta Garbo, the Marx Brothers, and Charlie Chaplin. He mentions Hollywood's influence on the work of a fellow Cuban author, the late Severo Sarduy, and on Argentine French directors Jorge Lavelli and Jérôme Savary. He moreover cites the addiction shared by Fidel Castro and Che Guevara. Manet reports that during the Cuban missile crisis in 1962, Castro and Guevara sought to escape the tension by viewing American Westerns (interview, Mambrino 361). The late Argentine novelist Manuel Puig, whose works are noted for their strong current of popular culture, similarly admitted to being raised on Hollywood movies (Puig).

Also among the traits listed by Montes Huidobro, Afro-Caribbean religions emerge in the novels and several of Manet's plays. The author recalls with affection his Haitian nursemaid—he calls her his second mother—and states that the spectacles of his youth included both Catholic masses and voodoo rituals (interview, Mambrino 361). Verbal humor, reminiscent of the Cuban *choteo*, is present in all of his theater with the exception of an occasional tragedy (*Mendoza, en Argentine . . . , Ma'Déa*).

At times Manet signals his Latin American origins through play settings or characters. Of the first ten plays published in France, six are set in Latin America or have direct Spanish connections: *Les Nonnes*, like Cuban-French author Alejo Carpentier's novel *El reino de este mundo*, has as its background the 1804 black revolt in Haiti; *Ma'Déa* is also set in Haiti, in the twentieth century. *L'Autre Don Juan* (The other Don Juan) is a metaplay based on Juan Ruiz de Alarcón's *Las paredes oyen*. The locale for *Madras, la nuit où . . .* (That night in Madras . . .) is unspecified, but could certainly be Latin American; at least some of the characters have Spanish names and the world without is in the throes of violent revolution. *Lady Strass*, 1977, is set in Belize; apparently concerned that readers in France would be unfamiliar with the little Central American country, the editors of *L'Avant-Scène Théâtre* prefaced their edition with a map and explanatory note, observing that English is the official language,

---

works of many French as well as Latin American dramatists. The current is obviously international and not by itself an indication of particular national roots.

but that the Indian, black, and mestizo population speaks Spanish. As indicated by their titles, *Un Balcon sur les Andes* (A balcony over the Andes) and *Mendoza, en Argentine* . . . (Mendoza, Argentina . . .) are situated in South America.

If Latin American settings explicitly point to Manet's Hispanic roots, so does his repeated use of the Spanish language. Often he interpolates Spanish expressions for comic effect so that they function as the kind of verbal humor that Montes Huidobro, Leal, and others have noted as characteristically Cuban. As a bilingual—or, to be more precise, a polyglot—Manet is personally prone to code-switching and readily creates characters who have the same tendency of shifting between languages, even within the same sentence. In *Lady Strass*, the characters represent three nationalities: British, French, and Guatemalan; words of English and Spanish lace the French-language text. At times all three of them mingle the languages, but of particular interest is Manuel. The stage directions indicate, quite realistically, that the mestizo from Guatemala is to speak with a slight Spanish accent. Equally realistic is the code-switching built into his speech. Whenever he is caught by surprise or reacting with emotion, he reverts to Spanish, blurting out exclamations ranging from the mild "madre de Dios" (10) to the colorful "puta y reputa de la chingada de su madre" (14). Spanish is introduced more extensively in *L'Autre don Juan*. The author/actor-character increasingly objects to the French version of his comedy and insists upon delivering lines of the original Spanish text; other actor-characters either clamor for a translation or provide one.

Manet reaches the peak of his bilingual games in *Un Balcon sur les Andes*. The episodic action revolves around some French actors who flee to South America. The South American characters all speak Spanish—or Portuguese—unless there is some justification for their knowing French. Early on, one Spanish American, who acquired his linguistic skills from a French prostitute, volunteers to interpret the actors' performances. Whole scenes are played in French with a running explanation in Spanish. Later, as the Frenchmen add Spanish Americans to their troupe, teach their new friends some French, and begin to speak Spanish themselves, their plays-within-the-play become bilingual, as are the posters announcing their performances. Code-switching becomes frequent.

A typical example is the following interchange when a local boy's goat interferes with the performance of the French actors who try to get the child and the animals to leave:

Blaise: Ah, Rodrigo . . . mon amant! Enfin seuls! Vete niño! Fuera chèvres!
Tarassin: Fuera cabritas . . . foutues chèvres . . . dehors . . . fuera . . . fuera . . . (1985: 41)

The characters' gradual acquisition of their second languages always rings true, but can yield comic results. At one point a Spanish innkeeper, who apparently assumes that she will not be understood by the Frenchman, tells the "rotten foreigner" not to sit down. Blaise responds in kind. When Tarassin does not understand, their bilingual friend Juan explains that the two have been insulting each other:

L'Aubergiste: No se siente! Váyase, podrido extranjero!
Blaise: Podrida extranjera tu misma, gallega de mierda!
Tarassin: Que se passe-t-il?
Juan: Ils se traitent mutuellement de sales métèques. (58)

Manet's bilingual/multilingual games have generally been acceptable to directors and audiences in France and abroad.[3] Any biased criticism in France against his theater or that of other Hispanics tends to be directed at them for being "baroque." Centuries ago the French employed the term "baroque" as a pejorative way of distinguishing an exuberant Spanish artistic style from their own neoclassicism, with its love of moderation. If one examines contemporary critical and audience response to Hispanic plays and Hispanic directors in France, even to those who have achieved considerable success, one readily discovers vestiges of the time-honored attitude. The stereotypical image of Spain in France—the famous *espagnolade* that was incorporated into the García Lorca myth on the postwar French stage—is that of a baroque, dark, violent, and passionate people. Not surprisingly, the adjective most frequently used to describe the Hispanic presence in contemporary French theater is, in fact, "baroque." It is the label of preference for directors, such as the

---

3. An exception was the initial planning for the October 1996 staging of my translation of *Lady Strass* at UBU Repertory in New York City. The theater's artistic director, Françoise Kourilsky, did not believe that her audience would accept the multilingual word games and requested that the script be modified. The author respected her judgment and approved the changes, but the play's director, André Ernotte, later suggested that at least some of the use of Spanish be reintroduced in the text. The casting of bilingual actor Robert Jimenez in the role of Manuel no doubt contributed to this decision.

Argentines Lavelli (until his retirement in 1997, head of the Théâtre National de la Colline), Savary (director of the Théâtre National de Chaillot), and the late Víctor García; for twentieth-century authors, including Manet and the Spaniards Lorca, Valle-Inclán, and Arrabal.[4]

The word is not always meant as praise. "Baroque" may encompass what some theater professionals in France—not just the Hispanics but also Patrice Chéreau, Daniel Mesguich, Ariane Mnouchkine, and others—have creatively sought in their spectacular stagings; nonetheless, certain critics deplore such performance texts for their "expense, waste, display, ostentation, and excess" (Guérin 31). Roger Blin indicated that he chose to direct Manet's *Lady Strass* precisely for its extravagant, irrational Hispanic baroque tendency, but critic Béatrix Andrade was not alone in finding that same tendency to fall outside "European good taste" (qtd. in *L'Avant-Scène Théâtre* 613:31).

Les Nonnes as Paradigm of the Hispanic Neobaroque

In the 1977 Rioduero dictionary of literature, José Sagredo observes that historically the baroque was not limited to Hispanic cultures but was in fact universal throughout Europe. The characteristics he identifies with baroque culture and considers particularly appropriate for theater may be more common in Hispanic texts but are also found in some French works. Among these traits are "fascination with the decay of life and with death; a view of the world as a universal stage and as a theatrical game; a conception of life as something changing and unpredictable . . . ; a general tendency toward contrast, dynamic expression, and allegory" (33).[5]

---

4. Michel Corvin labels all three Argentine-French directors as "neobaroque" and links them to Artaud and Arrabal. Among the characteristics he associates with them are "the fantastic, laughter, eroticism, and extravagance" (107–9). The term has also been used in reference to Manet's narrative; for example, in his favorable review of *Rhapsodie cubaine*, Jean-Noël Pancrazi tied the flow between past and present and between external and internal perspectives to a "baroque aesthetic" (Pancrazi 1996).

5. I am aware that Lezama Lima and others have identified differences between the European and the Latin American baroque, but such an analysis falls outside the scope of this study. It is worth observing, however, that the late Severo Sarduy, one of the foremost Latin American theorists on the baroque, lived in exile in France. The majority of the footnoted sources in the four groups of his essays (originally published 1969, 1974, 1982, and 1987) that were compiled in 1987 under the title *Ensayos generales sobre el barroco* are, in fact, French.

For Jorge Luis Borges, the baroque is not the style of a particular historical period but rather a "permanent category of the spirit" (Busquets 315). Similarly, for other Latin American writers—most notably the Cubans Carpentier, Sarduy, and Lezama Lima—the baroque is "a universal constant, a spirit" (Molinero 79). In his theoretical discussions, Sarduy goes beyond Bakhtin's concept of carnival and affirms that the baroque, or neobaroque sign, always contains a masking process (Molinero 85). Fittingly, Julio Ortega describes Sarduy's own novel *Colibrí* as containing "the carnavalesque code of the disguise, an illusionist transformation" (Ortega 212). It should be noted that Antonin Artaud's theater of cruelty and ritual was in part inspired by his trip to Mexico and serves as a bridge between the French stage and the Hispanic neobaroque.

From the Hispanic perspective, the most influential author of neobaroque French theater is undoubtedly Jean Genet. Genet's iconoclastic unmasking of decadence from the vantage point of the Other speaks directly to the Hispanic baroque. There are traces of Genet's metatheatrical games, with their emphasis on exploiter and exploited, not only in the Cuban exiles, Triana and Manet, but also in such Spanish playwrights as Arrabal and Francisco Nieva (b. 1927) and the Argentine Griselda Gambarro (b. 1928). Nieva, acknowledging the impact that reading Artaud and Genet had on his evolving theater, affirms that Genet revealed to him an appreciation of spectacle, of tragic nightmares, of the beauty rejected by a decadent civilization (Nieva 1978: 39–41). There is something essentially Hispanic in Genet's irreverent confrontation of taboos, in his insistent probing of the seamy underside of society, and in his baroque language, so far removed from classic French expression.

Among the native French directors who proved most influential in promoting Hispanic neobaroque theater was Roger Blin, who also directed works by Genet. In 1963 he played the role of Pedro Gailo and directed the flawed production at the Odéon of Valle-Inclán's *Divinas palabras* (*Divine Words*). Six years later he brought worldwide recognition to Manet for a macabre tragicomedy that illustrates well the characteristics of Hispanic neobaroque. Certainly *Les Nonnes* combines all of the traditional baroque elements in Sagredo's list and has close ties to works by Carpentier and Sarduy.

In addition to its obvious thematic link to Carpentier's *El reino de este mundo*, *Les Nonnes* reflects the *real maravilloso* that the older Cuban associated with the Hispanic baroque: "Carpentier characterizes as marvelous real an incredible reality, capable of successfully challenging the most vivid imagination and the greatest fantasy" (Márquez Rodríguez 108). Is this not what happens to the Mother Superior? Her vivid, metatheatrical imagination creates fictional scenarios that are transformed into incredible reality. Manet no doubt intended *Les Nonnes* to serve as a parable of revolutionary Cuba, but he also seconds Carpentier's amazement at the "incredible fact" that "the first socialist revolution on the continent took place in the country [Haiti] where conditions were the least conducive" (qtd. in Márquez Rodríguez 110).[6]

With Sarduy, Manet shares a number of characteristic strategies, including the use of parody, transvestism, and intertextuality. *Les Nonnes* parodies Catholic ritual and prayer. The grotesque scene in which the nuns convert the cadaver of the Señora into a saintly relic by decking her out in *peineta* and *mantilla* is strongly reminiscent of Valle-Inclán, perhaps pointing specifically to *Divinas palabras*.[7] Much has been written about Sarduy's interpolation of painting within his narrative; in Manet's case, the visual intertexts are more likely to be filmic. All of his plays contain elements of Hispanic neobaroque, but the critical and audience response that they receive is not always directly attributable to their "strange" and "eccentric" tendencies. Curiously, one critic who was dismayed by *Eux, ou la prise du pouvoir* (Them, or Taking power) faulted the 1972 production at the Petit Odéon–Comédie-Française because it lacked Lavelli's "baroque flair" (Gousseland). And a 1986 Paris revival of *Les Nonnes* was hailed precisely for its enduring magic, baroque quality (Marcabru).

Les Nonnes as Paradigm of the Latin American Theater of Crisis

In *Les Nonnes*, Manet introduced elements that are repeated, with variations, in much of his theater of the 1970s. At the personal level, the char-

---

6. A French-Cuban connection appears as even stronger if we realize that Carpentier first became aware of the Caribbean "magic world" in 1943, when visiting Haiti in the company of the noted French actor and director Louis Jouvet (qtd. in Márquez Rodríguez 109).

7. There are a number of scenes in Valle-Inclán's theater in which death and dead bodies are treated with grotesque humor. In *Divinas palabras*, a multiply disabled boy is used for begging even after he has died from an overdose of alcohol. Bradby finds obvious similarities between Manet's black humor and the early plays of Adamov or Ionesco (Bradby 237); the connection with Valle-Inclán in fact runs deeper.

acters, trapped in an enclosure, resort to metatheatrical games or rituals—often fraught with violence—either to control one another or to re-create an idealized past. Typically the unseen world outside that enclosure is one marked by the sounds of revolution or other danger. These early plays tend to small casts, single sets, and a highly theatricalist mode that features cinematographic acting style, lighting, and sound track; because of the enclosed space, movement comes solely through the interaction of the characters and their role-playing. In Manet's later plays, the cinematographic strategies, including spatial fluidity, will be enhanced and the external violence only implied here will take center stage: battle scenes and political assassinations in *Un Balcon sur les Andes*, physical torture of a political prisoner in *Mendoza, en Argentine* . . . The constant of violence, explicit or implicit, viewed from varying perspectives and theatrical modes, is as typical of Latin American drama in general as it is of Manet.[8]

Thematically Manet's first plays staged in France are linked to contemporary Cuban theater as discussed by Montes Huidobro and Leal, but the ties extend to a more general current that Diana Taylor has defined in her 1991 book, *Theatre of Crisis: Drama and Politics in Latin America*. Concentrating on 1965–70, a period of increasing political turmoil and oppression in South America and Cuba, Taylor posits that the theater of crisis in Latin America "differs from other kinds of crisis theatres—the theatre of the absurd or protest theatre—in that it formulates the objective manifestation of crisis as inseparable from the subjective experience of decomposition" (Taylor 9). She affirms that in the Eurocentric theater of the absurd, the outside is still a stable, bourgeois world and that in theater of protest, although the outside may be undergoing sociopolitical change, those in opposition remain firm.[9]

---

8. Severino João Albuquerque foregrounds this aspect in the title of his book *Violent Acts: A Study of Contemporary Latin American Theatre*. His analysis includes verbal and nonverbal violence and ways of representing repression and resistance, the unrepresentable, and the violent double.

9. In his earlier discussion of contemporary Latin American theater and the "French connection," George Woodyard traces the significant impact of Sartre and Camus, of the absurdists, and of Artaud and Genet. He points out the relationship between Genet, for example, and the ritual theater in Cuba and the persistent presence of metatheatrical games in the works of many French and Latin American dramatists. Taylor asserts that, because of external political reality, there are essential differences between the French models and Latin American works that fall into related currents; she identifies a process of transculturation. I am not convinced that the differences between Latin American and European theater are always as clear-cut as I believe Taylor suggests, but that point is irrelevant in the case of Manet. His plays from the French stage reflect Latin American experience.

Taylor's distinction between theater of crisis and theater of the absurd is open to debate. The external world for the European absurdists may not be stable at all. In her history of world theater, Felicia Hardison Londré points out that the existentialist theater of Jean-Paul Sartre (1905–80) and Albert Camus (1913–60), immediate forerunners of the absurd, were responses to the horrors of World War II and that the sense of absurdity that permeates the 1950s was related to the cold war and the testing of atomic and hydrogen bombs (Londré 1991: 439).

Whether or not Taylor is correct in her definition of the absurd, several of Manet's plays clearly fall within her category of Latin American theater of crisis. Manet seldom avoids external political reality. He has recently affirmed that from early childhood on he was affected by the always highly politicized environment of Cuba and that Latin American theater is always deeply rooted in social and political issues (interview, Leroyer 12).

For her study, Taylor combines social and scientific theories in order to examine simultaneously both internal and external worlds. Played against a background of crumbling beliefs and structures, "[t]he moment of crisis is one of rupture, of critical irresolution, the 'in between' of life and death, order and chaos" (56). The objects of attack at such times "are precisely the boundaries—physical, moral, legal or discursive—the previously maintained social hierarchies, family and personal integrity, law and order" (60). "In the theatre of crisis, both the objective context and the subjective consciousness threaten to collapse. The onstage worlds concretize the systemic shifts and ruptures by means of crumbling walls and fragile partitions between inner and outer, walls that neither separate nor protect. The onstage characters, who attempt to situate and define themselves in relation to disintegrating ideological frameworks and faulty social mirrors, appear as monstrous hybrids, as yet devoid of personal identity and incapable of self-government" (Taylor 9). Taylor applies her definition to selected works by Triana, Gambaro, the Mexican Emilio Carballido, the Colombian Enrique Buenaventura, and the Chilean Egon Wolff. In the case of Triana's *La noche de los asesinos*, she uncovers the play's political reading, thus effectively defending it from the charge of being ambiguous and hence antirevolutionary.

Many of Taylor's observations about theater of crisis in general and of *La noche de los asesinos* in particular could be applied equally well to Manet's *Les Nonnes* and to three of the works that followed in his early years of exile: *Le Borgne* (The one-eyed man), *Madras, la nuit où . . .* , and

Fig. 4. *Les Nonnes*. Amsterdam (photo courtesy of Eduardo Manet).

Lady Strass. The characters in the plays studied by Taylor, "have no safe home of their own" (56). Their houses are being taken over by someone else, and cease to shelter or protect them; "often they are prisons, with barred windows and locked doors" (57). The house may become a weapon; structures collapse; inner spaces merge with outer ones. There is no escape from the present and no future.

According to Taylor, in *La noche de los asesinos*, the characters and the audience are "trapped in a totalizing, closed world that refuses to let us see beyond the limiting discursive and perceptual frames" (68). The outside world of *Les Nonnes* is somewhat less impenetrable; the constant voodoo drums and the pounding at the door confirm that a revolution has begun. The open ending of the play leaves the two surviving nuns inside the closed space that has become a prison from which they desperately attempt to escape. Should the door cave in before they complete a tunnel, the chaotic outer world will merge with their inner one. That inner world, of course, is already in a state of chaos and decomposition—literally, in the case of the dead bodies of the Señora and Sister Ines. If in *La noche de los asesinos*, the family has become the locus of murderous hatred, in *Les Nonnes* the sisters of charity are given to violent acts against others and themselves. In both plays, social hierarchies have given way.

The hallmark of *La noche de los asesinos* is ambiguity. The stifling enclosure in which the action takes place may be a basement or an attic. The three characters embark upon a series of sometimes violent metatheatrical games. They are perhaps the victims of their parents' tyranny; they are perhaps their parents' assassins. The ending seems to give circular structure to the play; the events we have seen may merely be a rehearsal for an act that has not yet taken place. Whether the characters are in or outside the revolution is as unclear as what lies outside the closed space in which they find themselves.[10] Taylor explains this ambiguity as a reflection of the political context at the time of the play's writing: "When revolution offers no possibility of critical distancing, when there is 'nothing' outside the revolution, when all discourse is subsumed by the revolutionary frame, then the only *other* space is the area of ambiguity within the confines of the revolutionary frame itself" (84).

Les Nonnes is somewhat less ambiguous. The circular structure of *La noche de los asesinos* has been replaced by a linear frame play; Manet's characters function metatheatrically, but it is clear that the roles within their roles are not a ritual subject to repetition but rather part of a forward-moving story line. On the other hand, the reality of the male nuns is never certain, either in terms of their sexuality or religious status or in terms of their metaphorical position vis-à-vis the Cuban Revolution. More complex in this respect than Triana's play, in Manet's grotesque tragicomedy there are at least three social classes: the wealthy Señora, the nuns—who in turn, like Triana's family, have their own hierarchy—and the unseen forces outside the basement-convent. When the Mother Superior and Sister Angela invent variations on the story of their relationship to the Señora and her death, in effect they define themselves as being part of the revolution should the black Haitians defeat their former white masters, and part of the counterrevolution in the event that the white landowners are triumphant. But those are only their fictionalized stances; where do they really stand with respect to class conflict and

---

10. The question of one's position vis-à-vis the revolution was of crucial significance. In his *Palabras a los intelectuales* (Words to intellectuals) in June 1961, Castro raised the question of what rights authors and artists have as revolutionaries or nonrevolutionaries. He answered his own question by stating: "Within the Revolution: all rights; against the Revolution no rights." Castro added that authors had freedom of expression but that "we will always evaluate their creation through the prism of revolutionary glass" (qtd. in Leal 1980: 132).

social injustice? In the past, have they been among the exploited or the exploiters? And does the manipulative Mother Superior not represent forces that will inevitably abuse the evolving sociopolitical context for their own benefit? The equation of role-playing and farce with power underscores the Latin American subtextual reading of this and other Manet texts. In other words, the Mother Superior could be, as Bradby suggests, representative of "self-interested behavior" that is normally "masked by the repressive apparatus of Catholic ideology" (Bradby 237). That would make her part of a power structure that the Cuban Revolution would wish to overthrow. But given her histrionic skills and her desire to usurp assets belonging to the upper class, is she, like the One-Eyed Man, not also a possible stand-in for Castro, that is, for the revolution itself as it runs amuck?

Eux ou La prise du pouvoir and *Sur la piste*: Going at It One on One

Manet's second French-language play to be staged in France was *Eux ou La prise du pouvoir*; it premiered at the Petit Odéon–Comédie-Française, under the direction of Tony Willems, in February 1972.[11] In several respects, perhaps as a reaction to his recent exile, it is among the author's least overtly Hispanic works and stands at a distance from the theater of crisis. On several occasions over the years, Manet has suggested that *Les Nonnes*, *Madras, la nuit où* . . . , and *Lady Strass* form a triptych: a claustrophobic cycle, marked by grotesque humor and dealing with class struggle, in which the characters hope in vain to barricade themselves against a menacing external reality. *Eux ou La prise du pouvoir* differs from that pattern primarily because of the absence of the threat of outside violence and chaos; it might therefore be considered an absurdist work, similar to

---

11. In Manet's personal collection of reviews and programs there are references to productions of *Eux ou La prise du pouvoir* in Amsterdam (1972), Montreal (1974), Beirut (1983), Geneva (1984) and Brussels (1985). At Avignon 1991 Festival Off, three of his plays were revived, making him one of the most staged playwrights at that important theater event. The productions took place as follows: *Eux ou La prise du pouvoir*, Théâtre du Peuplier Noir (Ile-de-France), dir. Jean-Pierre Muller; *Madras, la nuit où* . . . , Compagnie Le Pantographe (Midi-Pyrénées), dir. Alain Igonet; *Lady Strass*, Le Théâtre du Bilboquet (Ile-de-France), dir. David Benda. Manet's files are incomplete; information on stagings is therefore inconclusive but gives at least a limited view of the wide impact of his theater.

Chilean Spanish playwright Jorge Díaz's *El cepillo de dientes* (The toothbrush; one-act version, Chile, 1961; two-act version, Spain, 1966), which also centers on the game-playing of a married couple. But *Eux ou La prise du pouvoir* is not unrelated to Manet's later plays of enclosure and entrapment; it is linked to *Madras, la nuit où . . .* and *Lady Strass* by its incorporation of psychodrama within the play and by an extensive use of cinematographic references. Taking advantage of the subversive potential in metatheater, these Manet texts, along with *Le Borgne*, reveal a connection between game-playing and power but ultimately suggest that nothing authentic remains behind the mask.

Díaz's *El cepillo de dientes*, subtitled "Castaways in the amusement park," is widely recognized as a foremost example of Latin American absurdist theater. It has also been criticized for being imitative of a European model and for being too superficial and comic. Leon Lyday describes it as "a hilarious farce that presents a day in the life of a young married couple" (Lyday 61). As Kirsten Nigro points out, because the farce bypassed political protest, some critics labeled it elitist and ideologically reactionary (Nigro 114–15). To be sure, it was also written when Latin American dramatists were trying to make their works universal. Díaz explained to Taylor in a 1988 interview that he was not conscious of his attitude at the time but that "Eurocentricism was characteristic of his progressive bourgeois Chilean background" (Taylor 13). Nigro observes, however, that *El cepillo de dientes*, by portraying a couple who speak in clichés and recite advertisement jingles, does make a valid criticism of Latin America: "He and She are clearly symbols of Third World economic and cultural dependency" (Nigro 115). This same criticism is also present in Manet's *Eux ou La prise du pouvoir*.

The two characters in Díaz's play act out what appears to be a daily, metatheatrical ritual. The set visually establishes their marital conflicts: on one half of the stage are pieces of old Spanish furniture, while the other half is decorated in ultramodern Danish. The neutral ground between them is the breakfast table. The action is accompanied at times by a musical motif that evokes the image of a carousel. Their fragmented, nonsensical conversation, which more closely resembles juxtaposed monologue than dialogue, eventually leads to violence: the man strangles his wife and then reads about the crime in the newspaper he already has at hand. In the second act, She reappears as Antona, the maid. With a series of farcical ploys, He attempts to keep her from discovering his wife's body hidden in the bedroom. Antona becomes the wife again, they fight, and She kills her husband with a fork. But He, too, comes back to life. The lights begin to dim and the scenery begins to disappear. As they are left on a bare stage, He and She declare that is has been a marvelous day but that tomorrow they will have to reinvent their amusement park.

It should be observed that the couple's "house" is just as unstable as the shelters that give way in the theater of crisis. In Díaz's absurdist farce, the collapsing outer walls are part of the game-playing space and there is no indication of what, if anything, lies beyond them. In works like Manet's *Madras, la nuit où* . . . and *Lady Strass*, characters within houses elect to live theatrically; they stage plays-within-the-play or act out roles, but there is a clear line of demarcation between the site of their fantasies and an outside world that poses a threat of violence or other "real" problems. Although the chaotic outer world does not encroach upon the couple in *Eux ou La prise du pouvoir*, Manet's play probes Latin American cultural dependence somewhat more deeply than does Díaz's farce.

Eux ou La prise du pouvoir is a physically demanding tour de force for two actors who, in their roles as Monsieur and Madame Arthur, engage in an exhibition of nonstop, ritualistic game-playing. Nothing is what it at first seems as they attempt to outmaneuver one another through the rapid assimilation of a variety of cultural clichés, adopted primarily from Hollywood movies. Stage directions underscore the shifting moods, ranging from farcical to erotic to violent, through carefully selected musical motifs. The single set is to be "convertible"; in most sequences it suggests model home décor from an American magazine, but it must also be rapidly changed into the viewing room of a funeral parlor.

Manet's stage directions, both in his early exile theater of enclosure and in his later plays, often include film terminology, suggesting, for example, that the actors' movements simulate a freeze, slow motion, or the projection of frames at double speed. It should be noted that Manet has been in the forefront in this use of cinematic devices. Mireille Willey has identified Lavelli as an innovator for the introduction in his staging of Arrabal's *Bella Ciao* at the Théâtre National Populaire in February 1972 of "slow motion, which up to then was exploited exclusively by movies and television" (Willey 32). Manet had already explicitly called for the varied rhythms of film in *Eux ou La prise du pouvoir*, published the year before. Nowhere in his theater is the deliberate acting out of film images more obvious than in this play. Moreover, it is intended to be performed without an intermission, another device that relates it to film.

Wearing a blond wig, Madame Arthur initially appears as a vamp of the 1930s (14); her gestures are to be vaguely reminiscent of Garbo or Swanson (19). With a change of hair and costume, she later becomes Ava Gardner of *The Barefoot Contessa* (70). Monsieur Arthur may adopt the voice and facial expressions of Jerry Lewis (43) or of the Hollywood stereotype of the smiling "black-boy" servant (44); at one point he pulls out a revolver and spins it, "like cowboys in the movies" (83). Stage directions continually refer to cinematic strategies. Monsieur Arthur interrupts his singing, in English, of "Happy Birthday," stops short, and stares at Madame Arthur "like a freeze frame of film" (14); Madame Arthur yanks off his fake moustache and burns it "in slow motion" (31). In a frantic, comic moment, he pushes a small player piano around the stage while she attempts to keep a serving cart out of his reach: the sequence is to evoke "the movement of silent films" (22). A few minutes later, the background music shifts to the tango, and the couple begins a languorous dance that turns passionate as Monsieur Arthur assumes the stance of the "professional seducer of Argentine films" (36).

The salient characteristic of *Eux ou La prise du pouvoir* is its very theatricalism. Two energetic actors are given the opportunity to show off all their performance skills as they change their identities with dizzying speed. At times they play roles within roles—adopting, for example, childish voices to narrate distant memories within a longer monologue. Perhaps the appeal of the text for a young theatrical group, like the one reviving the work at Avignon in 1991, is precisely this relationship to performance art. Indeed Manet recalls that he created this psychodrama as a kind of laboratory exercise for students in his private acting classes (interview, Mambrino 367).[12]

In the early sequences, *Eux ou La prise du pouvoir* appears to be a ritualistic struggle between two people who cannot or will not commu-

---

12. Manet examines the possibilities of psychodrama in several of his works, including ones discussed in this chapter and the later *Ma'Déa*. The most fully developed example of the subgenre is *Cahiers intimes*, a group of actor exercises that he wrote in 1980 based on the true story of a young woman in Paris in the early 1960s. The author considers this a minor text and it remains unpublished. Fragmented in structure with a strong narrative voice, it might not stage well but in some ways is reminiscent of Arrabal's *The Red Madonna*, which received its successful world premiere at INTAR in New York City (1986). Both works are documentaries that explore the motivation behind the irrational killing of a close family member. Manet's poetic use of voices in counterpoint anticipates *Ma'Déa*, as does the constant shifting of the three actors into the multiple roles they must act out in order to trace the stages of Verna's mental illness.

Fig. 5. *Eux ou La prise du pouvoir*. Beirut (photo courtesy of Eduardo Manet).

nicate with each other in the present. Thus they are impelled to act out scenes from their pasts or to evoke their inner phantoms and bad dreams. Monsieur Arthur is desperately seeking Madeleine, a figure who Madame Arthur assures him will never return (27). They enact erotic scenes and speak of the need for love. For their program notes at the 1991 Avignon revival, both author and director highlight this aspect of the text. Manet describes it as "a love story that turns out badly"; Jean-Pierre Muller calls it "a beautiful love story." But Manet also suggests that this couple could be anyone: you, me, our neighbors; and Muller alludes to a stifling atmosphere and a metaphorical set design: "The rays of the setting sun filter through, marking their pattern on the floor like the bars of a cage."

These comments, like the play title itself, point to another level of meaning in the text. "Taking Power" may refer to sexual politics, to the tug-of-war between Monsieur and Madame, but it has other connotations as well. When the convertible set is changed into the luxurious viewing room, the player piano is covered to become an altar. Monsieur Arthur

Fig. 6. *Eux ou La prise du pouvoir.* Finland (photo courtesy of Eduardo Manet).

dons a priestlike robe, and the couple enters into a ritual in praise of Power. In earlier scenes, the dialogue at times has parodied Christian prayer. In this scene, played against the sounds of nature, flutes, and percussion instruments, the parody shifts to Afro-Caribbean rituals. The couple's litany is aimed at a kind of empty seat, adorned by the figure of a virgin sculpted in black wood and wearing a blond wig. A veil around the bottom of the chair conceals a white cock, whose flying feathers ultimately signal a ritualistic sacrifice.

The blond wig on a black virgin provides a visual symbol of a melding—or imposition—of religions and cultures. Monsieur Arthur makes several direct references to himself as a mestizo, before he and his wife begin shooting a number of balloon sculptures identified as major figures of Western culture: Kant, Chopin, Rubens, Chaplin, Newton, Hegel, Petrarca, Cervantes... They then turn their guns on the audience but refrain from firing. "Why bother?" asks Madame Arthur: "There will always be someone to falsify History" (85).

While these scenes, like all the others, may be perceived as mere role-playing within the role, Jack Gousseland, writing for *Combat* at the time of the original production, found in them an underlying ideological message: "But this couple, crumbling and frayed, is also—metaphorically—the image of the old Western world in decline, a prisoner of its cultures, of its myths, of its representations of itself." It is precisely this message that will be foregrounded in *Madras, la nuit où . . .* and *Lady Strass*.

During the first decade after his return to France, Manet wrote several texts that remain unpublished.[13] One that received extensive press coverage, *Sur la piste* (In the ring), premiered in March 1972, almost simultaneously with *Eux ou La prise du pouvoir*. Manet wrote it as a theatrical exercise for two actor friends who needed a text that could be staged with minimal props and set. Although he was more pleased with a 1974 revival, which was given wide and mostly favorable critical coverage, the author considers the play unimportant, and the manuscript is no

---

13. Among unpublished plays from the period not mentioned elsewhere are *Mirage dans un miroir sans reflets* (a *Twilight Zone* kind of radio play aired on France-Culture, 12 March 1974, dir. Jean-Pierre Colas) and *Les Ménines de la mer Morte* (a collectively created script, focusing on Velázquez's painting and the impending death of Franco. *Les Ménines* was written for Véronique Petit, to whom Manet was married at the time. The couple worked collaboratively with the Groupe d'Expression Libre, which took the play on tour in Switzerland starting in April 1977).

longer available.[14] As described in reviews, the play is closely related not only to *Eux ou La prise du pouvoir*, but also to Díaz's *El cepillo de dientes*. It therefore is germane to our discussion.

The multiple themes of *Sur la piste* include love, hate, joy, anger, and life. The tone is predominantly comic, but the play's ironic perspective is tinged with melancholy. In a 1974 interview for the newspaper *Le Figaro*, Manet clarified that there was no story, merely a connecting thread that curved back to its point of departure after each episode; like variations on a theme, the numerous scenes revolve around the couple: "the relationship between two actors and, by extension, the relationship between a man and a woman" (interview, Varenne). Director Andréas Voutsinos stated in an interview for *Combat* that what interested him was precisely the battle between the sexes: "the reasons why each one constantly has to prove superiority; how the woman, instead of seeking her own identity, strives to grasp power and punish the man."

Critic Jacqueline Cartier compared the actors to dancers; Matthieu Galey emphasized their function as clowns: "[It's] a sad and yet funny little farce, played by Man and Woman, those two clowns who have been abandoned by God and who whimsically cavort about as best they can in order to forget the state of their souls." Along these same lines, Dominique Nores compared *Sur la piste* to Calderon's religious allegory, *El gran teatro del mundo* (*The Great Theater of the World*), and Dominique Jamet signaled a connection with paradise lost: both characters proclaim that they were once happy, free to enjoy the sky and the sea, and then they found each other.

Jamet provides the most detailed information on the content of *Sur la piste*. She describes the text as a juxtaposition of two series of monologues, not dialogues. The characters' roles and their relative positions of power shift from scene to scene, and the related costume changes are made in plain view of the audience. When Man is the master, Woman is a household drudge; when she is a vamp, he becomes a sex object. An allegedly "ideal couple" is composed of Madame Star and Monsieur Muscle. Disillusioned by their role-swapping efforts, generation after generation, Man and Woman eventually resign themselves to living together. Their performances "in the ring" as circus clowns and gymnasts

---

14. *Sur la piste* was first staged in Paris, 3–4 March 1972, at the Salle Jean-Cocteau. Performed by Hasol Carr and Jonathan Nerzer of the Maison de la Culture of Val-de-Marne, it was directed by the author. A Parisian revival at the Théâtre 13 opened on 9 April 1974. It was directed by Andréas Voutsinas and performed by Maria Laborit and Roger Mollien.

are a response to boredom. As Manet asks at the close of the *Combat* interview, would life not be unbearable if Man and Woman somehow resolved their fundamental conflict? The battle of the sexes in works like *Sur la piste* and *Cepillo de dientes* suggests that such game-playing is an inevitable and indeed essential part of life. The characters are entrapped at a personal level, but the absence of external conflict removes *Sur la piste*, even more than *Eux ou La prise du pouvoir*, from the theater of crisis.

Unmasking the One-Eyed Man

Contemporary critical theory teaches us that any literary text is open to multiple readings. The dramatic text in performance is notoriously polyphonic and polycentric; each spectator may shift the focus and find a different message. The play is both text and context, and the context of a revival can never be precisely that of the original staging. When, as in the case of an exiled playwright, the original staging itself is removed from the source of the text's inspiration, the text's original intentions may be concealed as its potential connotations change. Moreover, all theater may be seen as an expression, conscious or unconscious, of the playwright's inner world, of his or her own ghosts and demons. Thus we may give a particular play a subtextual (psychoanalytical, sociopolitical, or allegorical) reading that uncovers levels of meaning that would otherwise remain invisible. If we read *Le Borgne* this way, we will find that it goes well beyond the superficial interpretation given it by David Bradby, who describes the tragicomedy as a simplistic "demystification of Catholic ideology" (Bradby 238).

Bradby, of course, was not alone in giving to *Les Nonnes* an anti-Catholic interpretation, and some Parisian theater critics also read *Le Borgne* exactly as he did. André Alter, in *Témoignage Chrétien*, found in this new work the same obsession, black humor, and violence as in *Les Nonnes* but determined that it was not an attack on Christianity per se but on the manipulation of faith for profit and a warning about the danger of state religions. Jean-Jacques Gautier, who reviewed *Le Borgne* for *Le Figaro*, had a narrower view, expressing a dislike for Manet's treatment of Christianity as a fraud. Jean Vigneron, writing for *La Croix*, saw the text as conspiring against hope by alleging that Christ had "duped all humanity." Vigneron hastened to add that he had controlled his anger because "the Inquisition is no longer in style." On the other hand, Matthieu Galey of *Combat* wondered if the play might not be so simple after all, if it might also have a political message; and Robert Kanters in *L'Express* decided not only that it was not sacrilegious but that it was the "strongest, funniest and most stimulating" play to come along in months. Kanters also saw a comparison between Manet's Christ figure and Beckett's Godot, thus anticipating Judith Suther's groundbreaking 1975 scholarly essay *"Godot* Surpassed—Eduardo Manet's *Holocaustum ou le Borgne."*

Le Borgne rivaled *Les Nonnes* not only as a polemical piece inspiring multiple interpretations but, because of its fast-paced physical action, also as an exciting performance piece that quickly reached audiences in several countries. It received its world premiere at the National Theater in Brussels, Belgium, in November 1972 and was staged in Geneva, Switzerland, in January 1973. The Paris premiere followed in October 1973 at the Théâtre de l'Athénée, under the direction of Michel Fagadau.[15]

At first glance, *Le Borgne* is far removed from Caribbean reality. It ostensibly takes place in Rome when throwing Christians to the lions was a form of popular entertainment; Manet says he conceived the play while traveling in Italy (interview, Mambrino 367). In proclaiming *Holocaustum ou le Borgne* a "new masterwork," Suther reveals the text's ties to Beckett and the French theater of the absurd. J. L. Styan points out that Beckett's early plays "drew upon the content and techniques of mime, the music hall, the circus and the *commedia dell'arte* to represent the business of everyday living" (126); Manet's seemingly comic characters are also related to those traditions. The three clownlike characters (Tibulus, Martibus, Cumulus) do not have Spanish names; the Spanish language is reduced to one use each of "fiesta" and "adiós." Yet there is a use of the grotesque, a touch of the picaro in these clowns, and a biting parody of Catholic dogma that invite an Hispanic reading. Moreover, the juxtaposition of subjective decomposition and collective chaos relates the text to the Latin American theater of crisis; *Le Borgne* fits the paradigm just as closely as does *Les Nonnes*. By Taylor's definition, these Manet plays are not theater of the absurd at all, for the outside world is anything but stable.

The Borgne, or One-Eyed Man, is a Christlike figure who proclaims his willingness to sacrifice his own life to save the three friends. While Cumulus—in parallel to Sister Ines's positive response to the Señora—

---

15. In Manet's files there are references to stagings in Greece, Italy, Mexico, and Poland, to a Flemish version as well as the original French one in Belgium, and to a number of revivals throughout France, including a performance in Avignon during the 1981 festival.

attempts to defend the newcomer, the other two respond initially by physically mistreating him; finally they, too, are converted—and hoodwinked. They will achieve paradise by giving themselves to the lions. As they eagerly go off to martyrdom, beating their breasts and confessing aloud their sins, the One-Eyed Man removes his eye patch and smiles. The fake One-Eyed Man is, in essence, just as self-serving and manipulative as the Mother Superior. Are we to see a Castro look-alike behind the eye patch? Probably so, if we recall the dialogue from Manet's novel of the Cuban Revolution, *Un Cri sur le rivage*; for the counterrevolutionaries, Castro was the Antichrist. Demagoguery is the opium of the people, whatever the ideology behind the manipulation. The One-Eyed Man, like the Mother Superior, is a charlatan who dupes the gullible by holding out false promises.

The parallels with *Les Nonnes* are many. The single set is a cell-like cave in which three men are imprisoned. While the menace outside the nuns' basement-convent is signaled by offstage drums, here the sound track reveals the roar of the lions and of the enthusiastic crowd. The danger and instability of the external world is mirrored in the disintegration

Fig. 7. *Le Borgne*. Mexico (photo courtesy of Eduardo Manet).

of the three men's friendship, much like the verbal and physical conflicts that arose among the three nuns. The inability of the trio to work together in common cause once again decreases the possibility that they will be able to escape from the situation that entraps them.

As the two-act play begins, the prisoners are fighting: Tibulus and Martibus have ganged up on Cumulus. Only after minutes of rapid farcical action are the reasons for the dispute revealed to the audience. The men have been told that all three are to be crucified but that if one of them volunteers to be destroyed by the lions, the other two will go free. The men have been pitted against one another by the unseen outside forces, and Cumulus claims that, when they drew straws, he was tricked into becoming an unwilling volunteer.

Cumulus finds the courage to knock at one of the cell's two iron doors; it noisily opens and he bravely ventures forth to question the authorities. He returns with the information that the Roman emperor has converted and, after that day's event, will cease throwing Christians to the lions. The news does not alleviate the three men's problems but rather underscores a moment of crisis. The conversion means not that the prisoners will be pardoned but that the opportunity for one of them to save his two comrades is about to disappear. Crucifixions will still take place, but in secluded places away from public view. The new order will not end violence but will merely introduce a new secrecy.

Cumulus has also learned that the volunteer will be granted his last wishes. This information inspires Tibulus, whose gluttony rivals that of the Mother Superior, to volunteer. The series of scenes in which he acts out his desires are done with comic flair. The unseen authorities respond to his wishes as soon as he verbalizes them. The door opens automatically to allow entry to a dinner cart à la Maxim's, to a luxurious fur robe, and to a voluptuous young woman who disappears behind a curtain with Tibulus for a romp on a previously unseen bed. All anachronisms are deliberate. Aside from evoking laughter, they should also suggest that *Le Borgne* is not meant to be interpreted at the most obvious, literal level. This play has as little to do with the persecution of the early Christians as *Les Nonnes* has with the early nineteenth-century black revolution in Haiti or with a typical convent. While it is always somewhat ambiguous whether the nuns are, in fact, nuns, there is no indication whatsoever in the text that the three men, who admit to committing all manner of crimes, have ever heard of Christ.

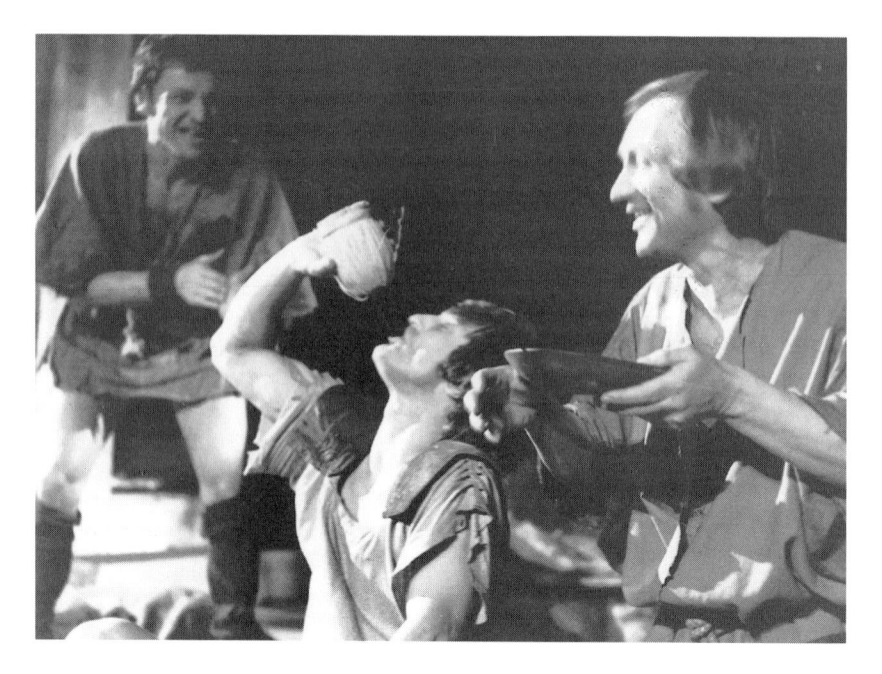

Fig. 8. *Le Borgne*. Poland (photo courtesy of Eduardo Manet).

After tasting of the pleasures of life, Tibulus retracts his offer to volunteer. At the end of the first act, as the three men face the same impasse with which the play began, the door opens and the mysterious stranger appears. With consummate skill, Manet lowers the curtain on a moment of surprise and anticipation. It is only in the second act that Christian dogma becomes the object of parody.

On the surface level, the initial dialogue in the second act presents a comic contrast between the incongruously courteous and formal speech of the three captives as they express gratitude to the stranger and the threat of impending violence. The scene, however, parallels the prelude to interrogation and torture as it is often chillingly depicted in theater and film. After the One-Eyed Man refuses to explain to the increasingly skeptical men why he is willing to give his life to save them, he passively submits to physical mistreatment. His reluctance to share his secret functions as reverse psychology. Once the men learn that being torn apart by the lions will keep them from the fires of hell and will gain their entry to paradise, where their every wish will be granted, they are eager to follow precisely the path that they had earlier resisted so vigorously. The paradise they anticipate is not the celestial one associated with New Testament teachings but, given the previous fulfillment of Tibulus's desires, no doubt a place offering wine, women, and song. Typical of the theater of crisis, there is no way out for these three men, but their particular downfall at the end is related to gluttony and lust.

In her comparison of *Holocaustum ou le Borgne* with *Waiting for Godot*, Suther suggests that Beckett's text brilliantly revealed the human condition, "its patterns, its limits, its temporality," but that Manet's text "goes farther, by rooting itself in the personal. The basic theme of *Holocaustum* is human nature, its vagaries, its solipsism, its ambiguity" (Suther 47). She asserts that Beckett's figures become less individualized over the two hours of performance time; on the other hand, Manet's tragicomedy "presents three personality sketches: Martibus the malcontent, Tibulus the pragmatist, and Cumulus the dreamer" (47). The individualized characters in combination with the surprise ending lead to a reexamination of human nature in an "ambivalent and violent world" (48). Beckett's characters, surrounded by nothingness, "are caught in the great web of their fate" (50); they remain passive. Manet's characters are "stupid, ignorant, greedy, and credulous, but for all their limitations, they are idealists" (50). They fall into the trap of a bogus promise of deliverance, but they are capable of change and of action. During Cumulus's absence Martibus and Tibulus vigorously attempt to escape from the cell.

Suther makes no effort similarly to analyze the One-Eyed Man and his function vis-à-vis the outside world of violence, but her comments on change hint at a liberal, if not Marxist, attitude toward history. If the individual can change, then there is hope that the outside world, too, can be changed. Unfortunately, there is no guarantee that the change will be for the better. If we set aside the possible religious connotations of the One-Eyed Man and his message, we discover that the old order has openly persecuted dissidents or misfits; under the new order, despite the surface message of "salvation," the persecutions will not end but will merely be conducted with greater secrecy. Assuming that Manet, consciously or not, is writing in response to his own disillusionment with an idealistic revolution that had deteriorated into political repression, *Le Borgne* is a clear example of theater reacting to a moment of crisis.

On the Brink of Revolution

While the power struggle in *Eux ou La prise du pouvoir* remains, at least superficially, at the individual level, *Madras, la nuit où . . .* belongs to the group of early plays that readily lend themselves to a collective, political interpretation. Like *Les Nonnes* and *Le Borgne*, the sound track indicates from the beginning the chaotic conditions in the external world. The sounds of gunshots, explosions, sirens, and church bells are immediately clarified by Alcibiar, the first character onstage, who excitedly announces that the revolution has come.

Madras, la nuit où . . . was first performed at Avignon in 1974, under the direction of Lucien Attoun. Along with *Eux ou La prise du pouvoir* and *Lady Strass*, it was also revived at the Avignon Festival Off in 1991.[16]

The locale for *Madras, la nuit où . . .* is unspecified but might be a Latin American country; of the five characters, three have names in Spanish (Alcibiar, Aya [governess], and Jilguero [goldfinch]). The play clearly meets Taylor's criteria for Latin American theater of crisis: internal decomposition and external chaos. The action takes place amid baroque clutter in the living room of a once grand house that is now dilapidated. Outside may be heard the sounds of revolution. As the play begins, Alcibiar is at the window, delightedly watching buildings explode, as if he were the audience for a spectacular show. The program notes for the Avignon revival aptly describe him as "degenerate, deceitful, and vicious," but within the dramatic world he is not alone in his bizarre view of life as theater. To varying degrees, all of the characters engage in role-playing, often assuming the attitudes and even the dialogue of stock cinema types.

Alcibiar's mother, known only as La Dame (the lady), like the title character of *Lady Strass*, is the widow of a British administrator in the colonies. From her days in India, she remembers an idealistic young poet and revolutionary, Emile, whom she loved. She constantly anticipates his return. In the meantime, her house is a stage set and, in Lionel Abel's terms, she is the would-be dramatist: she times her entrances, dons costumes from her youth, calls for lighting and sound effects, and despotically commands the others to play their designated parts. In honor of her long-lost love, she insists upon calling her son Emilio, a name he rejects.

---

16. *Madras, la nuit où . . .* reached Paris in 1977. It has also been performed in Iran (1977) and Holland (1978), and was revived in Nice in 1984.

In the culminating play-within-the-play, a scene reminiscent of its counterpart in *Hamlet* and directed not by La Dame but by the servant Aya, it is revealed that Emile was executed by La Dame's husband with her approval, as a jealous response when she discovered he loved someone else.

That La Dame and her household are intended to symbolize the decline of imperialism is evident. La Dame, unaware of present reality or practical concerns, lives in the past; she insists upon game-playing, even while the world outside is aflame, and she calls upon Aya's skills with Tarot and voodoo to predict the return of "l'homme" (the man). It is Aya who handles the finances, finding ways to keep the household going after La Dame's money is gone. The younger servant, little Jilguero, is the object of Alcibiar's sexual harassment and cruelty.

Parodying the structure of the well-made play, Manet has L'Homme appear shortly after La Dame announces his impending arrival. The Man in this case is not an idealistic poet and revolutionary, but rather a grade-A charlatan who recalls the devious male nuns in Manet's first French stage production and the demagogue behind the eye patch in his *Le Borgne*. Masquerading as a priest, L'Homme had seduced Aya into giving him the last of La Dame's money, then abandoned her for another lover. Aya in turn has used her voodoo skills to cause the rival's death. Fearful of the revolutionaries, L'Homme now seeks refuge and quickly changes into a soldier's uniform as a more appropriate costume. Later he will don a white suit that belonged to La Dame's husband and will be the government official in the play-within-the-play who will lead Emile (played by Jilguero) off to his execution.

The identification of Jilguero with the martyred poet is not gratuitous. Within the frame play, she represents the victims of imperialistic exploitation and is the one character who does not engage in game-playing to deceive others or herself. The Avignon playbill describes her as "taking revenge, in her own way" for having suffered the tyranny of La Dame and Alcibiar. "Poetic justice" might be a more appropriate term. Reversing the fate of Emile in the play-within-the-play, Jilguero does lead L'Homme to his execution at the hands of the triumphant revolutionaries, with whom she makes common cause, but she also arranges for her decadent ex-masters and Aya to remain "free"—that is, unharmed within the enclosed space of their escapist world. In the final moments of the play, as darkness descends and we hear gunshots from the firing squad, an anguished Aya discovers that her incantations have no effect against the power of the people.

Fig. 9. *Madras, la nuit où* . . . Théâtre de l'Epée du Bois, Paris (photo courtesy of Eduardo Manet).

The ideological underpinning of the text is readily apparent. The decadent forces of imperialism—and of voodoo—can lead only to stagnation and death. As represented by L'Homme, with his rapid costume changes, the church and the military have been mere facades for exploitation. The humble Jilguero, in her relative innocence and authenticity, is the hope of the future.

The Old Order in Decay

Despite a shift in political focus, *Lady Strass* also nicely fits the theater of crisis paradigm. The central character is Eliane Parkington Simpson, an older, upper-class Englishwoman in Belize (formerly British Honduras). Like La Dame in *Madras, la nuit où . . .* , Eliane is a remnant of British colonial rule. Barricaded from the outside world of political unrest in Central America, she lives in a remembered or imagined past. As two would-be thieves readily discover when they break in, her isolated, boarded-up house is a prison; a guillotine-like contraption closes off the window by which they have entered, thus trapping them. To explain their intrusion, Bertrand, a middle-aged Frenchman, and the younger Manuel, a mestizo from Guatemala, tell the rifle-toting lady that they are escaping from the latest coup d'état in Tegucigalpa. Bertrand will eventually recall his experiences in a real crisis, namely the German occupation of France, and both men have lived chaotic existences because of economic and political problems. In this case, the external revolution is a fiction: a story quickly made up to justify their intrusion. It is from the perspective of Eliane that external chaos must be judged.

The world Eliane once knew is crumbling; the boarded-up house is her defense against the ruptures and shifts of that external world. Initially it appears that the thieves are trapped; in fact the real prisoner is Eliane. The barricade she has built around herself, at both physical and psychological levels, loses its sheltering capacity once the men intrude upon her space and her imagined past; in the end, after Manuel turns her game of theatricalized life into psychodrama, her only refuge is madness.

First staged under Blin's direction at the Théâtre de Poche-Montparnasse in 1977, *Lady Strass* has since become one of Manet's most performed texts internationally. It was given a major production at Brussels's Théâtre Royal du Parc in 1990, was revived at the Avignon festival in 1991, and received its American premiere at UBU Repertory in New York City in October 1996.[17] The New York production led critic Rosette Lamont to declare the play a "masterpiece" (53) and its author "one of the great dramatists of our generation" (54).

With only three actors and a kaleidoscope of metatheatrical games, *Lady Strass* is a demanding tour de force on a par with *Eux ou La prise du pouvoir* but with the clearer story line and political message of *Madras, la nuit où* . . . The three characters, individualized like those in *Le Borgne*, transcend the series of stereotypical images they portray both to take on a life of their own and to reflect, through the cultures they represent, the relative decadence of old Europe and the vitality of Latin America.

Lady Strass is explicitly metatheatrical. When the two men first illuminate the room with their flashlights, Manuel says it looks like a church. Bertrand corrects him: "No. A theater" (10).[18] Suddenly the darkness is broken by spotlights. The living room before them not only has a stage—a reminder of grander days when this house was the scene of amateur theatricals—but also a balcony. Viewing them from above is Eliane, a superior markswoman who becomes a would-be dramatist with the aid of her trusty gun, her enviable collection of costumes, and, finally, her false promise of payment for the reenactment of a melodramatic love story from her days in India: a tale that partially repeats the play-within-the-play of *Madras, la nuit où* . . . But the melodramatic stories she tells of her two marriages, her life in India and Belize, and her tragic love stories are all reminiscent of films, as is her own hybrid image. The first words she speaks, trilingually, over loudspeakers, are pure Hollywood: "Don't move! Ne bougez pas! No se muevan! You are under surveillance!" (10). When she later asserts her loyalty to England and her sharpshooting skills, the lines juxtapose two distinct intertextual references to film: "Wherever one finds an Englishman and an Englishwoman with a stout heart, there the British Empire lives and shall live in all its glory. And you should know that I can hit a fly at a hundred paces. One more insult, and it'll be curtains for you" (12).

---

17. The Théâtre Royal du Parc program indicated that *Lady Strass* had been translated into various languages and staged around the world, including Holland, Italy, Japan, and Norway. I am also aware of productions in Canada (1982), Portugal (1982), and Switzerland (1989).

18. Page numbers are to the original French text; translations are taken from the slightly revised version I prepared for the UBU production, included in the anthology *Playwrights of Exile*.

Fig. 10. Susanne Wasson in *Lady Strass*. Ubu Repertory Theater, New York, October 1996 (photo by Johnathan Slaff).

Manet's baroque tragicomedy begins with the rhythm and tone of farce.[19] Bertrand and Manuel engage in comic quarrels and name-calling and express exaggerated fear; perhaps at first they are slightly reminiscent of the clown figures in *Le Borgne*. Eliane's sometimes genteel British speech contrasts incongruously, and hence humorously, with her Western garb and her love of good cigars and whiskey. The comic effects are enhanced by the lines that are drawn from the discourse of film. Manet's film images may be somewhat less explicit here than in *Eux ou La prise du pouvoir* but are used with greater comic and, ultimately, dramatic impact as the role-playing assumes psychological and sociological connotations.

Manuel, wearing a costume Eliane has provided, overtly evokes film images. Bertrand says he looks like "Fred something or other" from an American movie he saw in Tegucigalpa (18). Later in the scene, the stage directions indicate that Manuel is to look "more like 'Valentino' than ever" (20). Although not explicitly a film image, Manuel's subsequent appearance as a Nazi officer is likewise drawn from the movies. The German uniform Manuel has found in a closet would be familiar to Manet himself and to most spectators, not directly through memories of World War II, but indirectly through the cinematic portrayal of the period. The same is true of "Lili Marleen," the musical background that accompanies Manuel in his new role as Hans.

In *Lady Strass* there is an almost constant use of music, ranging from Wagner's *Tristan and Isolde* to that played on a flute from India. In the central scenes, when Eliane stages a party for her unexpected visitors, the music is readily associated with movies: "Ramona," "Smoke Gets in Your Eyes," a "Charleston genre *Gold Diggers 1933*" (20). The effects created by this background music, alternately sentimental and lighthearted, are important to the development of the action. Eliane at first is delightfully eccentric, a comic combination of two contrasting film stereotypes. In the party scene, she is still the aristocrat, albeit one who smokes cigars and drinks whiskey; she blithely changes Bertrand's name to one she likes better—Gabriel—and is vivacious enough to teach the overweight, out-of-shape Frenchman to dance. Throughout these early scenes, the

---

19. In her preview of *Lady Strass* for the *Village Voice*, Ana Puga highlights the humor of Manet's "surreal drama" by quoting artistic director Françoise Kourilsky. Kourilsky had chosen Manet's play "in which a woman goes crazy rather than the one in which a corpse is dug up and given a beauty makeover" (*The Nuns*) because the "former is 'more of a fun play'"; according to Kourilsky, "of course both works are hilarious" (qtd. in Puga).

rapid costume changes, representing comic role reversals for the two men in particular, coupled with their visible hunger and greed, contribute to the light tone.

The advertising blurb for the Avignon revival pointedly asks, "But can memories be manipulated according to the fantasy of our imagination and our desires?" The answer is no. In the final scenes, when Manuel takes control, directing a cruel psychodrama that forces Eliane to confront the grotesque truth of her past, she retreats totally from reality. Early in the second act, she makes a surprising and elegant entrance, reciting Keats's poem "La Belle Dame sans merci." Her final appearance, strewing flowers, evokes Ophelia's mad scene from *Hamlet*.[20] In the end, Manuel prepares to leave while Bertrand stays behind with Eliane in her escapist enclosure. Perhaps he does so out of pity, from his old-school sense of chivalry, but more likely he is influenced by his desire to have guaranteed room and board.[21]

The dominant musical motif of *Lady Strass* proves not to be the Charleston or "Smoke Gets in Your Eyes" but rather "Lili Marleen" and the Wagnerian opera that underscores the beginning and end of the play. "Lili Marleen" is a song frequently associated with the German military. *Tristan and Isolde* has a double intertextual reference. The opera story deals with tragic love; Isolde, like Eliane in both tales from her past, is married to an older man but loves a younger one who is killed. In that Wagner's works were appropriated by the Nazis, his operas have also

---

20. *New York Times* reviewer D. J. R. Bruckner also emphasizes the humor of the Manet production: "And Mr. Ernotte so skillfully emphasizes the comic aspects of the dreamlike scenes that the shock at the end comes like a sudden shot from one of the woman's pistols" (Bruckner).

21. A revival of *Lady Strass* in Fall 1987 at the Théâtre Marie Stuart in Paris highlighted the importance of Manet's cinematic intertexuality—by eliminating it. Perhaps because of budget restraints, perhaps because of the director's unfamiliarity with the references, the production did away with Eliane's Western garb and guns, with her elegant pre–World War I gown in the party scene, and with Manuel's dressing up as Valentino. It likewise replaced "Smoke Gets in Your Eyes" and the Charleston with indistinguishable, loud contemporary music. The dance became violent instead of funny. All the intertextual humor of the early scenes had disappeared. Rather than Eliane's degenerating from eccentricity to madness, with associated changes in linguistic registers, she simply reflected a monochord madness throughout. Bertrand's gallant French gesture, his apparent decision to stay with her and care for her, became inexplicable. Additionally, in losing its series of historical allusions evoked through film images, the play also lost its subtextual message: its implicit criticism of Western materialism and imperialism, including cultural imperialism, as exemplified by various nations in the course of the twentieth century. The richness of Manet's theater is dependent upon cinematic techniques and film images both for its brilliant technical effects and for its implicit ideology. To ignore these aspects of his work is to impoverish it.

come to be identified with them. Linda Hutcheon affirms in her recent book on irony: "The fact that Wagner died well before Hitler used his work for his own purposes is not the point here: the point is that the context in which I hear or see Wagner's music today has to include Hitler, and that is a fact with which I (and perhaps you too) must deal" (Hutcheon 1994: 6). Manet's introduction then of Wagnerian music at the beginning of the play for at least some spectators will already announce the story of Hans.

Eliane, with the same nostalgia for a lost love that La Dame conveyed for Emile, begins talking idealistically of Hans, an allegedly loyal, brave and noble Nazi who fled to Central America after the war solely in order to seek out his superior officers. Her reminiscences are triggered in the first act by the startling entrance of Manuel, who appears in Hans's menacing SS uniform. Near the end of the second act, he forces Eliane to relive the German's departure: his violent assault of her husband, his flight with her jewelry and money, her denunciation of him to the police, and his death in prison.

Manet may have chosen voluntary exile from Castro's Cuba, but there is no indication in these plays from the 1970s that he left behind his own leftist garb in exchange for a cloak of rightist rhetoric. If Jilguero, representative of the people, is the one sympathetic character in *Madras, la nuit où . . .* , Manuel, the sometimes hostile mestizo, is the counterpart figure in *Lady Strass*. Bertrand and Eliane symbolize the decadence of the Old World; Eliane, quoting her two deceased husbands, gives direct expression to European racist attitudes toward the natives of colonized lands. The play-within-the-play about Hans reveals not only Eliane's repression of her personal truth but also a criticism of economic imperialism being imposed upon Latin America by capitalists, both British and German, with or without past Nazi connections. In his review of the original production, Alain Leblanc summarized the ideological message: "Fascinated by the almost hypnotic power of money, the Indian Manuel finally realizes that Lady Strass's splendor, all of it fake, is nothing but lies and encroachment. For false Western values he will substitute his own new, different values that will permit the peoples of tomorrow to rise from the ashes of yesterday."

In *Eux ou La prise du pouvoir*, Monsieur and Madame Arthur are doomed to repeat their meaningless rituals. La Dame, Alcibiar and Aya, in *Madras, la nuit où . . .* , as well as Eliane and Bernard in *Lady Strass*, are representatives of the decadent old order who will remain on the stage set of theatricalized life rather than confront the changing reality of the external world. The only characters able to break out of the enclosures are the representatives of the people, Jilguero and Manuel.

Although these plays are not bereft of hope for change, the dominant motif remains enclosure. The entrapment of characters within cave- and cell-like structures (*Les Nonnes*, *Le Borgne*) or houses isolated from the outside world (*Madras, la nuit où* . . . , *Lady Strass*) not only foreshadows the metonymic prisoners' cages of *Mendoza, en Argentine* . . . but gives metaphorical expression to a more general condition of alienation. Alienation may result from exile, either inner exile of the individual estranged from the regime in power, or political exile in a geographic sense. The Spanish Civil War and its aftermath gave rise to countless dramatic texts built on the metaphor of enclosure. That the Cuban Revolution should do the same is not surprising. Manet consciously develops the metaphor when he places the decadent aristocrats of *Madras* and *Lady Strass* within enclosures, isolated from the indigenous society, where they can relive the past through a kind of theatricalized life. Leblanc has not missed the target in observing that in *Lady Strass* the

Fig. 11. *Lady Strass*. Théâtre du Parc, Brussels (photo courtesy of Eduardo Manet).

spectator is led to accept the indigenous Manuel's new values in place of the false ones of the two European characters. But it is quite possible that the repeated use of metaphorical enclosures also responds, unconsciously, to the playwright's own circumstances, to his alienation from his native land and his status as "rotten foreigner" elsewhere. In that respect, it is interesting to note that the motif all but disappeared from his work some years ago, about the time he became a French citizen.[22]

---

22. Manet's French citizenship dates from 1979. The one work after that date that is closely related thematically to texts discussed in this chapter is *Sacrilèges*. The staging of this play November–December 1981 at the Théâtre Marie Stuart in Paris was, in Manet's opinion, a disaster, and the work remains unpublished. The action takes place in a sanctuary, in ruins, somewhere in the tropics. Outside a battle is raging. The war has destroyed everything, turning paradise into a desert. Except for Quatub, who is part savage, part robot, the characters have Hispanic names. Indio and Yoyo are soldiers; María is a kind of intermediary between Quatub and the believers in the old religion. In the end, María and Yoyo agree that the totem they have worshipped is a meaningless prop. They elect to leave their refuge and seek a new paradise somewhere beyond the no-man's-land that surrounds them; Indio decides to stay within the enclosure. Typical of Manet's work in general, the text calls for extensive musical and lighting effects, acrobatic stunts, and comic word games. The basic situation recalls the earlier works of entrapment and enclosure but also serves as a link to later plays, discussed in Chapter 6. *Les Chiennes* and *Mare Nostrum* also take place after cataclysms. The use of the robot anticipates one element of *Deux siècles d'amour*.

5

A Postmodern Breaking Out

EXPERIMENTS IN

HISTORIOGRAPHIC

METATHEATER

During the first decade after his return to France, Manet concentrated on plays of enclosure and entrapment: works with small casts, single sets, and claustrophobic atmospheres. Of his published texts from this period, the one exception is *L'Autre Don Juan* (The other Don Juan, 1974), a creative reworking of *Las paredes oyen* (The walls have ears) by the seventeenth-century Mexican-Spanish author Juan Ruiz de Alarcón. We shall consider the Alarcón version in the chapter on multicultural metatheatricalism, but I mention it here because in its effervescent farce and playful mingling of languages, cultural discourses, and historical moments, it is closely related to the dominant current in Manet's postmodern, historiographic works.

Manet has periodically revealed his abiding interest in political history, particularly that of Latin America. As we have seen, his quasi-autobiographical novels are set against prerevolutionary Cuba. Although these novels use historical background in a fairly conventional way, Manet's writing for the theater does not include traditional history plays; rather he tends to blend history with metafiction. Similar in this respect to the stage works to come is an unpublished television play, *Bolívar et le Congrès de Panama*. Written in 1976 for Antenne 2, the script is structured as a film-within-a-film. The frame story centers on a movie director who initially does not know much about Simón Bolívar and mistakenly believes that he can use the format of a spaghetti Western to relate the nineteenth-century South American liberator's life and death. Interspersed within the movie about Bolívar are contemporary film clips, giving contrasting images from Brazil of carnival and military parades and from Chile of the dictator Pinochet in parallel with poet Pablo Neruda's funeral.

The blending of cultural discourses and technological advances is characteristic of postmodernist art. In his *Theatre, Theory, Postmodernism*, Johannes Birringer affirms that theater has lagged behind the other arts and cultural practices: "One could argue that the theatre itself . . . has diminished its historical consciousness because it seems not to live within the image-ridden and hysterical world of postmodern consumer capitalism" (x–xi). Because of his extensive involvement with film and a Marxist concern about the excesses of capitalism, Manet's theater surely lags less than that of many other playwrights. The four works considered in this chapter incorporate filmic techniques or other rapidly changing images and, albeit in different ways, they criticize capitalist activities. In parallel with Linda Hutcheon's definition of historiographic metafiction in the novel (*A Poetics of Postmodernism*), three of them make extensive use of parodic intertextuality. All of them call into question the validity of official versions of historical figures or of the ideological bases for political action.

Politics as Metatheater

Bradby, viewing *Un Balcon sur les Andes* (A balcony over the Andes, 1979) from the perspective of a specialist in French theater, labels it as "ubuesque" (238) and compares it to Mnouchkine's *Méphisto* (239). It might be better appreciated in its Latin American context. Indeed nowhere is the Hispanic presence in Manet's theater more visible than in this overtly Latin American metaplay. An exuberantly Brechtian text, ostensibly set in the mid-nineteenth century at a time of great political turmoil, it presents an episodic account of a French theatrical troupe's travels through Peru, Bolivia, Paraguay, and Brazil. Continuing the use of bilingual and multilingual dialogue found in *L'Autre Don Juan* and *Lady Strass*, the playwright exploits his basic situation by introducing extensive passages of Spanish and, to a lesser extent, Portuguese. Some of the plays-within-the-play are done in French with a running consecutive interpretation to Spanish.

To varying degrees, Manet's works are always metatheatrical. According to Richard Hornby, the most fully developed kind of metadrama, the play-within-the-play, surfaces when society becomes cynical. Theater functions as a metaphor for life. If the play is but an illusion, then "by extension, the world in which we live, which also seems to be so vivid, is in the end a sham" (Hornby 45). It is this full-blown approach to metatheater, with its concomitant cynicism, that we find in *Un Balcon sur les Andes*. The dual subject, as the title suggests, is theater and Latin American politics, or, more precisely, the theater of politics and the politics of theater. We, as spectators, shall have our balcony seat to enjoy the spectacle: a contredanse of power. Bradby finds the Manet work, in contrast to *Méphisto*, "rather simplistic . . . because neither the characters nor the situation have precise historical referents" (239). Those more connected to Latin American history may feel that the referents are multiple and all too real.

If it is the playwright's intention to tear away the mask of political power and reveal the face of tyranny beneath, then metatheater is a splendid vehicle for doing so. In his comparative overview of possible French influence on contemporary Latin American theater, George Woodyard has correctly pointed out the persistent use of metatheatrical games in the works of many dramatists of both stages. But metadrama obviously antedates the twentieth century, and its use by Hispanic playwrights may also be readily traced to Spain's Golden Age. It is the potentially subversive impact of metadrama that explains its appeal for many Latin American playwrights, whatever their country of residence. Few French playgoers recall that the late Copi was Argentine, but his corrosive 1969 text *Eva Perón* would doubtless never have been written by a non-Latin American. Copi's title character feigns her illness and death and has an unwitting double buried in her place. The historical Evita's physical suffering is presented as a farce. Even if the spectator rejects this premise as fiction, the suggestion remains that Latin American politics is a world of sham in which the citizens are manipulated and victimized. As in Gabriel García Márquez's novel *El otoño del patriarca* (*The Autumn of the*

Patriarch) those in power have their doubles so that they may never die. Manet, too, introduces the dictator and his double in a key episode of his complex political satire *Un Balcon sur les Andes*. Although there are no references in Manet's text to real historical figures, the overall situation has obvious associations with much of South American history.

The play consists of forty-four scenes. For purposes of performance, these are divided into two parts, with the break occurring between scenes 19 and 20. The written text is divided into three sections, respectively labeled "The actors" (scenes 1–15), "The politicians" (scenes 16–26), and "The guerrilla fighters" (scenes 27–44). A multileveled set facilitates rapid changes of scene and, as the rhythm increases, simultaneous action. There is a Brechtian use of placards to indicate shifts in historical time and geographical location and to announce the plays-within-the-play. A small orchestra provides further narrative commentary through the kinds of ethnic music they play and the accompanying changes of costume.

The action begins in Paris in 1848. Erroneously believing that the revolution has triumphed, Blaise and Tarassin present a proliberty farce. They are imprisoned, manage to escape, and flee to South America. By scene 8, Blaise and Tarassin are in Peru, and up to their old theatrical tricks. Their troupe prospers. They add local talent to the cast, begin to learn Spanish, and, in a burst of capitalist inventiveness, sell food and the services of prostitutes. Because of the subversive content of their performances, they are in constant trouble with the authorities; thus, like Brecht's Mother Courage with her wagon, they keep moving on. They continue to do so even after their wagons are confiscated by thieving soldiers. (Instead of the traditional "Hide the hens, the actors are coming," the actors learn they must hide their belongings when the soldiers are coming.)

Finally the troupe falls into the hands of General Palomares, the Francophile dictator of a not yet existent nation. Palomares, who controls a vast amount of land, is in constant war with Paraguay, Brazil, and Argentina—not to mention the indigenous guerrillas. Tarassin (alias Tarrasco) adapts happily to the luxurious lifestyle of Palomares, but Blaise leaves, taking part of the troupe with him, and eventually joins the revolutionaries. Palomares is assassinated by Colonel Zaldivar, who replaces the general and is assassinated by Gutierrez, who is assassinated by Ramiro. Tarassin serves each general in turn, typically joining the conspiracy when the general is still a colonel, and thus is able to save his friends Blaise and Jacques when the guerrillas are destroyed. In a final scene, General Ramiro accepts the support of the United States; Tarassin, now a colonel himself, visually covets Ramiro's seat of power; and the MGM lion flashes on the backdrop screen. Versailles has been replaced by Hollywood. Imperialism, cultural or political, has shifted from Europe to North America. And the game of musical generals goes on.

Throughout *Un Balcon sur les Andes*, there is a constant interplay between the theatrical and political worlds. The former is clearly one of "let's pretend." For example, in the opening play-within-a-play, Tarassin's role in the farce is established by his costume: he is "absurdly, poorly dressed as a king" (1985: 15). Blaise is the queen, by virtue of his costume and the comic, high-pitched voice he assumes to establish his character's gender. By association, the external political world is seen to be equally theatricalist, reminiscent of Alfred Jarry's *Ubu Roi*. Palomares's throne is but a prop, and Zaldivar, Gutierrez, and Ramiro can become the ruling general merely by usurping the previous dictator's uniform and medals. The transfers of power, in which each survivor in the chain of command puts on the uniform of his new rank, are handled as spectacle: a Versaillesque carnival or a ritual ceremony carried on before a bank of mirrors. Even Palomares's imposition of the French language is but a kind of role-playing, a superficial assumption of culture that can no more turn the Indians into Europeans (Palomares's stated intention, 73) than Blaise's stage voice can make him female.

As George Szanto has shown, theater is always political, whether the political message is overt (agitation propaganda), covert (integration propaganda), or more subtle and hence thought provoking (dialectical propaganda). Repressive regimes may fear theater because of its subversive potential but they also tend to exploit the stage to promote their own ideology. In Manet's work, General Palomares hopes to use Tarassin's troupe to enhance his self-image. He commands Tarassin to create a text extolling his life and deeds. Tarassin, who places greater value on creature comforts—and personal safety—than on freedom of expression, is happy to oblige. He will become the dictator's double in order to play the role. But Zaldivar manipulates Palomares's script to meet his own ends; he takes advantage of the double's presence at a public function to sequester and kill the real Palomares. The political stage is thereby set for the arrival of the new dictator.

The visual signs establish clearly that the uniform makes the general, but the equation *politician = actor* is given verbal expression as well. Colonel Gutierrez explains that Tarassin has been chosen for an international mission precisely because of his acting skills: his ability to memorize texts, to create a character, to disguise himself, and to pretend. Great diplomats are, Gutierrez says, part clown, part actor. In each country he visits, Tarassin-Tarrasco will speak their language and, as needed, lie with panache (97). To be sure, this is what Tarassin has been doing all along with the series of colonels and generals and what they have been doing with everyone. From the opening scene, the stage directions indicate the audiences for the plays-within-the-play should consist in part of life-size dolls. The technique not only underscores the text's essential theatricalism but implies that the spectators of the larger political stage may also be reduced to mannequins. Manet's theater repeatedly calls for dolls to supplement the live actors. The strategy may have its origins in Artaud; Styan points out that Artaud, working with his assistants Barrault and Blin, intermingled dummies in his famous 1935 staging of *Les Cenci* "in order to suggest a bizarre society" (Styan 110).

In the series of episodes dealing with the generals, there is a dehumanizing quality, reminiscent of Valle-Inclán's *esperpento* (grotesque tragicomedy) and Goya's expressionistic paintings. Palomares is described as being a little thin man with a large bald head. The dark glasses he wears are small and round, making him look like a death's head (*Un Balcon* 1985: 67). (Tarassin's portrayal as Palomares's double is thus simplified by an appearance that is basically a mask.) In the stage direction describing the execution wall set up by General Zaldivar, Manet acknowledges the Hispanic influence when he specifically cites the memory of Goya (82). The ceremonies marking the transfer of power to a new general coincide with the sound of the firing squad. All of those associated with the generals' repressive regimes, including Tarassin, are subjected to the deforming effects of the *esperpento*. Whether they are playing the role of puppet or are temporarily pulling the strings, they are all charlatans. They are further dehumanized by the use of doubles for flashbacks and recorded narrative voices in scenes that juxtapose two moments in time. Significantly, these staging techniques are never used in portraying the guerrillas. If the spectators, like Blaise and his companions, are ultimately led to take the side of the guerrillas, it is because the revolutionaries are free of role-playing and project a humanity and authenticity totally lacking in the world of the politicians.

Un Balcon sur les Andes, true to its Brechtian antecedents, is political theater. But it is also political metatheater, that is, a treatise on political theater as well as a political satire. Eschewing the tenets of socialist realism, in his text Manet suggests both that theater for entertainment's sake has a value and that any play, no matter how frivolous it seems, may be laden with ideological significance. For that reason, any play may prove dangerous to the health of the actors or of those in power.

Some of the defense of political theater is directly expressed by Blaise, whose committed stance is diametrically opposed to Tarassin's willingness to collaborate with whoever is in charge. Back in France it was Blaise who urged the agitprop farce defending liberty and attacking absolutism. Once in South America, he promotes an underground theater that will focus on the problems of the peasants; he states that such a theater existed among the Indians before the Spaniards came (58). He later convinces the guerrillas that theater can provide the relaxation they need after a day of battle. Everyone will laugh, and laughter will make them all feel better (94–95). Not surprisingly, he creates a script that they can easily interpret to their satisfaction: "A celui qui vole un voleur tout sera pardonné" (For him who steals from a thief all will be forgiven; 98).

Through the plays-within-the-play and the audience response to them, Manet foregrounds the subversive potential of theater. The dramatic text in performance is a censor's nightmare. Not only may the director or actors change the written dialogue or, through other sign systems, alter its meaning, but each spectator may shift the focus and find a different message. The play is both text and context, and the context of any one performance may differ from previous ones, thus affecting the meaning received by the audience. Manet demonstrates these principles by providing examples of texts in performance that give rise to unpredictable reactions.

The agitprop play-within-the-play in the opening scene is a case in point. The queen usurps power from the ridiculous king and proclaims liberty for the people. This is harmless propaganda as long as it is consistent with the dominant ideology. But, as the police in the audience for the play-within-the-play forcefully reveal, the dominant ideology has just changed. Yesterday's harmless propaganda is today's punishable, subversive act.

The equally agitprop play ordered by General Palomares also proves to be a text out of the control of its creator. The final curtain to his idealized biography is not one he planned. Moreover, even before Zaldivar provides his ending to the real Palomares's script, Blaise sets aside the planned dialogue relating to the fictionalized general. Arriving drunk to the performance, he begins to ad lib a satire of the dictator. The other actors, terrified, drown him out with trumpets and drums.

The meaning of any dramatic text is subject to the multiple readings the spectators may give it. Manet illustrates this polycentric aspect of theater through clever variations on the bedroom farce: the eternal triangle of deceived husband (Tarassin), faithless wife (Blaise), and treacherous lover (Jacques). It is the "safe," nonpolitical text that Tarassin recommends in Peru after their escape from the French prison. In their first performance, the actors discover that the Peruvian spectators do not react to the text in the expected way. They throw rotten fruit at a surprised Tarassin and, taking the side of the adulterous wife over the cuckolded husband, insult him—in Spanish, of course—and tell him to go away: "Fuera, tarrudo! Abajo los maridos cornudos! Deja joder tu pobre mujer, cabrón! Vivan los amantes! Fuera! Fuera!" It is a reading of the text encouraged by the native interpreter: "El cobarde y asesino marido llega para golpear su dulce mujercita. Duro con él! Duro!" (The cowardly, murderous husband enters and starts to beat his sweet little wife. Let him have it! 38). The audience effectively imposes a reversal in the anticipated good guy/bad guy roles and the legitimacy of marriage is called into question.

Nor is the bedroom farce, epitome of bourgeois comedy, necessarily nonpolitical. In *The Field of Drama*, Martin Esslin recounts an episode in the former Czechoslovakia after the Soviet invasion that illustrates the ever present metaphorical overtones in any dramatic text. Czech theater people found it unwise to stage almost anything: either their own classics or Western plays would be read by the censors as anti-Soviet statements. So they settled on the safety of the bedroom farce. "But then, when in one of the cliché farce scenes, the husband opened the cupboard and found the lover hiding there, the line: 'You have no business in my cupboard' brought the house down" (Esslin, *Field:* 167). The eternal triangle had become a political allegory with the treacherous lover in the role of the Soviet invader.

Despite Manet's ties to the theater world in Czechoslovakia—it was his opposition to Castro's pro-Soviet stance in 1968 that precipitated his departure from Cuba to France—he had not heard this anecdote. By coincidence, then, in *Un Balcon sur les Andes* he exploits the metaphorical potential of the bedroom farce. In its several variations among the plays-within-the-play, the husband, portrayed as a soldier, comes to symbolize the repressive military. The wife, and, in an expansion of the cast, her son as well, are victims whose cause is championed by the heroic lover-bandit. The popular audiences identify the cuckolded husband with the soldiers they hate. Even Palomares reads the text his way; the military that is satirized is not his private army but rather the regular armies of the countries he is fighting. The stock bourgeois comedy has become an agitprop farce open to shifting identifications of the political symbolism.

In the fast-paced *Un Balcon sur les Andes*, there are no fewer than nine plays-within-the-play, that is, scenes that are wholly or partially focused on a performance in progress. As we have seen, the reception to these plays-within-the-play varies from spectator to spectator, and the plays themselves are subject to change. However, although Blaise and Tarassin create new scripts to meet new circumstances, the deep structure of Blaise's texts in particular remains more or less unalterable: the subservient individual sides with the outsider in rebellion against the oppressive authority figure (e.g., the queen joins the people in rejecting the king; the wife joins the lover-bandit and rejects the husband-soldier). Downtrodden people and the cause of freedom triumph. The political world within Manet's text provides an inverted mirror image of this theatrical world. Politics and theater reflect each other faithfully in the sense that each political scene is subject to different interpretations by the citizen-spectators and that the script may change (a monarchy is restored, a general is assassinated, etc.). Even when the geographical or historical scene shifts, the deep structure remains unalterable: power remains in the hands of the exploiters and the people continue to be victimized. If the play is to be given a subversive meaning, the message (that is, the answer to the political mess) lies in Blaise's plays-within-the-play: it is time for the bandit-lover to unite with the people and overthrow the bad marriage with the military dictator.

Un Balcon sur les Andes and *Mendoza, en Argentine* . . . : Plays or Movie Scripts?

Twenty-five years ago Susan Sontag called into question the traditional dichotomy between movies and the stage. She astutely observed both that "theatre can emulate and incorporate cinema" (355) and that, by the late 1960s, in France and other European countries there was a notable influence of movies on theatrical stagings (352). In *The Field of Drama*, Esslin affirms that cinematic types of drama and live theater now share signifying systems to such an extent that they should be studied within a single concept of dramatic performance (91). He notes the influence on live drama of such cinematic techniques as "the flashback, the dynamic montage of long and short scenes, frequent change of the place of the action, the use of recorded voice-overs" (100). Such filmic strategies are characteristic of the postmodern stage.

In his theater, Manet reflects a cinematic influence in various ways, ranging from intertextual references, to the use of specific devices, to the fluid structure of his texts. As his work evolved structurally and thematically in the late 1970s and early 1980s, he began to incorporate on the stage the kind of sweeping, cinematic narrative structure that he had earlier used in his novel of the Cuban Revolution, *Un Cri sur le rivage*. Two plays dealing directly with Latin American political history, *Un Balcon sur les Andes* and *Mendoza, en Argentine* . . . (Mendoza, Argentina, 1983) could readily be transformed into film scripts. The former, in its farcical treatment of a metatheatrical Latin American political reality, including the use of a double, might even be considered an Hispanic precursor to the 1988 Hollywood movie *Moon over Parador* (dir. Paul Mazursky).[1] *Mendoza, en Argentine* . . . , on the other hand, is a serious treatment of political torture and class struggle; its tone is tragic.

Both plays are conceived more as movie scripts than as conventional play texts. They are written in sequences, calling for rapid shifts in time

---

1. For a critical analysis of *Moon over Parador* as Hollywood's facile view of Latin American politics, see Juan Bruce-Novoa's 1991 article. Although the satirical American film has a closed, happy ending not present in *Un Balcon sur les Andes*, it has a number of points in common with Manet's work, including the extensive use of metafictional and multilingual games. The film begins with a movie-in-the-movie. When Parador's English-speaking dictator, Alfonse Sims (Richard Dreyfuss), dies unexpectedly from a heart attack, Jack (also played by Richard Dreyfuss), an American movie actor on location, is pressed into service to assume the dead man's role. (The translated title in Spain fittingly was *Presidente por accidente* [President by accident].) In a dramatic world marked by role-playing within the role, all of the characters have chameleon-like qualities. Jack, whose real name is Noah, soon discovers that Sims wore lifts and a wig; the "real" dictator's public image was no less theatrical than the actor's professional persona. Roberto (Raúl Julia), the evil head of the secret police, is a theater buff of Germanic origins who runs a nightclub. Madonna (Sonia Braga), the president's lover, is leader of the oppressed lower classes and a dancer. The CIA agent (Jonathan Winters), who in large part pulls the strings of the puppet dictator, poses as a retiree who exports hammocks to cover up his true function. Jack rehearses for Sims's speeches in the same way that he would prepare any role; Dreyfuss changes voice to make rapid shifts between the two characters. When Jack muffs his role as Sims, Sims's personal staff acts as if they had not noticed. When Jack does well, Roberto elatedly declares that their play is a hit. At the film's end, when Jack stages his assassination as Sims so that he can go home to New York, Roberto is killed by the people and Madonna is elected president of a liberal democracy.

and space. The critical response to *Un Balcon sur les Andes* in performance specifically discussed this aspect; the complex set, designed by Patrice Cauchetier and Alain Baliteau to facilitate the forty-four scene changes, led some reviewers to compare the production with a cartoon. While the action of this episodic farce is generally linear, *Mendoza, en Argentine . . .* makes extensive use of flashbacks, calling for fluidity both in space and time. It also shifts passages of narration and interior monologue to a sound track and calls for projections on a backdrop screen.

In these plays, as well as in his farcical view of a medieval battlefield, *Histoire de Maheu le boucher* (The story of Maheu, the butcher, 1986), Manet deliberately blurs the line between cinema and theater. He expressed his intentions clearly in an October 1979 interview, preceding the world premiere of *Un Balcon sur les Andes*: conceived as a film script, the play relies on "the impact of the image"; the mise-en-scène, rather than the verbal text, is the vehicle for conveying the message (interview, Salducci). The tendency to construct his work in sequences—that is, as images in motion against a changing background—also underscored Manet's early novels. The assertion that Manet foregrounds images in his texts is somewhat paradoxical, for one of the principal strengths of his theater is his ingenious dialogue. Nevertheless, whenever he wishes to privilege the historical context of his characters, he is apparently influenced by film's potential for rapid movement and for panoramic or simultaneous views. He exploits the latter effect when the action in *Un Balcon sur les Andes* shifts back and forth between Blaise in the jungle and Tarassin in the theatricalized world of political power.

Manet's dominant filmic strategy, to use Esslin's terms, is "the dynamic montage of long and short scenes" but he introduces various other cinematic techniques as well. The orchestra, whose costumes and placards signify the changing scenes, provides the equivalent of a musical score. There is frequent use of a sound track to suggest offstage action. In one notable scene a voice-over, with the recorded dialogue of Tarassin and the dictator Palomares, allows for a split-screen effect: on one side of the stage Tarassin tells his friends Blaise and Jacques of his recent encounter while, simultaneously, on the other side, we can see and hear the flashback he evokes. (The stage directions indicate that Palomares faces the audience, while a stand-in for Tarassin has his back turned.) At the play's end, the guerrillas have been crushed and the dictator of the moment is making a deal with American capitalists. The familiar icon of the MGM lion, projected as a final image, symbolizes cultural imperialism from the North and the debt of Manet's own text to filmic structures.

Manet's text is Brechtian both for its political message and for its staging.[2] Jacques Desuché has described for us the impact of the revolving platform utilized by Brecht, coupled with placards to mark the scenes. He observes that rhythm is fundamental to epic theater and that Brecht made the playing space itself participate in that rhythm (Desuché 83–84). Spanish playwright and set designer Francisco Nieva clarifies to what extent Brecht's own stagings were cinematic: "Dancing images pass rapidly before our eyes. During a single scene, through the shifting of actors and scenic elements, we see effects like different shots. And the little white curtain that goes across the stage, at mid height, could serve as a screen for projecting short, informative sentences while, at the same time, suggesting a theatrical equivalent to a dissolve. Even in the speed of opening or closing the little curtain there could be an intentional effect" (1980: 35). Manet, too, envisions such a rhythm of images in motion for *Un Balcon sur les Andes*.

Manet's episodic farce, with its elaborate set design, premiered in Nice in October 1979. The same production was then taken to Paris in January 1980 for staging at the Odéon National Theater.[3] In the French capital, it ran into "technical" difficulties: Manet recalls that the unionized Odéon crew objected to their heavy assignment. The play, with all its scene changes, went smoothly in Nice; in Paris the dress rehearsal ran twenty-five minutes longer than it should have. Not surprisingly, some Paris reviews found that the play dragged or that the reliance on machinery was excessive.

Such problems notwithstanding, the cinematic staging of *Un Balcon sur les Andes* yielded interesting results. In reviewing the Nice production, Jacques Deslandes described the theater as a "vast cinematographic complex" and emphasized the "magic of the spectacle." In response to the Paris staging, Guy Verdot acknowledged that the set changes were

---

2. In his 1979 interview with Salducci, Manet declared that he had given up on Brecht because of the rigid attitude of Brecht's followers. In my discussion of Manet's theater, I have chosen to ignore the author's passing comment.

3. *Un Balcon sur les Andes* was first presented as a radio play on France-Culture, 24 January 1979, under the direction of Georges Peyrou. The original stage production, opening in October 1979 at the Nouveau Théâtre de Nice, ran 25 January–2 March 1980 in the large auditorium of the Théâtre National de l'Odéon. It was directed by Jean-Louis Thamin and starred Pierre Forest (Blaise), Wladimir Yordanoff (Tarassin), and Jean-Jacques Moreau (Jacques). A filmed version of the Odéon staging was prepared for French Television, under the direction of Jacques Audoir. It aired on Channel 1 on 8 January 1981 and was rerun in 1990.

"not always perfect" but applauded the blend of cinema into theater; he likewise commended the "eminently Latin spirit" of the text, with its characteristic "agility of thought and word."

Such "agility" was, of course, underscored by the rhythmic use of the playing space. That rhythm was nicely described by critic José Barthoneuf: "The clever combination of horizontal and vertical curtains frames images and creates cinematographic effects and optical illusions, while facilitating the substitution of sliding sets. In short, it's a real spectacle. Tenderly naive, perhaps, but pleasing to the eye." Giles Sandier, on the other hand, saw that "tenderly naive" aspect as unsatisfactory cartoon: "Tintin aux Amériques." Even Sandier's negative review gives us the flavor of a highly cinematic staging: Director Jean-Louis Thamin "uses scenic space like a photographic apparatus with constantly changing apertures: screens of all types allow him to toy shamelessly with the framing of images" (Sandier).

Manet's experience with machinery and crews in *Un Balcon sur les Andes* may well explain his somewhat simplified approach to cinematic theater in *Mendoza, en Argentine . . .*[4] His stage directions call for a large, empty space, with a backdrop screen. The stage is to be divided into several platforms of varying heights. The action—which takes place in Mendoza, near the Chilean border, in 1933—is divided into twenty-nine sequences of unequal lengths. The transitions do not require set changes but are facilitated through projections on the screen; a sound track, including suggestive offstage noises, music, and voice-overs; telephone calls, sometimes with accompanying split-screen staging; and special lighting effects, equivalent to cinematic fades and dissolves.

The structure of *Mendoza, en Argentine . . .* is somewhat related to that of *Un Cri sur le rivage*: the individual situation is foregrounded and the past, with its sociohistorical context, is run in episodic fashion as a series of flashbacks. Labeled near the end as "the tragedies of the house of Montalvo" (203), *Mendoza, en Argentine . . .*'s central story—of personal jealousy and vengeance as catalyst for political torture and death—is indeed reminiscent of Greek theater. In addition, the methods used by

---

4. *Mendoza, en Argentine . . .* has not yet had a major professional stage production in France. It was presented as a radio play on France-Culture on 29 September 1983, under the direction of Evelyne Freny. The stage premiere followed in 1984 at the Théâtre Populaire de Champagne with a cast of acting students. Manet's files include clippings from a second provincial production, in 1985–86 by the Atelier de Créativité Théâtrale des Prémontés at Pont à Mousson (Lorraine). It has been translated into English by David Graham-Young and was presented in Hammersmith, England, in January 1986.

the military figure to make the protagonist reveal the whereabouts of the guerrilla leader recall a classic French-language text of Latin American revolution: Emmanuel Roblès's *Montserrat* (1948). On the other hand, Manet's cinematic text breaks with the Aristotelian mode favored by Roblès; in that respect, it is much closer to a play such as Arrabal's *Et ils passèrent des menottes aux fleurs* (*And They Put Handcuffs on the Flowers*, 1969), which similarly contrasts the suffering of a political prisoner with memories of tender love.

The fictional present—Baptiste's torture, culminating in his suicide—is juxtaposed with his narration of scenes from the past, including happier moments and idealistic hopes for social justice. Simultaneously on the backdrop screen, images of barbed wire and of blue sky are projected in ironic alternation. The nightmarish, threatening world of running shadows, marching boots, and gunshots, is created on the screen and through the sound track, in contrast to serene afternoons of listening to opera music or projections of the family photo album that Lorna shows to Baptiste during their courtship days.

The juxtaposition of Baptiste's personal past happiness and the events that converted the couple into committed revolutionaries is intensified through another filmic device. Within the flashback sequence of their marriage, the stage directions call for a "fondu enchaîne" (140), a dissolve that blends the wedding dance into the army's merciless expropriation of Indian property. Later, when both Baptiste and Lorna are held prisoner, a split-screen effect heightens the pathos of their situation: Baptiste's voice-over reads the letter he attempts to write to his pregnant wife while Lorna, cramped in a cage, speaks tenderly to their unborn child.

In other sequences, Manet creates the equivalent of cutting to achieve the kind of rapid rhythm of images that Nieva identified in Brecht's cinematic stagings. Such is the effect in the sequence that reveals a succession of separate actions of several key characters just before Baptiste is taken prisoner. The resulting dramatic tension, with its increasing audience expectation, is typical of adventure or war movies.

Looking at Torture

In *Stages of Terror: Terrorism, Ideology, and Coercion as Theatre History*, Anthony Kubiak traces a symbiotic relationship between theater and terrorism from Greek tragedy to Artaud and postmodern performance art.

He identifies "the operation and objectification of terror as a first principle of performance, from thought, to *mise en scène*, to terrorist act" and affirms that the "history of theatre's filiation with psychic and political terror is the perfect twin of terror's own history as politics" (2). Although Kubiak convincingly presents his case for the pervasive relationship between theater and terror, his thesis might have been further strengthened by including Hispanic authors.[5] With good reason, Severino João Albuquerque has given his book on contemporary Latin American theater the title *Violent Acts*; he emphasizes such subjects as repression and resistance and representing the unrepresentable. In her *Theatre of Crisis: Drama and Politics in Latin America*, Diana Taylor examines the work of Argentinian author Griselda Gambaro under the specific heading "Theatre and Terror" but also generally relates theater produced in Latin America in the 1965–70 period to a historical context of "violent political transition and ideological crisis" (6). She notes how those in power use spectacle to destabilize and control the population: "Dramas of terror and oppression can paralyze the audience by means of real, though highly theatrical, acts of public execution, torture, and terrorism" (19). "Oppression," "torture," and "violence" are key words in her study. Had Taylor concentrated on the period following Pinochet's rule in Chile and the Dirty War in Argentina, her emphasis on torture would doubtless have been even greater.

Manet places the action of *Mendoza, en Argentine . . .* in 1933, when Fascism was a growing, repressive force in the Southern Cone as well as in Europe. His brief preface refers to the series of military regimes preceding the rise to power of Juan Péron and to the system of *desaparecidos*: political opponents "who disappeared from the face of the earth as if by magic" (119). But Manet wrote his play in 1983, after Argentina's seven-year Dirty War, with which the term *desaparecido* has now become associated. Moreover, he not only links his text to Greek tragedy but also has Baptiste recite speeches of Simón Bolívar. Through these strategies, the author encourages us to see class struggle and political violence as ongoing phenomena in South America and the underlying forces of hatred and vengeance as universal.

---

5. Kubiak cites the theory of Brazilian Augusto Boal in a footnote and makes a brief reference to *Fefu and Her Friends* by Cuban American author Maria Irene Fornes. Unmentioned is Fornes's disturbing treatment of torture, *The Conduct of Life*, which would have been an excellent example to support his thesis. He might also have considered any number of works by such authors as Griselda Gambaro and Eduardo Pavlosky (Argentina), Ariel Dorfman (Chile), Antonio Buero-Vallejo (Spain), and Fernando Arrabal (a Spaniard residing in France).

Kubiak describes the productions of Samuel Beckett as moving "silently and inevitably into a theatricalized terrorism, a 'theatre of torture,' which surreptitiously re-creates the torture chambers of state in the agony of waiting and the pain of being bound" (133). He quotes H. Porter Abbot as pointing out that Beckett in essence tortures his actors through the treatment they are subjected to on stage (qtd. in Kubiak 133). Manet's visualization of torture in *Mendoza, en Argentine . . .* is anything but surreptitious. A stand-in for Baptiste is repeatedly on display as the tortured man. At first, he is attached by a diabolical system of cords and pulleys to a board, mounted on two wheels. The board goes up and down as four soldiers move it about the stage. With each movement, the cords are drawn tighter. The actor's clothes are torn and bloodstained; his moans form part of the sound track. In later scenes, both Baptiste and Lorna are in prisoners' cages; although the pregnant Lorna is temporarily protected from beating and other torture by her brother-in-law captor, Dr. Miyares warns her that a week more in her cramped quarters will mean her death and that of her baby.

To Baptiste's intense physical suffering, Manet adds the psychological torture of becoming responsible for a loved one's death. In discussing Gambaro's theater of terror, Taylor reminds us that "family torture"—"raping, brutalizing, and killing the woman in her own home in front of her children and husband"—is "a well-known form of torture used in Latin America" (128); the dehumanized woman victim is but an object used to extract information from the man. Manet's dramatic situation is devoid of such traditional machismo in that husband and wife are treated as equals. Both Baptiste and Lorna have allied themselves with the revolutionaries, both have information on the whereabouts of the guerrilla leader Puma, and both are told that they must confess in order to save the other's life and that of their child. The elderly family doctor is drawn in through a related psychological blackmail: he can save the victims if he can get either one of them to confess.

Manet's use of psychological torture relates *Mendoza, en Argentine . . .* to Roblès's *Montserrat*. The title character of that existentialist tragedy is a Spanish officer in South America who allies himself with Bolívar's revolutionary struggle for independence. In an attempt to force Montserrat into confessing Bolívar's whereabouts, his commanding officer takes six hostages and executes them one by one. Through his silence, Montserrat is made responsible for the deaths of these innocent people, who have pleaded with him for their lives. Deeply grieved, Montserrat yet holds firm and goes bravely to his own execution; for him, the cause of freedom transcends individual rights. The emotional level of the drama is excruciatingly intense, but, in keeping with the French tradition of *bienséance*, the brutal physical action takes place offstage.[6] By contrast, Manet forces his audience to witness Baptiste's torture and suicide. Lorna resists the coercion and Baptiste has the mental and emotional strength to do so as well. Miyares yields; he injects Baptiste with a kind of truth serum. When Baptiste realizes that he has confessed while drugged, he addresses a poetic monologue to his absent wife and slashes his wrists with a blade provided him by a compassionate guard.

Taylor points out that torture sequences may include a false element of choice: "if the victim *chooses* to suffer rather than answer or 'confess,' we (as spectators) are relieved of the moral responsibility of interfering with that choice" (111). The victim, not the victimizer, is to blame for what transpires. Montserrat could have prevented the deaths of six innocent people by betraying Bolívar; some spectators might well find his actions abhorrent and forget that the real executioner is the Spanish commander. Baptiste could have answered the questions and avoided both his torture and the danger to his wife and unborn child. Roblès and Manet prepare the audience for sympathizing with their martyr figures, however, by first establishing the terrible atrocities perpetrated by those in power. Violence on the part of the revolutionaries is justified by the violence previously and consistently done to the people. Manet reinforces this perspective in *Mendoza, en Argentine . . .* through an epilogue that reveals the psychological aftermath suffered by those who betrayed Baptiste and Lorna: a guilt-ridden Dr. Miyares withdraws from the world; Lorna's older half sister retreats to madness. Baptiste could not live with the knowledge that he had involuntarily confessed, but those who placed him in jeopardy cannot easily live with their guilty deeds either.

Manet is also careful to place blame for the violence on greed. Foreign investment spurs the expropriation of Indian lands. Asunción, an illegitimate mestizo, achieves status in society by making a profit on the ranch that she controls after her half sisters, Raquel and Lorna, are orphaned. The ruthless Colonel Sanchez's military actions are closely linked with his own materialistic goals and those of the capitalists in

---

6. Emmanuel Roblès (1914–95) was born in French Algeria of Spanish parents. He spoke fluent Spanish, was well versed in Hispanic literature and history, and often dealt with Hispanic themes in his narrative and dramatic works. In form his plays generally remained within the classic French conventions.

power at the national level. Because she needs his protection and monetary support, Asunción forces Raquel into marrying Sanchez.

The subjugation of the young, beautiful Raquel is treated within the text as another example of torture. She is painfully aware of being reduced to an object of exchange in order to cement the bonds between Asunción and Sanchez.[7] Lorna escapes this traditional "traffic in women" because of a physical deformity that causes her to limp; as damaged goods, she is not for sale and hence is free to marry a poor schoolteacher for love. Lorna and Baptiste conspire, unsuccessfully, to save Raquel from legalized rape and enslavement. Dr. Miyares, too, is aware of Raquel's suffering; the most he can contribute is an abortion so that she is not forced to bear the child Sanchez so desperately wants.

Manet's play deals overtly with the exchange of women fostered by a patriarchal society and with Asunción's willingness to ally herself with white male hegemony. In the process of overcoming her own disadvantaged situation, she adopts white culture and spurns her indigenous heritage. While she stages opera gatherings in her home for which she dresses elegantly in order to listen to the radio with her guests, in her daily life she runs the ranch like a man. Her self-hatred, as defined by Sander Gilman, encompasses the rejection both of her Indian roots and of "feminine" weakness that might have led to solidarity with her sisters.[8]

The tale of passion that turns *Mendoza, en Argentine . . .* into "the tragedies of the house of Montalvo" avoids falling into melodrama through Manet's narrative strategy: the series of flashbacks in which the tale is told are juxtaposed with the visible suffering of Baptiste and Lorna. Emilio Laguardia, who is none other than the infamous Puma, is given refuge in the Montalvo house after being found wounded by some of Asunción's laborers. Handsome and charming, able to play multiple roles, he wins Baptiste and Lorna to his cause and seduces both Asunción and Raquel. Asunción, perhaps pretending not to know Emilio's secret iden-

---

7. Eve Kosofky Sedgwick points out that in the patriarchal traffic in women, women are used "as exchangeable, perhaps symbolic, property for the primary purpose of cementing the bonds of men with men" (qtd. in Austin 47). In Manet's play, Asunción has taken on the role of the "man of the house."

8. As a mestizo born out of wedlock, Asunción is doubly the Other in her society. Gilman observes: "Self-hatred results from outsiders' acceptance of the mirage of themselves generated by their reference group—that group in society which they see as defining them—as a reality" (2). The reference group holds out the illusion that the outsiders can belong by rejecting their difference. However, "as one approaches the norms set by the reference group, the approbation of the group recedes. . . . For the ideal state is never to have been the Other, a state that cannot be achieved" (3).

tity, justifies her lover's continued presence at the ranch by making him her administrator. Raquel, equally enamored and rebellious as well, learns to feign affection for her husband in order to gain information of use to the guerrillas. It is only when Asunción discovers Emilio's relationship with Raquel that she unleashes Sanchez's wrath. Asunción's sacrifice of her sisters' happiness, and perhaps their lives, is not unlike Medea's revenge when she similarly learns of her man's betrayal. The cuckolded colonel, who otherwise would have released his in-laws with a mere warning, orders Baptiste's torture precisely because of Emilio's attack on Sanchez's honor. From his machista perspective, Raquel is once again but an object, not the subject of her actions.

The tone of *Mendoza, en Argentine* . . . is diametrically opposed to the farcical *Un Balcon sur les Andes*. Nevertheless, the underlying structure of the central love triangle remains the same: the subservient wife sides with the lover-guerrilla in rebellion against the oppressive authority figure, her husband-soldier. The sympathies of the audience should be with the adulteress, whose forced marriage has clearly placed her in the position of victim. That Emilio is an unwilling partner in his relationship with the authoritarian Asunción is underscored by the legends Dr. Miyares relays at the play's end. Emilio and Raquel together, along with Lorna and her baby, have become the illusive leaders of the rebel forces.

Given the complexities of torture, plays revolving around the theme may foreground one or more of a variety of elements. *Mendoza, en Argentine* . . . is a particularly complete text in that it includes several of these possibilities: the personal, rather than ideological reasons for becoming a torturer; the exploitation of psychological as well as physical torture; the psychological aftermath both for the person who confesses under torture and for those who facilitate the torture. Among the play's strengths is its presentation of the victims as sympathetic human beings with whom the spectators may identify.

A Cartoon Approach to the Medieval Battlefield

Unlike *Mendoza, en Argentine* . . . , *Histoire de Maheu, le boucher* is a return to the irreverent, animated cartoon approach to history that Manet had developed in *Un Balcon sur les Andes*. Temporal and spatial fluidity and the elaborate set changes found in Manet's fanciful view of Latin

American dictatorship have disappeared; they are replaced here by a structure far more typical of French theater: a single set and the classic unities of time and story. Such surface traits aside, this work is as wildly comic, as subversively satirical, and as prone to anachronistic reference and incongruous discourse as the more complex play. In a Bakhtinian sense, it is a carnivalesque parody that, by maintaining a dialogue with an incredible variety of antecedent texts, calls into question the official discourse of the dominant society. Because of its parodic intertextuality—or, as Linda Hutcheon would have it, its interdiscursivity (1988: 130)—with both popular and high culture, Manet's historical farce is also typically postmodern: a clear example of theater equivalent to Hutcheon's definition of historiographic metafiction.

The Roseau Theater's production of *Histoire de Maheu, le boucher*, directed by Jean-Claude Broche, opened on 11 July 1986 in Avignon and was subsequently awarded that year's René Praile, the grand prize for the "Off" Avignon Festival. The following October the same group staged the work at their own theater in Paris. Favorable critical reaction identified the play's raucous humor as being reminiscent of everything from medieval farce to Monty Python. Writing for *Libération*, Henry-Jean Servat affirmed that the text, unleashing as much crazy laughter as fake blood, provided a constant seesaw "between the grandiose and the outlandish, the sublime and the ridiculous, sniggering and tenderness."

The action of *Histoire de Maheu, le boucher* takes place near a French battlefield in 1429, during the Hundred Years' War. The title character has long dreamed of being a knight despite his humble origins and the discouragement of Mathilde, his stereotypical Jewish mother; she prefers that he tend the family business and take advantage of a burgeoning Parisian market. On this eventful day, the thirty-five-year-old first learns that he is the bastard son of Count Thibault de Blois. As the battle progresses, the butcher; his friend Jehan, the hunchbacked tanner; and finally Mathilde, too, amputate limbs and sew up the wounded. Although his much amputated biological father has at last dubbed him a knight, Maheu is ultimately dismayed by the blood and gore and opts to go off and save souls rather than enter the fray. At the rollicking farce's conclusion, Mathilde and Jehan quickly improvise ways to get rich by selling relics of the would-be saint, among them photos, T-shirts, and the Editions Papiers text of the play just staged. The ending's emphasis on contemporary commercialism readily recalls the final image of the MGM lion in *Un Balcon sur les Andes*, and the actors' transformation into vendors who mingle with the audience repeats the strategy of *L'Autre Don Juan*.

The simple set for *Histoire de Maheu, le boucher*, represents an area adjacent to a battlefield. In the semidarkness at one side of the stage, a ladder provides a vantage point for viewing the offstage action; Jehan climbs up and narrates from there what he sees, sometimes in awe and sometimes in crude detail, as if he were witnessing a theatrical spectacle. (He becomes so enthralled in his role as towering spectator that when Maheu and his mother hug each other, he applauds.) Among the minimal props are the items necessary to create a makeshift operating table—along with large quantities of ketchup. To allow the "amputations" to take place out of audience view, there are curtains, reminiscent of children's puppet shows, and screens. The stage directions, following Manet's typically extensive use of sound track, call for a wide range of musical motifs. These include trumpet fanfares and drumrolls, to announce the impending battle; a choral rendition of "La Marseillaise," to underscore Maheu's idealistic, patriotic speech, inspired by the example of Joan of Arc; and a choir of angels, with organ accompaniment, when Maheu sets off on the path to would-be sainthood.

No doubt the salient aspect of *Histoire de Maheu, le boucher* is its cartoon or puppet-show-like violence and bloodshed. The wounded Count Thibault enters, has his right arm amputated, and goes back to battle, pausing only long enough to jauntily thank his impromptu surgeons for their good work: "Merci les gars! Bon travail!" (21). Two clownish soldiers come in, with multiple arrows protruding from their bodies; Maheu and Jehan pull out the arrows and patch them up with adhesive bandages in the form of a cross—imitating the emblem of a knightly order. Hugues de Champagne staggers in, clutching his intestines to him with his cloak, and leaves feeling like a new man as soon as Mathilde, in a scene of shadow play projected on the privacy screen, stitches him up with an exceedingly long thread. Thibault returns, with multiple injuries, and Mathilde amputates his remaining arm, both legs, and his genitals. Wrapped like a baby in swaddling clothes, he rides on a cart that his warrior wife Marguerite energetically pushes back out on the battlefield where she personally beheads their archenemy who, as her exaggerated hostility reveals, had once been her lover.

There is nothing subtle about Manet's substitution of a butcher-tanner team for the traditional barber-surgeon. The result is a satirical equation of the manly art of war with the slaughter of animals: Maheu merely transfers his skills at cutting up carcasses to cutting off human limbs. The theme could, of course, be dealt with naturalistically; here Manet presents it with macabre, grotesque humor—and the audience predictably laughs.

In his classic study on laughter, French theorist Henri Bergson clarified that ugliness and physical deformity are comic only if the distortion is one that can easily be imitated (398). It is this principle that Manet follows in introducing hunchbacks as figures of fun. In the earlier *L'Autre Don Juan*, the author/actor-character openly adopts the costume of deformity when he assumes a role within the role; the theatricalism of his actions emphasizes that the hump is but artifice. In *Histoire de Maheu, le boucher*, Maheu proclaims himself a self-made man as a result of lifting weights: "I'm the one who made this body!" (9). He suggests to Jehan that he could have followed the same exercise regimen and also have become a perfect specimen. Maheu's anachronistic devotion to bodybuilding is intended to make spectators see the character's imperfection as something under his control and hence not a real or permanent impairment.

A similar phenomenon occurs with the amputations in *Histoire de Maheu, le boucher*. In that they are performed in overtly theatricalist fashion, they are no more real than puppet show violence: the spectators of course realize that the actors are faking. Thibault's severed arm, displayed at one point by Jehan, must be an obvious prop, and the copious amounts of blood must not hide their tomato sauce origins. When the injured men undergo hasty major surgery and cheerfully head right back to battle, there is a further foregrounding of the nonrealistic intent of the scenes. In her 1993 study on comedy as discursive exchange, Susan Purdie observes that in cartoons the overt artifice of the medium "retards sympathetic 'realisation' of the (considerable) harm its victims experience," a delay enhanced by the fact that "no one in the cartoon world—including the victim—reacts as if sympathy were appropriate" (67–68). Equally applicable to Manet's outlandish approach to the Hundred Years' War is Purdie's analysis, based on *Tom and Jerry* cartoons and those characters' vitality in the face of mayhem: "effortless resilience is actually likely to be funny, because it is the ultimate 'discursive manipulation'" (70).

Another clue to the comic success of Manet's use of gruesome injury in the series of battlefield operations is provided by Bergson's theory of acceleration or snowballing action as a source of laughter (Bergson 424). Adopting the rapid rhythm that characterizes farce, the wounded warriors arrive one after another, each requiring more invasive treatments than the one before. Moreover, their unexpected responses and those of the medieval MASH squad are filled with incongruity. Several decades ago, Stephen Leacock conjectured—no doubt erroneously, considering the atrocities of recent history—that, while primitive people laughed at others' misfortunes, civilization has modified this source of laughter from injury to incongruity (1938: 17); building on a theory of laughter that dates back at least to Kant and Schopenhauer, he suggested that laughter is provoked by incongruities, contrasts, and disharmony (1935: 12). It is on this surefire comic strategy that Manet builds both his wild action and his dialogue. When Maheu and Jehan undertake their first operation, passing their "surgical" instruments from one to the other, their parody of the typical surgeon-nurse interchange is immediately apparent and unquestionably ludicrous:

Maheu: Pick.
Jehan: Yes, chief.
Maheu: Tongs.
Jehan: Here, chief.
Maheu: Hammer.
Jehan: There you are, chief.
Maheu: Hatchet. (20)

If the sight and out-of-sight gags of violence and bloodshed are the farce's outstanding feature, Manet's usual linguistic games are not far beyond in their audience impact. I have already alluded to Mathilde's unexpected, anachronistic portrayal as a stereotypical Jewish mother. Following Manet's pattern of foreign language use for insults and terms of endearment, her sporadic Yiddish expressions, generally aimed at the grown son she treats like a child, are guaranteed to evoke laughter. The opening scene, between Maheu and Jehan, presents the former's defense of knighthood and his own ardent desire to continue in the paths of the national epic heroes he so admires: to be a second Cid Campeador or a new Roland (9). Thus he is in the process of donning his homemade suit of armor. Mathilde's eruption onstage is marked, in Leacock's terms, by the contrast and disharmony of her speech: "Maheu, schnook! Que fais-tu, malheureux! Oy-oy-oy! Qu'est-ce que c'est que ce fils que Dieu m'a donné? Enlève ça immédiatement, Maheu! Et je dis bien im-mé-dia-te-ment!" (Maheu, you schnook! What are you doing, you miserable wretch? Oy, oy, oy! What kind of a son did God give me? Take that off immediately, Maheu. Im-me-di-ate-ly! 12).

In addition to employing the recurring use of Yiddish whenever Mathilde is present, Manet gradually adds occasional, unexpected expressions in Spanish and English. One of the grateful soldiers praises Jehan for the healing quality of his hands, his "manitas de plata" (26). Mathilde calls for a miracle from the "Virgencita . . . macarena," the much-loved statue of Mary found in Seville (38); but she also worries about "cash-flow" and accuses some nobles of acting like "gangsters" (31). Jehan proposes the unseemly activities of the kings of France as subjects for "best-sellers" (26). Although the expressions in Spanish might not be accessible to his French audience, Manet's anachronistic English ones, drawn from the worlds of business and cinema, no doubt will evoke laughter because of their obvious incongruity.

Even more extensively, Manet exploits his medieval setting to make French expressions seem just as opaque and strange as the foreign ones. In effect he defamiliarizes expletives by introducing them as words invented by Maheu that shock or confuse Jehan. Simultaneously, he emphasizes that Maheu's social status is based on roles that can be either adopted or set aside. For example, after exclaiming, "Oh, merde, ne me fais pas chier, Jehan!" (Oh shit, don't be such a pain in the ass, Jehan), Maheu agrees with the nonplussed Jehan that this is not the language of chivalry but clarifies: "I'm still a butcher. I won't be a knight until after the dubbing" (10). Maheu both "invents" obscenities and explains what a word like "brigand" will mean in the future, after the Hundred Years' War is over (10–11). The defamiliarization process continues when Mathilde reacts to her son's new slang, even slapping him for speaking so crudely in her presence (13). Then, in a comic reversal, the offended mother herself introduces unexpectedly coarse language: saying to Jehan, "TA GUEULE, LE BOSSU!" (Shut up your mug, you hunchback; 16); calling Thibault's wife "cette chienne" (that bitch; 17). The contrast between contemporary colloquialisms and the lofty ideals of medieval chivalry espoused by Maheu in the opening scene serves as a comic device that foregrounds the anachronistic use of language.

Language becomes directly self-reflexive in the scene with Hugues de Champagne. Given the nobleman's severe injuries, he can barely talk and thus has an elliptical style, which he describes even as he speaks: "Short phrases. Suppression articles. If possible. Syntax. Reversed. If phrases too long. Obliged breathe. Deeper." (33). At once, however, while still clutching his dislocated intestines—or, as he explains, "Tripes tombent" (guts falling)—he radically shifts in tone, softly reciting a rondeau by Charles d'Orléans: "Le temps a laissié son manteau / De vent, de froidure et de pluye" (Time has left its mantel / Of wind and cold and rain; 33). The juxtaposition of the lovely medieval lyric with the previous comic speech and Hugues de Champagne's grotesque appearance creates the incongruity between subject-matter and style that John D. Jump has defined as the essence of burlesque.

If insults and obscenities are time-honored comic devices, so are the ribald and the taboo, elements that abound in *Histoire de Maheu, le boucher*, with particular emphasis on incest. Hugues de Champagne promises his virgin daughter in marriage to Jehan if the latter will heal him; once cured, he admits that he is keeping the girl for himself. (Jehan's despair at this turn of events will lead him to Sartrean existentialism, including his quotation of the famous line from *Huis clos* [*No Exit*], "Hell is other people.") While Mathilde is energetically amputating Thibault's various parts, Marguerite—recalling the obsession of Racine's Phèdre with her stepson—attempts to rape Maheu. The parting kiss of Mathilde and Maheu is more passionate than one might expect from mother and son.

The comic techniques discussed thus far function at a superficial level and will be easily captured by the audience in performance. Perhaps more interesting from a literary point of view is the dramatic text's pervasive use of parody and intertextual references to a wide variety of discourses. Some aspects of this use, like Mathilde's assimilation of the discourse both of the Jewish mother and of the modern capitalist, are also part of the surface humor. Allusions to such works as *Huis clos* and *Phèdre*, for those who recognize the sources, will cause pleasurable laughter from their incongruity. Other uses of intertextuality, as we shall note, are somewhat more complex.

From the outset, Maheu's infatuation with chivalry, his extensive reading on the subject, and his impossible dream of becoming a knight make him a quixotic figure. Nor is he without a sidekick who contrasts with him in physical appearance; as Servat observes, Jehan plays Sancho Panza to Maheu's Don Quixote. Like Don Quixote, Maheu hopes to be immortalized in a book on his life and adventures. And just as Cervantes's idealistic hero must confront the grotesque realities of his world, Maheu discovers that the glory he seeks, in his mother's words, is "dying in a pool of crap" (15). Despite the obvious parallels, the only direct reference within the dialogue to Cervantes or his masterpiece comes within a long speech of Mathilde in which she relates—in the patter format of a stock, vaudeville-style Jewish joke—a conversation she has had with her grocer friend Sonia Potocki about their respective concerns as mothers (29–30). In theatricalist fashion, the actress is to move back and forth on the stage, assuming a different stance for each character (30). No doubt she will also adopt a comic Jewish inflection in both voices in order to draw attention to the popular discourse she is imitating. The reference to the Quixote in this context will be doubly parodic: a parody of the books of chivalry alluded to within a parody of a particular kind of twentieth-century popular humor.

The juxtaposition of high and low culture is even more notable with reference to the *Chanson de Roland* (*Song of Roland*), source of the most extensive direct citations in the text. Maheu quotes some dozen lines from the poem in the scene preceding Mathilde's narrated dialogue between the two Jewish mothers (26–27); he quotes another two dozen lines in a subsequent argument with his mother about chivalry (31–32). In both cases, as with the severely wounded Hugues de Champagne's rendering of the lyric rondeau in the following scene, the lofty verse is totally debunked by the context in which it is recited and the various theatrical signs with which it comes into play.

Prior to his first recitation from the *Chanson de Roland*, Maheu has been steadily drinking whiskey as a response to the shocking news he has been given by the two clownish soldiers: that Thibault is an incorrigible womanizer and that he has lured hundreds, perhaps thousands, of lower-class men to their deaths on the battlefield by stories and promises similar to those that Maheu has heard. Jehan follows this revelation with references to the scandalous love lives of the kings of France. Thus it is at a moment of drunken disillusionment that Maheu turns to the beloved epic for inspiration. As he tells Jehan, "That is the France I love, Jehan. Those are my heroes! (26)" Jehan responds in an unexpected, scholarly tone, casting doubt on the historic validity of the literary text and referring to the Oxford manuscript. As Maheu continues his recitation from the epic, he simultaneously floors Jehan with a series of karate chops.

Maheu's savagery, however, is not at all inconsistent with the content of the *Chanson de Roland*: the lines he quotes are filled with references to massacre and bloodshed. His blows to Jehan coincide with the description of Olivier's cracking open a man's skull and having the eyes and brains fall out. The slapstick scene will doubtless make the audience laugh, but it also calls attention to the exaltation of violence in the French national epic.

Maheu's longer citation from the *Chanson de Roland* starts with the verse "Roland sent que la mort est proche pour lui" (Roland feels that his death is near), and then jumps to an idealized view of the battlefield with its conclusion that the struggle itself and men's deaths cannot be avoided: "Rien n'empêchera cette lutte désormais. / Sans mort d'homme elle ne peut s'achever." The protagonist summarizes his own position thus: "I . . . I chose chivalry out of devotion, of love . . . to defend France, the idea of France . . . that I hold here, in my heart" (32). Maheu's ideals are juxtaposed with the opinions of his practical mother, with whom he continues to argue about chivalry and honor. She claims that chivalry has become commercialized, that prisoner exchanges are but a business transaction arranged between those with power. To Maheu's four knightly duties—defend the church, fight for truth, protect the poor, preserve peace—she counters with three quick routes to making one's fortune—marry a rich heiress, enter the king's service and take advantage of what power brings, take a rich enemy knight prisoner (30).

It is at this point in the play's action that history, rather than literature, finally becomes the source of intertextual reference within the fictional world. Maheu's day of revelation comes shortly after the early triumph of Joan of Arc. The story of the Maid of Orleans inspires Mathilde's materialism: she erroneously, and hence ironically, predicts that Joan will become a powerful duchess and urges her son, too, to become a "victor, not one of the vanquished" (32). After the interruption caused by Hugues de Champagne's entrance, Maheu returns to his idealistic interpretation of the *Chanson de Roland*, combining it with the story of the peasant girl who would crown the Dauphin at Reims. Repeating his faith in chivalry, he now affirms as well that he, like Joan, hears voices, and that his voices proclaim peace and happiness for the beautiful country of France, whose people will serve as a model to the world for grace and intelligence (36). The response to his stirring speech is a chorus singing "The Marseillaise," the French national anthem.

Maheu's moment of exaltation ends as Hugues de Champagne emerges from the operating area. Stage directions call for an abrupt cutting off of the anthem and "return to reality" (37). Now healed, Hugues reneges on all his promises to Jehan: there will be no marriage to his daughter, no acquisition of a castle. Joan of Arc, of course, will also not receive any long-term rewards for her heroic intervention; rather she will be burned at the stake. The anthem that underscores Maheu's patriotic fervor for France was written in 1792, at the height of the bloody and vengeful French Revolution. For some members of the audience at least, the anachronistic music, coupled with the references to the historical Saint Joan, will provide a satirical commentary on militarism, exaggerated patriotism, and, as foregrounded in the final scene, the commercial exploitation of a nation's heroes and saints.

As previously observed, *Histoire de Maheu, le boucher* may be identified with postmodern theater. Although it does not offer the multimedia approach that Manet used in the Latin American plays that link them to the kind of technological transformation that Birringer envisions for the postmodern stage, the extensive use of parody here does relate this "medieval" farce to Hutcheon's definition of postmodern historiographic metafiction. She places under this rubric a contradictory doubleness in which "the intertexts of history and fiction take on parallel status in the parodic reworking of the textual past of both the 'world' and literature" (1988: 124). When connected with satire, such parody may "take on more precisely ideological dimensions" (129). By situating his text in 1429 and placing Joan of Arc on the same discursive plane as the *Chanson de Roland*, Manet calls into question the validity of popular representations of heroic figures, both historical and fictional. Maheu's infatuation with chivalry is subjected to a burlesque treatment; by extension, his conversion to the path of sainthood is similarly viewed through a transgressive, distorting lens. Even as she wishes for her son the same success that she expects for the Maid of Orleans, Mathilde devalues the future saint's image by quoting Sonia Potocki's belief that Joan is guided, not by an archangel but by Gilles de Rais, a notorious pedophile. Like Charlemagne's knights from the epic poem, Joan of Arc is deflated to the level of Maheu's slapstick, farcical world. On the surface, audience laughter is aimed at transparent comic devices, both physical and verbal, but Manet's burlesque is aimed as well at Maheu's naive battle against "evil, injustice, and ignorance" (46). The force that triumphs in the end, as Maheu heads off to Jerusalem, is not chivalry, but postmodern consumer capitalism.

A Madcap Satire of Castro

Manet's identification with Latin America often underscores his theater. Cuba, however, has generally been the direct subject of his novels, not his plays. Indeed, he was involved not as playwright but as director in his first theatrical project to foreground current Cuban political reality:

Fernando Arrabal's *The Extravagant Triumph of Jesus Christ, Karl Marx and William Shakespeare*. The title notwithstanding, the object of the Spanish-French author's wild satire is Fidel Castro. It had its English-language premiere in New York City in April 1982 at INTAR, an off-off Broadway theater run by Cuban exile Max Ferra.

Writing for the *New York Times*, Richard Eder affirmed that Arrabal had once again turned his "weapon of unhinged absurdity against oppression: against its pretentiousness as much as its cruelty." As an anarchist, Arrabal felt free to point his outrageous humor, his "demented, fanged frivolity," at the leftist Castro as he had earlier done against the rightist dictator of Spain, Francisco Franco (Eder). In a contemporaneous interview with Amei Wallach, Manet expressed his personal disillusionment with Castro's socialist regime and with the general failure of communism to right social wrongs. This political concern, coupled with the fact that the play "was very badly received in Paris because it was very badly done," led Manet "to direct Arrabal's madcap critique of dictators like Castro."

A decade later, with Castro still in power despite the disappearance of the USSR and the Communist bloc in Eastern Europe, Manet returned both to the subject and to the farcical approach of Arrabal's work to create, in collaboration with Gilles Hertzog, an equally madcap satire, *Poupée Fidel, Papa Marx, Buffalo Bill et la femme à barbe* (Puppet Fidel, Papa Marx, Buffalo Bill, and the bearded lady). While the result might be compared to the Spaniard's 1982 play, it bears strong ties to Manet's own previous agitprop criticism of Latin American dictatorships, the 1979 *Un Balcon sur les Andes*.

Poupée Fidel... was published in French in a 1993 issue of *La Regle du Jeu* but has yet to be staged in that language. Manet's Spanish translation, *Papa Fidel, Papa Marx, Buffalo Bill y Taïna, la mujer barbuda* was given a staged reading in Madrid on 23 July 1992. It should be noted that for several years, starting in 1991, Manet served as founding president of Cuba Démocratique, an anti-Castro association formed at the request of a high official in the French government to provide a vehicle for dialogue with Cuban exiles.[9] In that capacity, Manet made several trips to Madrid to establish contact with Cuban exiles in Spain, a

---

9. Other members of Cuba Démocratique's original executive committee included Gustavo Sánchez, Guy Ruiz de Zarate, Jacobo Machover, Lászaro Jordana, and Ramón Alejandro. A Committee for International Relations, also identified on the group letterhead, consisted of Felix Hernández, José Triana, Juan Arcocha, Maydee González, and Nestor Almendros.

group that forms a natural audience for his satirical barbs against Castro and communism.

Like *Un Balcon sur les Andes*, *Poupée Fidel* . . . is overtly theatricalist: marked by staging techniques that call attention to themselves. Written in one act, the play runs about an hour and may be done with minimal set and props; it is hence readily transportable.

The play begins with the projection of film clips tracing thirty-three years of Castro's regime and the concomitant decline in the Supreme Leader's physical appearance and the situation in Cuba. At center stage is a huge puppet, from which emerges Fidel's head. In his wild enthusiasm at his own history, Fidel does not notice the arrival on stage of a wheeled cart bearing the coffin of Karl Marx. The elderly Marx sits up in the coffin and, after considerable effort, convinces Fidel of his identity. He begins to offer practical (i.e., capitalist) advice on saving Cuba from economic ruin: the "zero option" in Cuba has taken the form of "zero milk, zero bread, zero condoms" (*Poupée Fidel* . . . 103). Marx would have Fidel exploit prostitution, gambling, and the drug trade. His practical bent is reinforced by a new arrival, Buffalo Bill, but the latter offers a less risky and more entertaining proposal built on his own show business experience. When the Old West was dead, there was money to be made from the theme; now that revolution has gone the way of the buffalo, he suggests having Disney build a Revolution Land in Cuba. The only opposition to the Karl Marx–Buffalo Bill economic solution comes from the militant Bearded Lady—who loses her beard after an "erotic-kitsch" interlude under Fidel's cloak. The arrival of Akiramoto, a Japanese samurai cum entrepreneur, seals the bargain between Fidel, his allies, and big business.

As was true in *Un Balcon sur les Andes*, *Poupée Fidel*, *Papa Marx, Buffalo Bill et la femme à barbe* joyously coalesces time and space. Not only may Marx and Buffalo Bill return from the dead to offer counsel to Fidel, but Cuba's recent history, the presence of the Shining Path in Peru, and the fall of the Soviet Union are melded with the displacement of American influence by the economic triumph of Japan. Lenin and P. T. Barnum are dead; long live Sony. *Poupée Fidel* . . . may be linked to Manet's theater in general in additional ways. Like the title characters of *The Nuns* and *Lady Strass*, the now beardless lady appears smoking a cigar. The original text is written in French, but there is an extensive use of Spanish throughout: as occasional insults and particularly in songs.

Some of the Hertzog-Manet satire is aimed at events that had already taken place by 1992; other aspects are surprisingly prophetic. At the time the play was written, Paris subway stations had been lined with large posters intended to promote tourism to Cuba: suggestive, bikini-clad models, conveying an unveiled message to potential male visitors. Many of the posters had been defaced, perhaps by feminists who resented the exploitation of the female body, perhaps by Cubans who resented apparent attempts to turn their homeland into a brothel. The Japanese takeover of landmark American businesses, cited in the play's text, are all based in fact. More curious is the whimsical idea of a Disney amusement park tracing the rise and fall of revolutions, for the satirical fantasy foreshadows the 1994 controversy over the Disney empire's ill-fated plan to establish a history theme park in the Piedmont region of Virginia.

In its overt criticism of Castro's Cuba, *Poupée Fidel . . .* is clearly intended as agitation propaganda, but the ideological stance is tempered by rapid, often hilarious stage action and the use of classic comic devices, ranging from mistaken identities (Fidel's confusion of Karl Marx first with Carlos Gardel and then with Gabriel García Márquez) to repetition (repeated, unanswered calls for help to Fidel's brother Raúl). The filmic review of recent Cuban history and Puppet Fidel's chanting of political slogans is broken by the arrival of the coffin on wheels. Before the dialogue between Fidel and Karl Marx can flounder, the two are interrupted by the arrival of the Bearded Lady, a Peruvian militant dressed in a Cuban rumba costume and bearing a machine gun. The men are rescued from her by the timely entrance, on roller skates, of Buffalo Bill. The Western hero twirls his traditional lasso but also has a portable phone and a headset with microphone: "*Bref, le parfait disc-jockey à la sauce cow-boy*" (*Poupée Fidel* 114). The fast pace of the various scenes culminates in a finale structured as a grand ballet set to a mambo rhythm.

Among the salient farcical elements of the Hertzog-Manet text is the juxtaposition of incongruous items. Sometimes these are visual: a rollerskating Buffalo Bill in his traditional cowboy role combined with that of contemporary disk jockey; a bearded lady combining ultrafeminine signs (the sexy rumba dress) with masculine ones (beard, machine gun). More basic to the political satire are verbal incongruities: Marx preaching the benefits of capitalism; Buffalo Bill offering to talk to Ronald Reagan, cowboy to cowboy; Fidel expressing greater recognition of and admiration for Buffalo Bill than for Karl Marx.[10] A related comic aspect, which also high-

---

10. In the context of this satirical farce, Fidel's characterization here would function as humor from incongruity but it may be an intentional biographical comment, based on Manet's knowledge of the real Fidel Castro. Manet has commented on occasion that Castro—like many other Cubans of his generation, including Manet—has been a lifelong fan of Hollywood

lights the satire's Brechtian theatricality, is the constant flux in various characters' roles. The elderly Marx insists that he is who he says, that he is not simply someone disguised as Karl Marx; nevertheless, he eventually loses his beard and becomes a youthful Karl who proclaims, "On est tous double" (Everyone is a double; 127). Similarly, the Bearded Lady converts to a pregnant Beardless Lady who expects to save Cuba by bearing a number of little Castros, and the samurai turns into a businessman. In keeping with Manet's postmodern view, the not so subtle implication of the shifting roles on stage is that people in the real world, including the true-life counterpart of Puppet Fidel, are also capable of game-playing, of the deliberate assumption of multiple identities.

---

movies; in that respect, his admiration for Western movies and Buffalo Bill would antedate his familiarity with Marxism. Manet also affirms that Castro was not an orthodox Marxist, that he was primarily a nationalist who held anti-Communist views at the time of his first trip to the United States following the triumph of the revolution (interview, Mestiri 150).

6

Variations on Multicultural Metatheatricalism

The metatheatrical impulse is a constant in the plays of Eduardo Manet, and there are understandably many points of contact between those grouped in this chapter and the rest of his theater. There is no clear line of division between my categories of historiographic metatheater and multicultural metatheatricalism. *Un Balcon sur les Andes*, analyzed in the previous chapter as historiographic metafiction, is a fully developed example of theater-within-theater comparable to *L'Autre Don Juan* (The other Don Juan, 1974), *Les Gozzi* (The Gozzi family, 1981), or *Le Primerissimo* (The superstar, 1988). On the other hand, *Pour l'amour de Verdi* (For the love of Verdi, written 1992), with its panoramic view of modern Italian history, is closely related to the historiographic plays. Regardless of the somewhat arbitrary selection, the works considered as examples of multicultural metatheatricalism are distinguished by their extensive incorporation into French of texts from other languages, their transplanting of a text from one national culture to another, or, in the case of the Italian trilogy, of their development of theater-within-theater in a context beyond Manet's more typical Hispanic and French spheres.

L'Autre Don Juan, an exuberant performance-within-the-text of a comedy by Juan Ruiz de Alarcón, falls chronologically in the period dominated by plays of entrapment and enclosure. Manet wrote it in response to an invitation to prepare a French adaptation of a Spanish Golden Age play for an international theater festival; it paves the way for the equally playful and flamboyant *Un Balcon sur les Andes.* Structurally, the four-character *Le Jour où Mary Shelley rencontra Charlotte Brontë* (*The Day Mary Shelley Met Charlotte Brontë,* 1979) resembles the entrapment plays that precede it, but its fanciful portrayal of the two nineteenth-century English novelists and their most famous characters represents a new cultural dimension to Manet's approach to metatheater.[1] *Ma'Déa* (1986) is set in Haiti in the twentieth century; it introduces voodoo ceremonies and Haitian Creole chants in its retelling of the Greek tragedy of Medea.

Pour l'amour de Verdi, Manet's tribute to Verdi's operas, is as yet unstaged. Among Manet's other works in progress are several that are linked to the texts chosen for analysis in this chapter.

Pierre, Esmeralda et Quasimodo dates from 1986. Manet wrote the female role for Fatima Soualhia, his future wife, who had recently appeared in *Ma'Déa.* Repeating to some extent the metafictional strategy of *Le Jour où Mary Shelley rencontra Charlotte Brontë,* the play explores what happened to the characters at the conclusion of a nineteenth-century novel: Victor Hugo's *The Hunchback of Notre Dame.* The beautiful Esmeralda, who yearns for her Prince Charming, and Quasimodo, the hunchback who loves her, have lost their memories; they are caught in a world of dreams. Pierre, a eunuch who used to be a goat, maintains the household through his talents as cook, magician, and thief; the role calls for a demanding level of gymnastic skills. Pierre's efforts to bring the couple together take five hundred years and a total transformation of Quasimodo's physical appearance. The final scenes, reminiscent of other Manet texts, incorporate Hollywood film references and dance sequences, featuring the Charleston and tango.

Juan y Teresa en busca de Dios (written 1987) draws on the writings of Spain's mystic saints Teresa of Avila and John of the Cross to recount the story of their lives. *Pierre, Esmeralda et Quasimodo* is a French farce deal-

---

1. The Shelley-Brontë play had its stage premiere in January 1979, but, like many of Manet's stage plays, was previously heard on France-Culture. The radio version aired 16 October 1978 and was directed by Jeanne Rollin-Weisz. For broadcast on France-Culture 15 November 1979, Manet prepared another radio play based on a novel: Alain Robbe-Grillet's *Topologie d'une cité fantôme.* *Ma'Déa* was aired on France-Culture on 22 September 1985.

ing with a French novel and hence not bicultural. On the other hand, Manet's respectful treatment of the Spanish historical figures was intended for American audiences. He wrote the script in Spanish, at the invitation of Max Ferra, director of New York's INTAR theater, which specializes in English-language productions of Hispanic plays.[2] The frame action of Manet's work is set in the elderly Mother Teresa's convent. As she dictates the story of her life to a younger nun, the scenes from the past are evoked expressionistically. Temporal shifts are facilitated by music, special lighting, and extensive doubling by three of the actresses in the cast of five.

At the request of Princess Caroline of Monaco, Manet has recently prepared a libretto based on the classic Cuban novel *Cecilia Valdés*. The opera, with music by Charles Chaynes, is scheduled to open in Monte Carlo in May 2000. The co-production by opera companies from Nancy, France, and Liège, Belgium, will be performed in these two cities in 2001.

Interlingual Metatheatricalism: The Blurring of Borders

In the prologue to his *L'Autre Don Juan*, Manet recounts that when he was invited to prepare a French adaptation of a Spanish Golden Age play, he began reviewing texts by the best-known dramatists of the period, Lope de Vega and Calderón de la Barca. Setting these aside, he selected instead Juan Ruiz de Alarcón's *Las paredes oyen* (The walls have ears), "a minor, but charming work" (8). Neither the request nor Manet's response is surprising. Spanish Golden Age theater has enjoyed considerable popularity in France over the centuries. That popularity has often been related to the perception of the classic Spanish stage as "popular theater," that is, one aimed not at an elite audience, like French neoclassic tragedy, but rather at the masses. The postwar decentralization of theater in France, followed by the student revolt of 1968, therefore renewed French interest in Golden Age texts.

---

2. The cover of the original typescript gives the title in French: *Jean et Thérèse a la recherche de Dieu*. Manet tentatively titled his revised version *Les Chemins et les nuits*, playing on the references to "way" and "night" in the poetry of the two mystics. From my conversations with Manuel Duque, then literary manager at INTAR, I believe that the perceived problem with Manet's text was the dominance of words over visual action or image. In this respect, the text leans toward the conventions of the French stage, rather than the Cuban or American one.

Manet's choice of Ruiz de Alarcón has a special dimension, for this particular "Spanish" author was actually Mexican, a fact that struck a responsive chord in his Cuban-born French adapter. Manet's prologue makes clear that his comedy is intended as a vindication of a Mexican-born writer whose important influence on Corneille and Goldoni has not always been recognized and whose Latin American origins have often been obscured. The "very free version" of *Las paredes oyen* was completed in December 1972, published in France in 1973, and premiered in Montreal in 1974. It is among Manet's most frequently staged works, especially by young theater companies.

As we shall see, *L'Autre Don Juan* is not merely a French translation or adaptation of the Spanish-language comedy but rather a complex meta-play that blurs geographical and chronological borders by introducing Don Juan Ruiz de Alarcón both as an author-character within the frame play and as an actor-character within *Les Murs ont des oreilles*, the play-within-the-play. (This despite the fact that the performance is ostensibly taking place in France in 1800 and the historical Alarcón died in Spain in 1639.) Eventually, the author and actor facets of the character merge as Don Juan, much to the consternation of the French troupe, insists upon delivering his lines verbatim from the original Spanish text.

The strategy of placing the original author as a character within the adapted text is not unique to Manet in the 1970s. Earlier in 1972 in France it was tried by Denis Llorca in his revival of Corneille's *Le Cid* at the Théâtre de la Ville in Paris. Llorca added to the cast the figure of Guillem de Castro, the often unrecognized author of Corneille's source text, and had him speak lines in Spanish. The production "provoked passionate and contradictory reactions" (Willey 93).[3]

Although Manet is surprisingly faithful in his scene-by-scene re-creation of the Ruiz de Alarcón play-within-the-play, he interpolates dances and songs, some in Spanish and some in French. Exuberantly Brechtian in its theatricalism, *L'Autre Don Juan* also introduces traditional elements of French farce, repeated cinematic images, a parody of the typical French approach to Spanish culture, and a running commentary on theater and the theater world. Richard Hornby defines five manifestations of the metadramatic: the play-within-the-play, ceremony within the play, role-playing within the role, literary and real-life reference, and

---

3. I have not been able to verify Denis Llorca's family background. His surname suggests a Catalonian ancestry, a factor that might give a personal reason for his vindication of the Valencian dramatist.

self-reference. *L'Autre Don Juan* contains examples of all of these, carried to farcical extremes.

As is often true with this kind of metadrama, the text that becomes the play-within-the-play is itself a metatheatrical work that foregrounds role-playing within the role. Alarcón's didactic comedy is filled with examples of role-playing and self-serving fictions: noblemen disguised as coachmen, lies used in amorous pursuits, false tales spread to discourage rivals. The result when such a text is placed within the frame of a theatrical troupe's performance is a dizzying *mise-en-abîme*: actors playing actor-characters who play characters playing someone else. Manet further complicates this structure with real-life references: extratextual allusions to the historical Alarcón and, through the figure of the Alguacil, or constable, who becomes the audience within the play, to external censorship.

In the published dramatic text, Manet carefully separates his frame play from his version of Alarcón's text. *Les Murs ont des oreilles* is presented in acts with numbered scenes: act 1 has twenty scenes, act 2 has thirteen, and act 3 has fourteen. The scenes and their basic action coincide quite closely with the original play. Manet merely omits an occasional brief scene or combines two into one until he nears the end of Alarcón's third act. He then eliminates the ending of the play-within-the-play. In place of Alarcón's scenes 17–19, Manet creates a musical number in which the singers offer several possible endings and invite the spectators to choose among them. This grand finale lightheartedly also ignores the resolution of the intrigues of the frame play.

The frame play, dealing with Marius, his troupe of French actors, and their interactions with the author-character Don Juan (including the rivalry of two actresses for Alarcón's affections, a situation mirroring the love intrigues of the play-within-the-play), is presented in specially designated sections: prologue, supplement to act 2 (divided into a bullfight and an intermission), and supplement to act 2. Given this structure, there are no real intermissions. In Pirandellian fashion, the disjunction between actors and spectators, performance and rest period, disappears. One of Marius's repeated themes is that his "poor" troupe will only survive by selling food and drink on the side.[4] Manet suggests in the stage directions

---

4. Although Marius literally means "poor," in the economic sense, he may also be alluding to Jerzy Grotowski's concept of "poor theater." Grotowski's internationally acclaimed version of Calderón's *El príncipe constante* (*The Constant Prince*) reached the Théâtre des Nations in Paris in 1966 and had a significant impact on theater practitioners there. At that time Manet was in Cuba, but he had already met Grotowski in Warsaw in 1963 and found the concept of

that the actors follow Marius's advice by hawking refreshments during the prologue and "intermission."

In his preface to *L'Autre Don Juan*, Manet describes the language of Alarcón's text as brilliant and his versification as graceful and resonant; he declares himself incapable of recreating the same effect in French. Recalling the old Italian expression "Traduttore, traditore," he says that he will not half betray the original through a deficient translation but will rather "trahir *tout à fait*," betray it completely, by adopting only the internal action and sense of spectacle that attracted his own interest (8). In spite of his prose rendition (with occasional rhymed couplets at the ends of scenes), in some ways Manet is far more faithful to the original dialogue than his comment would indicate. On the other hand, he systematically subverts Alarcón's dramatic text through the other signs that make up the performance text. The Golden Age play limits stage directions essentially to exit and enter; Manet creates extensive stage directions, including detailed instructions to the actors for their gestures.

Among Golden Age dramatists, Alarcón was the one with the greatest affinity for the decorum of French neoclassicism. His comedies not only avoid the swashbuckling action of Spanish cape-and-sword plays but also have a moralistic bent.[5] In contrast to the rather austere *Las paredes oyen*, Manet's *Les Murs ont des oreilles* is a bawdy French farce—or a return to Renaissance Spain's own *La Celestina*—filled with sexual innuendoes and exuberant physical action. In particular, the servants in the play-within-the-play, from the first scene on, add meaning to their lines by obscene gestures. They appear laughing at upstairs windows while their masters are delivering serious lines and they engage in love play behind the protagonist's back.

Mendoza, the character played by Don Juan, is physically deformed—a hunchback, like the historical Alarcón. The maid Celia wickedly suggests that he has other, less visible, physical attributes that her mistress Doña Anna should consider in choosing him over his rivals. Interference from the frame play grows throughout the play-within-the-play, in part because the author-character becomes increasingly angry at

---

poor theater especially relevant for revolutionary Cuba (interview, Mambrino 364). At a later point in the play, Grotowski's theories, like various other contemporary theater movements, are mentioned directly in the dialogue and stage directions.

5. In his 1972 book on Alarcón, Walter Poesse establishes that the author's works were neither as classical nor as moralistic as they are generally labeled. To the extent that these tendencies are present in *Las paredes oyen*, Manet has subverted them.

Marius and the blatant change in the tone of his comedy. Don Juan's anger is also treated as a stock device of farce.

To facilitate rapid physical action, Manet calls for a stylized set, made of lightweight boxes. These are to represent houses with two or three levels for doors and windows. Characters not only enter and exit quickly and eavesdrop with ease but also appear at windows to add their comments to the scene in progress. Marius and three other actors from his troupe double in two or more roles of the play-within-the-play; the multiple houses speed costume changes—some of which take place in full view of the audience—and, through association of particular units with particular roles, help identify the emerging character. As a playful reduction in Alarcón's cast, Manet substitutes a puppet for a human actor; a house window becomes a puppet theater for the intervention of that servant.

The obvious use of doubling functions metatheatrically in several ways. In one sense, it is a Brechtian technique that winks at the audience, calling attention to the play as fiction. This function is akin to the direct narration—supplied by Marius, Don Juan, or occasionally another actor-character—that informs the spectators about the work to be performed or about the scene in progress. In a self-referential way, the doubling allows the actors to reveal their histrionic tricks. And, because the doubling involves cross-gender acting, it prompts the Alguacil to voice a traditional bias against theater.

Martin Esslin, in his "Actors Acting Actors," has pointed out the metadramatic implications for the audience of an actor-character within the text. He states that the attraction of all the variations on actors acting actors resides precisely in the chance to compare and appreciate the levels of "theatricality" and "naturalness" displayed side by side (Esslin, "Actors": 75). The technique inevitably "highlights the problem of acting itself" (77); it thus breaks the illusionism of the performance by calling attention to theater as theater. Manet fully exploits this potential. In his metatheatricalist approach, spectators not only "see double"—Hornby's requisite—but triple. For example, Marius is not only his "natural" self (the troupe's director) but also his "theatrical" roles: the Count and the Duke. When Marius plays the Count, we see double. But the Count in act 1, scene 16 relates to Doña Lucrèce a conversation he has had with Don Mendo; in so doing, he changes his voice to reenact their dialogue. We "hear triple" as Marius plays the Count playing Don Mendo. Manet expands upon the strategy in act 2, scene 9. The actress-character Lola normally plays Don Mendo; in this scene, she simultaneously assumes the role of Léonardo, Don Mendo's friend. Through changes of voice and stance, Lola moves back and forth between her two characters. Lola's Léonardo and Marius's Don Mendo will be noticeably more theatrical than their respective interpretations of Don Mendo and the Count, which, in turn, will be less "natural" than their portrayals of the actor-characters themselves.

Manet incorporates a related progression in cross-gender acting. In act 3, scene 3, the servant Beltran thinks that Mendoza has gone mad when he overhears him having a conversation with himself, using his natural voice (that is, the voice Don Juan has assumed for playing Mendoza) and his imitation of Doña Anna's female voice. Later in act 3, the actress-character Eunice, who has played the maid Celia up to this point, suddenly appears in scene 11 in a male role, that of Marcello. After slipping out of character entirely—becoming again the actress-character Eunice—she reappears in scene 12, back in the role of Celia. At the same time the actress-character Lola continues to play Don Mendo, but wearing her own female costume. The snowball effect in the rapid role/gender changes leads to a total breakdown of the play-within-the play: that is, to the kind of disruption that Hornby has identified as essential to metadrama.

It should be noted that Manet does not overlook the possibilities presented by the cross-gender acting for comic irony in his dialogue. For example, in a scene between Doña Anna (played by the actress-character Bella) and her cousin Lucrèce (played by the actor Pascual), Lucrèce welcomes the opportunity to chat "woman to woman." When Lucrèce confesses that she is burning with passion, Doña Anna expresses in an aside her shock at a lady using such language (69). The audience, fully aware that the "lady" is being played by a man, will doubtless laugh at such double-edged comments.

The two characters within the frame play who are most distressed by the doubling are the author-character Don Juan and the Alguacil. One of the catalysts for Don Juan's reverting to the original Spanish text is excessive doubling, which, he says, destroys his intended comic rhythm. He accuses Marius of greed: "You could have hired another actor for the role of the Duke" (114). Hornby informs us that self-reference is an extreme, intense form of metatheater, even more so than the play-within-the-play. Don Juan's complaints about Marius's handling of the play in progress are among many self-referential commentaries on *Les Murs ont des oreilles*; he affirms that his text has been so distorted that he will not defend it to the censor. The Alguacil is particularly offended by the erotic elements and by the cross-gender acting; he only allows the play to go on because of Lola's physical charms and Marius's bribes.

Beyond the satire of censors and censorship (implicitly Hispanic-style censorship, given the Spanish word used for the law enforcement officer), the Alguacil's discomfiture reflects an important aspect of Manet's theater about theater. With respect to role-playing within the role, Hornby alerts us that cross-gender acting raises questions of sexual identity and that bisexuality, traditionally viewed as a threat, therefore is one reason for an antitheatrical prejudice (68–70). When the Alguacil enters in the supplement to act 2 to close down the show, he labels the production "subversive and porno." He complains that the nobles are portrayed as idiots and the servants as wise, but he is even more alarmed that Marius has "changed the men into women and the women into men" (97). After Lola reveals her breasts (the stage directions allow a peep but recommend a full view), he expresses his admiration for the actress's femininity and accepts her playing a male role. (From this point on, Lola will play directly to the Alguacil, who will applaud her repeatedly.) In act 3, he becomes enraged again at Pascual's portraying Lucrèce; he shouts insults at the actor, questioning his sexual orientation. The constable's response is realistic; as the production history of Manet's *Les Nonnes* attests, Western theater audiences and society in general are less threatened by women in pants—who may be seen as sexy—than by men in skirts.

When Lionel Abel created the term "metatheater," he identified Calderón as one of the earliest exponents of this theatrical mode. Manet cites the baroque master to justify the deliberate anachronisms in his own metatheatrical farce: "La vie (le temps) n'est qu'un songe et les songes ne sont qu'illusion" (12). Time, like life, is but a dream, an illusion. Manet's playful twisting of the famous line from *La vida es sueño* (*Life Is a Dream*) ("que toda la vida es sueño, / y los sueños, sueños son" [all life is a dream / and the dreams are dreams]) nevertheless reveals a recurrent characteristic of metadrama. In Llorca's *Le Cid*, Guillem de Castro (1569–1631) becomes a character in a contemporary production of a play written five years after his death. Manet, too, places his author-character out of his original historical context, but the most consistent anachronism in *L'Autre Don Juan* is found in the performance text's intertextuality with film. The use of cinematic techniques is, along with the superimposed eroticism and cross-gender acting, a key method of subverting Alarcón's *Las paredes oyen*.

Film imagery in *L'Autre Don Juan* at times is incorporated in the actors' movements, which are intended to simulate camera and editing effects. For example, at Don Juan's first entrance, during the prologue, there is a drumroll and the five members of the acting company become immobilized, as if in a freeze-frame (20). Similarly, at the beginning of act 3, Marius narrates what had occurred at the end of act 2, and the actors return to that moment first by freezing and then by coming out of the freeze with the associated jerky motions (103). At other times, specific gestures recall stock film images. In act 1, when Don Mendo promises to ask Doña Lucrèce's father for her hand in marriage, the two engage in a long kiss in the style of Hollywood films of the 1930s (47). When the Duke intervenes to prevent a sword fight between Don Juan and Don Mendo, the stage directions indicate that the pantomimed scene should recall silent movies (59). The sudden reversal in the Alguacil's attitude when Lola bares her breasts should be inspired, not by Stanislavsky, but by cartoons (98).

Another of Manet's favorite cinematic strategies that underscores *L'Autre Don Juan* is the use of a sound track. There is a musical motif associated with Don Juan: a soft theme played by flute, harpsichord, and guitar (20). The stage directions specifically call for a sound track to accompany the bullfight that takes place in the supplement to act 1 (61). When Don Mendo plots to kidnap Doña Anna by bribing her coachmen (really Don Juan and the Duke in disguise), Marius intervenes with a narration that evokes captions from silent movie melodramas: Will the villain succeed in his dastardly plans? (85) The chase scene itself, of the horseman pursuing the carriage, calls for a sound track from an American Western (86).

Some of these cinematic elements may also be related to Manet's parody of *espagnolade*. The French stage has not always welcomed contributions from Hispanic countries and has tended, in the case of Spain, to superimpose on plays imported across the Pyrenees all the stereotypical trappings of Andalusia, whether or not they were appropriate. In her review of fifty years of production history of Lorca in France (1938–88), Felicia Hardison Londré observes that the commercial success of major stagings could be attributed to a "tourist-bureau vision of Spain." To be sure, Federico García Lorca came from Andalusia, placed the action of his major tragedies there, and thus invited flamenco background music and traditional costumes from the south. Valle-Inclán, on the other hand, came from Galicia, and his northwestern region with its green forests, coastal mists, Celtic superstitions, and bagpipe music is far removed from Andalusia's parched plains and gypsy dancers. The Parisian premiere of

Valle's *Divinas palabras* in 1946 gratuitously shifted the action from Galicia to Andalusia in order to exploit *espagnolade*. In his study of Spanish theater on the French stage (1935–73), Francisco Torres Monreal asserts that playwrights whose works could not be molded into the accepted folkloric images were doomed to failure. Manet's free version of *Las paredes oyen* is a reaction to this cultural context.

As already noted, Manet suggests a leitmotif for the Alarcón figure: the soft blend of flute, harpsichord, and guitar subtly evokes Spain, not flamenco, of course, but perhaps the music of Manuel de Falla, whose impressionistic "Night in the Gardens of Spain" will later underscore *Mendoza, en Argentine* . . . The costumes for the play-within-the-play are logically Spanish: Lucrèce carries a fan, and several characters will wear capes. Other elements are more exaggerated. The swordplay, which the neoclassical Alarcón would not have presented on stage, is added by Manet and doubtless meets audience expectations for a swashbuckling Spanish play. The most blatant example of *espagnolade*, however, is the bullfight: it has no relationship whatsoever to either the play-within-the-play or the frame play. Understandably, the furious author-character emerges on stage, waving his text and shouting at the director.

The brief bullfight scene, done in pantomime to the accompanying sound track, is described in the stage directions as satirical but carefully structured. The actress-character Eunice appears as the bullfighter and Marius, with an appropriate mask, is the bull. Their movements are to follow the rhythm of the castanets associated with the clicking heels of flamenco dancers. Significantly, the death of the bull is to be played against the music of Bizet's *Carmen* (61). That French opera, based on Mérimée's French story, is the epitome of *espagnolade*: a Gallic fictionalization of Andalusia that has come to be a universally accepted image of Spain. By parodying it, Manet anticipates Carlos Saura's ingeniously metafictional 1983 film in which he effectively reclaims *Carmen* for Hispanic culture.

That France has freely borrowed from Spain's creative genius is an overt theme of *L'Autre Don Juan*. In the prologue, Marius introduces Alarcón as the source for Pierre Corneille's *Le Menteur* (*The Liar*). "Pierre who?" asks the author-character. He expresses mild surprise but generously agrees to lend his intellectual talents to France. After all, there is an obligation to help "underdeveloped" countries (25). The dialogue inverts French pride in Corneille and ignorance of the original Hispanic author. Eventually Don Juan can no longer tolerate the way his text is being distorted by the French theatrical troupe. At that culminating point in the action (act 3, scene 9), he announces that the play will go on, but only in Spanish, in order to put an end to his anxiety (115).

The linguistic strategy Manet develops here is similar to the one found in his *Un Balcon sur les Andes*; in the later play, French actors perform in their native language to Spanish American audiences, with the aid of a running consecutive interpretation by a bilingual character. In *L'Autre Don Juan*, Alarcón delivers his character's lines verbatim from *Las paredes oyen* (lines 2506–7, 2526, 2529–36, 2538, 2543–44, 2546, 2573–75). Marius instructs Pascual to respond in French with Beltran's lines and at first attempts to provide a rapid consecutive interpretation to Alarcón's dialogue. In a snowball effect, Marius then switches to a simultaneous mode, partially drowning out Alarcón's Spanish. When Pascual gives up, Marius takes over the role of Beltran, becomes hysterical himself, and begins responding with the original Spanish lines to Alarcón's speeches (lines 2545, 2547–48). Lola and the Alguacil call out for a translation, Pascual spouts Grotowski's theories on the need for a laboratory theater, and the scene finally ends on the brink of chaos.

The extended bilingual scene is built on the accelerating rhythm of farce and should provoke laughter from the audience for that reason. The use of the foreign language within the dialogue may also have a comic effect. Those who understand Spanish will receive pleasure from their linguistic skills and those who do not will be pleased to discover how well they can follow the action anyway. When Marius switches from French interpreter to Spanish-language actor, his reversal functions as another stock comic device. Although the scene at some deeper level satirizes French appropriation of Spanish-language intellectual property, on the surface it entertains through its linguistic games. There is a related comic effect from the occasional interpolation of familiar French literary quotations and, even more so, in act 3, scene 11, from Pascual-Lucrèce's adoption of a tragic style. Audiences will receive pleasure from recognizing the familiar, superimposed lines, and they may be expected to laugh at the inappropriate use of a Racinian mold to convey a Spanish comic message.

L'Autre Don Juan is a metatheatrical *mise-en-abîme*, starting with its very title. Spectators may well think initially of the legendary womanizer. Don Juan Ruiz de Alarcón is clearly not that Don Juan, but another one. Moreover, Manet's text deals directly with the question of Alarcón's identity. The playwright has stated that his work is intended as a kind of "fanciful biography," and in that context he attempts to uncover the Mexican-born author's inner world as revealed in his text.

At the author-character's first entrance, he delivers a verse soliloquy rich in intertextual references to the philosophical ponderings of Descartes ("How can I know that I am / when I think . . ." [20]), Calderón's Segismundo ("Let the dream not be a dream nor life a lie" [22]), and Shakespeare's Hamlet ("to be oneself or not to be" [22]). He concludes that life would be a heavy burden without the hope that others might see him as he wished to be: Juan Ruiz is the shadow of another Don Juan (23). The author-character of the prologue is not the deformed hunchback described by history but rather a romantic leading man. To become the character Mendoza for the play-within-a-play, he must don a jacket with built-in humps and a boot with a special heel to create his limp. His transitions follow the reverse path of the one adopted by the hunchback of Notre Dame in the unstaged *Pierre, Esmeralda et Quasimodo*.

In theatricalist fashion, Don Juan's transformation takes place in front of the audience, and the visible use of a mirror here, as in other scenes throughout the play, draws attention to the mirroring effect of the metaplay itself. The physically deformed Mendoza is a false reflection in two ways. The outward appearance of the character in the play-within-the-play conceals his moral and—in Manet's bawdy farce—physical virtues. At the same time, the audience will see double, realizing that this Mendoza is but the creation of Don Juan, an actor-character with the physical appearance of a romantic hero.

The historical Alarcón very probably created the Mendoza figure of his *Las paredes oyen* as an idealized self-image. As Walter Poesse states, the victorious protagonist is poor, luckless, deformed, and homely: "In this character, appropriately called Don Juan de Mendoza, Alarcón is undoubtedly portraying himself, and wishes to 'prove' that nobility of family and soul should triumph over wealth, handsomeness, and a mean spirit" (Poesse 42). Manet takes this idealization process one step further, inventing a Don Juan whose handsome body matches the soul that Alarcón imagined as an expression of himself. In the process, the Cuban-French Manet places the anxieties of the Mexican-Spanish playwright at center stage in his modernized version of *Les Murs ont des oreilles*. *L'Autre Don Juan* may be a French farce, but the constant presence of the author-character and the interlingual games are guaranteed to keep audiences aware of the original source of this complex metatheatrical text.

Two Characters in Revolt Against Their Authors

As we have seen in *L'Autre Don Juan* and *Un Balcon sur les Andes*, Manet's metatheatricalism and fascination with language sometimes lead him to incorporate whole passages of Spanish within his French texts. He is not merely bilingual and bicultural: he is a polyglot who, in plays as dissimilar as *Lady Strass, Histoire de Maheu le boucher*, and *Ma'Déa*, may introduce dialogue, poems, or songs in Italian, Portuguese, German, Haitian Creole, Yiddish, or English. In the specific case of English, he reflects an abiding affection not only for Hollywood movies but also for British literature. Nowhere, among his thirty plays to date, is this tendency more apparent than in *Le Jour où Mary Shelley rencontra Charlotte Brontë*. As the title indicates, this Gothic horror comedy is also one of his most overt examples of intertextuality.

Manet's imaginary meeting of the two nineteenth-century English authors and their inseparable companions—Frankenstein's Monster and Jane Eyre—was first staged at the Petit Odéon in Paris, under the direction of Yves Gasc. The co-production with the Comédie-Française ran 9 January–18 February 1979 to full houses. In his preface to the *Avant-Scène Théâtre* edition, Gasc expressed the hope that all those turned away when seats ran out would be able to read the text and hence experience "an exceptionally sophisticated, intellectual pleasure" (4). Excerpts from theater critics, published along with the play, were unanimously enthusiastic. They found Manet's work to be witty, stimulating, ironic, and humorous: a tragicomic blend of violence and tenderness (19).

Les Nonnes, ostensibly set in early nineteenth-century Haiti but referring metaphorically to Cuba, quickly traveled from Paris to the English-language stage. It was produced in England in March 1970, within a year of its world premiere, and reached off-Broadway by the early 1970s. *Le Jour où Mary Shelley rencontra Charlotte Brontë*, in spite of its obvious ties to Anglo-American culture, was to take far longer before being staged in English. Director Louis Fantasia first became interested in Manet's play in 1979, when he read it in *L'Avant-Scène Théâtre*, but he had to wait a dozen years before finding a theater (telephone interview). The American premiere, in a version by British author and producer Vivian Cox, finally took place in Los Angeles, at the Burbage Theater Ensemble, in winter 1991. An immediate critical and popular success, Fantasia's production was chosen by the *LA Weekly* as its theater "Pick of the Week"; originally scheduled for a six-week run, it was extended for sixteen weeks. The four-character comedy, now subtitled *The Monster & Jane Eyre, Vol. II*, was staged a year later, in April 1992, at Philadelphia's Society Hill Playhouse, under the direction of Jay Kogan.

At its most obvious level, *Le Jour où Mary Shelley rencontra Charlotte Brontë* deals with two autonomous, fictional characters who decide to rebel against their authors. Such is the thrust of Society Hill Playhouse's advance publicity: "Join Mary and Charlotte on the day their 'creations' demand that the novels be . . . rewritten!"; the play "tells of a fictional meeting of the two women authors on the day of Mary Shelley's death during which their 'monsters' take them hostage and demand that the writers pen sequels depicting them as happy, beautiful free spirits." The play has many levels of meaning. It raises not only the question of the relationship between author and character but also between God and his creations. The Monster in particular protests that he was cast in the role of "Other," but all four characters reveal a sense of alienation and a search for self-identify. Consistent with contemporary theories of fantastic literature, both source texts, *Frankenstein* and *Jane Eyre*, contain a double who externalizes a repressed, taboo aspect of the protagonist's inner nature; Manet's play emphasizes a similar function of characters from these novels vis-à-vis their creators. The probing portrait of the two women writers and specifically of women's roles in nineteenth-century England is also surprisingly close to recent feminist analyses; indeed, according to actress Deen Kogan, it was Manet's illuminating treatment of his female characters that prompted the choice of his play for production.[6]

The action takes place in Mary Shelley's sitting room on the night of 1 February 1851. As the lights come up, the Monster, his back to the audience, is reading to Mary from *Frankenstein*. In the ensuing dialogue, he expresses his existential anguish, and she comforts him. His momentary peace is interrupted by a loud ringing of the doorbell. In his capacity as Mary's servant, whom she calls Percival, he goes to answer. Alone on stage, Mary speaks of her own anguish.

Mary's unexpected visitor is announced as "Currer Bell" (Charlotte Brontë's masculine nom de plume). Once Mary recovers from her surprise at having a woman enter, she and Charlotte discuss literature and their lives. The Monster, reading from *Frankenstein*, and Charlotte, reading from the Book of Job, create a counterpoint of laments. Mary con-

---

6. I am grateful to Deen Kogan for sending me the theater's press releases and answering my questions. She created the role of Mary Shelley in the production directed by her late husband.

Fig. 12. *The Day Mary Shelley Met Charlotte Brontë*. Philadelphia, 1992 (photo courtesy of Society Hill Playhouse).

fesses her own rage and then comforts Charlotte. The latter's momentary peace is interrupted by a loud ringing of the doorbell.

The Monster ushers in a drenched Jane Eyre. The two authors, on the one hand, and their characters, on the other, recognize their respective common plights. The rebellion of the creatures leads to insults and physical violence. Mary asks Charlotte, who is planning to marry, to take her away with her to her new home where they might be free of their creations. The conspiring Monster and Jane exit and then return, carrying lighted candelabras and the outside key; Mary and Charlotte realize that they are now trapped. In parallel actions, the authors are forced to write the sequels dictated by their characters. Charlotte and Jane leave, and the clock strikes twelve. The Monster puts out the candles and discovers that Mary has died in her chair. Carrying her in his arms, he faces the audience for a moment, then turns and exits.

As we shall observe, in his text Manet reveals considerable knowledge of the source novels and their authors' lives.[7] Nevertheless, the play also makes a number of references to familiar film strategies and images. Classic Hollywood movie versions of nineteenth-century novels often begin with a verbatim passage, represented graphically or read in voice-over. Patrice Kerbrat in the original Paris production was made up to resemble Boris Karloff as the Monster (*Frankenstein*, 1931, dir. James Whale); in Manet's descriptions, the Monster, duplicating Karloff's lumbering gait, is to walk with difficulty, dragging one of his legs (1979: 5).[8] When Manet's stage directions describe Charlotte as wearing "Jane Eyre's famous black dress with the immaculate white collar" (8), one may well envision Joan Fontaine so attired (*Jane Eyre*, 1944, dir. Robert Stevenson). Mary's apparently isolated house becomes the prototypical place of enclosure of Gothic movies. It is, after all, a dark and stormy night: the unexpected caller at the door recalls similar scenes of visitors arriving at Frankenstein's mill, at Heathcliff's estate (*Wuthering Heights*, 1939, dir. William Wyer), or at any number of other desolate spots. The two creatures entering the room, candelabra in hand, will surely remind spectators, however vaguely, of horror movies, and the final image of the

---

7. In the 1995 novel *Habanera*, Mario tells anecdotes of Byron and the Shelleys as he escorts the American tourists around Geneva. The American women are "very excited to learn that the author of the famous *Frankenstein*, which had made them tremble so in the movies, was a woman" (37).

8. In the Society Hill production, no effort was made to have the actor resemble Boris Karloff and the Monster's portrayal lost much of its comic effect.

Monster, holding Mary in his arms, has a direct correspondence in Whale's film.

Some of these same Gothic elements, functioning as obvious parody, will have a comic effect: the Monster's appearance will initially evoke laughter, as will the entrance of the two creatures bearing lighted candelabras. Manet likewise makes use of stock elements of farce, from name-calling and fighting to comic contrasts, incongruity, repetitions, and role reversals. When the primly dressed Charlotte and Jane begin to exchange insults and to wrestle, the audience will be amused. The physical contrast between the huge Monster and petite Mary, who orders him around, is funny, as is the foppish name Percival by which she calls him. The three women's preference for whiskey instead of tea—the latter the beverage of choice of proper British ladies—and Jane's smoking a long, slender cigar are examples of humor from incongruity.[9] The repeat scene of spiritual peace, interrupted by the jangling doorbell, will elicit laughter both from repetition and from comic irony: Charlotte's exaggerated nervousness and the audience's knowledge of English literature create the expectation of Jane's entrance, however surprised Mary and the Monster may be. Mary's coquettish preparations for her "male" visitor, with her sudden about-face when Charlotte enters, as well as the creations turning the tables, or, more precisely, switching the chairs on their creators— Mary's comfortable padded one for the Monster's hard straight-backed —are role reversals typical of classic comedy.

To some extent, the intertextuality with the Shelley and Brontë novels is in parallel with Manet's playful parody of Gothic movies and use of stock comic devices. Physically, the Monster and Jane Eyre are to resemble the familiar characters, but their inner reality provides a comic, incongruous contrast with that outward appearance. In rewriting his fate, the sensitive, misunderstood Monster dictates—in exaggerated, boss-to-secretary style, complete with punctuation—the beginning of *The Return of Prometheus, or The True Story of Karl-Gustaf Schwartz* (16). Under a new identity, he will be transformed by a plastic surgeon into a slender and handsome young man, with blond curls. Jane titles her sequel *The Story*

---

9. Manet is repeating here some of his favorite characters, situations, and comic techniques. Lady Strass is also a proper British woman who drinks whiskey and smokes cigars. The physical fighting of the two women recalls the sisters of charity wrestling in *Les Nonnes*. In more general terms, this play is related to those of entrapment and enclosure whose characters either create fictions to deceive one another (*Les Nonnes, Le Borgne*) or attempt to change their past by acting out fictionalized memories (*Madras, la nuit où . . . , Lady Strass*).

of a Liberated Woman: Jane Eyre, Part II (16). She decrees the death of Rochester and their son, and sends herself off to Louisiana, where she will establish an estate named Harenton Earnshaw. As Mary exclaims, the Monster dreams of being Lord Byron (a real-life friend of the Shelleys), and Jane imagines herself as Heathcliff (the romantic hero in *Wuthering Heights*, by Charlotte's sister Emily, and created in the classic Hollywood film by Laurence Olivier) (17–18). Spectators will doubtless recognize the literary—or film—references and derive pleasure and amusement from mentally casting the hulking, hideous creature and the poor, plain governess into their chosen roles.

Typical of Manet's theater in general, the superficial humor in *Le Jour où Mary Shelley rencontra Charlotte Brontë* is underscored by a variety of serious concerns. The author-character rivalry is sometimes comic, sometimes violent, but always self-consciously connotative of literary and philosophical issues. Specialists in French theater have understandably found the play to be Pirandellian (Bradby 236; Temkine 1979: 19).[10] Charlotte confesses to Mary that all the Brontës wrote to achieve immortality, as if impelled by inner demons (10). When the Monster contends that the creations will live on, while their authors will be nothing but ashes and dust, Mary offers Charlotte the consolation to be found in their achievement: where Byron and Scott had failed, these two women gave immortality to characters of mythic stature on a par with Don Quixote, Don Juan, and Hamlet (12).

Neither the rebellion of the characters nor the anguish of their creators can be assuaged by immortality. None of them is happy with the role he or she has been assigned in life, with the restraints that have been placed on them by their creators or by society. Each seeks some level of self-fulfillment or freedom. That there are philosophical parallels with the human condition in general is made readily apparent. The set calls for a tripod in the corner, on which a Bible is prominently displayed. When the action begins with the Monster reading from *Frankenstein*, visual and audible signs point to a correlation between the two texts, between two levels of creators and their respective creations. Later, when Charlotte reads from the Book of Job in counterpoint to the Monster, the

---

10. Hispanists will surely perceive a relationship as well with Miguel de Unamuno's autonomous character. The various aspects of the author-character debate cited in the paragraph that follows may be found in the Spaniard's 1914 novel *Niebla* even more directly than in Pirandello. Manet states that he had not read *Niebla* and does not believe that Unamuno has influenced his work.

parallel is clearly marked: to feel betrayed by one's maker, to suffer bitterness in one's soul, to call out for pity, are part of universal experience.

In their landmark feminist study, *The Madwoman in the Attic*, Sandra Gilbert and Susan Gubar affirm that the Monster's perspective, although generally overlooked by critics and filmmakers, should be considered central to Shelley's novel: "the drastic shift in point of view that the nameless monster's monologue represents probably constitutes *Frankenstein*'s most striking technical *tour de force*, just as the monster's bitter self-revelations are Mary Shelley's most impressive and original achievement" (235). Rosemary Jackson, in her analysis of the fantastic mode in literature, similarly identifies the monster's narration as an essential component of a prototypical work: subsequent to its acquisition of language, the monster describes "pain, guilt, and *difference* from others" (100). Manet focuses precisely on this aspect of his source text. In so doing, he underscores the Monster's function as an outer expression of Mary's sense of alienation and otherness.

Mary Wollstonecraft Shelley's creation has become part of our lexicon: a Frankenstein is someone who creates a monster that ultimately destroys its creator. Jackson identifies the Frankenstein pattern as a basic myth of post-Romantic culture, noting that "self becomes other through a self-generated metamorphosis, through the subject's alienation from himself and consequent splitting or multiplying of identities" (59). In this respect, the monster is Dr. Victor Frankenstein's "grotesque reflection . . . his parodic mirror image" (Jackson 99). In Manet's version, the Monster does voice Victor Frankenstein's thirst for the absolute, including absolute control over others, but he does so in the essentially comic first scene. Far more interesting, as the play develops, is the relationship with Mary herself.

In her initial monologue, as well as her later confession to Charlotte, Mary expresses her own rebellion and rage. Her outward conformity had hidden "the violence of all the world's volcanoes" (8). Manet's Mary evokes a physical image not unlike Gilbert and Gubar's description of Jane Eyre: "little, pale, neat, and quiet" (361). At heart, she is the Monster. As she tells Charlotte, she engendered her vile creature to free her of her demons. Through her creation, she had briefly triumphed over her husband and Byron by becoming "the Archangel of anger, of vengeance, of death" (14). While Charlotte suggests that Mary has had a "full life," Mary complains that her libertarian father was tyrannical in the home, that her mother was too busy with her feminist causes to have time for her daughter, and that in her struggle for existence as a writer after her husband's death, she had no identity of her own: she was always Percy Shelley's widow.[11]

The search for self-identity is the basic theme of *Le Jour où Mary Shelley rencontra Charlotte Brontë*. It is the underlying cause both of the characters' rebellion against their authors and the authors' desire to escape from their characters. Because of the visual signs (size of the actor, gestures, makeup, etc.), the Monster's situation may be observed most readily, but the same contrast between outer role and inner desire exists in all four. The conflict is not one easily resolved, for over time the outer role has also been internalized. In the first scene, the Monster, standing behind Mary's chair, makes an impassioned plea for social justice: "How can we fail to tremble with impatience and anger at the mere sight of the poverty of the world? How can we stand idly by when faced with injustice, with ugliness, with wickedness? How can we not raise our voices and cry out for change" (6). As he speaks, his huge hands approach Mary's throat, as if to strangle her. The contrast between his idealistic words and the threat of physical violence is superficially comic but hints at the several characters' inability to reconcile their dreams with their prior socialization.

For women in the nineteenth century, the socialization process was clear: they should desire to be virtuous wives and mothers while repressing personal ambition and passion. Elaine Showalter has identified *Jane Eyre* as an extraordinary attempt at depicting a complete female identity, including the aspects previously silenced in women's literature. Through the characters Helen Burns and Bertha Mason, Charlotte Brontë externalized the forced division of "the Victorian female psyche into its extreme components of mind and body"; through these two and Jane Eyre—the "three faces of Jane"—she formulated "the deadly combat between the Angel in the House and the devil in the flesh" that has become a recurrent theme of later women writers (113). Manet, too, is aware of this Victorian division: the basis of Jane's complaint is that Charlotte is unable to break away from the Angel in the House mold and hence destroys Jane's freedom because of her own ambivalence.

---

11. Mary's impassioned speech to Charlotte introduces the theme of a generation gap between daughter and parents but is historically inaccurate. The mother of Mary Wollstonecraft Shelley (1797–1851), the famous feminist Mary Wollstonecraft (1759–97), died in childbirth.

On the recommendation of Mrs. Gaskell—Charlotte Brontë's real-life biographer—Charlotte has come to Mary for advice. As Mary intuits, the advice Charlotte seeks is to set aside her identity as Currer Bell, the writer, and conform to society's expectations: "To enter the anonymous life of the couple as one enters religion. And who knows? Some women find in marriage the happiness of the convent" (10). It is this promise of peace that Jane Eyre interrupts with her abrupt appearance.

Manet's Jane incarnates the side of Charlotte's personality that would be denied by her opting for the traditional gender role. She accuses Charlotte of having betrayed Jane and Charlotte's own convictions by opposing free love, by marrying her character off at the novel's end, and by giving her a "firstborn child," hence implying a growing brood and increasingly passive role. To prove her point, an angry Jane quotes Charlotte Brontë's feminist rhetoric against the rigid restraints placed on women and finally declares, "I would have preferred death, madness. Nothing is worse than mediocrity!" (13). Gilbert and Gubar have labeled their chapter on *Jane Eyre* "A Dialogue of Self and Soul." Manet similarly envisions the impassioned dispute between Jane and Charlotte as a battle of the author with herself. For Mary, this inner battle is not without value; she finds the Charlotte/Jane contradictions to be "creative, enriching, exalting," particularly in contrast with her own struggle against the demons represented by the Monster she created in her youth (14).

In one sense, *Le Jour où Mary Shelley rencontra Charlotte Brontë* may reflect another level of intertextuality, with Manet's own "youthful" creations. Robert Kanters concluded his favorable review of the original production by raising just that question: should we imagine Eduardo Manet, withdrawn from the world in a convent, "held hostage by the characters from his earlier plays, tormented by mocking nuns and being watched over by a one-eyed man?" Perhaps not, but Manet's frequent portrayal of characters trapped within enclosures and subject either to their own self-deception or to the cruel games of others suggests an abiding empathy with Mary, Charlotte, and their situations. From a variety of perspectives, the author's experience as political exile may well have raised his consciousness on such matters as alienation and otherness. More to the point of Kanters's comment, Manet cannot escape from the fame of his first French-language play. Unlike Mary Shelley and Charlotte Brontë, he has had many successful works to his credit—novels as well as plays; nevertheless, he will always be known as the creator of *Les Nonnes*, just as surely as these nineteenth-century writers are identified with their first published novels.

Les Nonnes is marked by a *mise-en-abîme* of metatheatrical games, of role-playing within the role. By the same token, *Le Jour où Mary Shelley rencontra Charlotte Brontë* includes multiple layers of metafiction, for Mary and Charlotte, as we know them here, are both the creators of the Monster and Jane Eyre and the creations of Eduardo Manet. As Manet's creations they may well reflect his own ambivalence, as a Hispanic-French author, between competing identities. The attraction of the play for audiences, whether French or American, relates not to Manet's demons, or even to Mary and Charlotte's, but to our own. Manet's Gothic horror comedy ultimately provides insights into the lives of his women writers and their characters but it also presents an entertaining and illuminating commentary on universal human experience: on every person's search for identity.

Voodoo Becomes Medea

Ma'Déa, written in 1984 in collaboration with the actresses Michèle Armand Barthélemy and Fatima Soualhia, opened in April 1986 at the Théâtre de la Poche-Montparnasse in Paris, under Manet's direction. Along with *Mendoza, en Argentine...*, the work that immediately precedes it, *Ma'Déa* is Manet's only exploration to date of the tragic genre. In his comprehensive inventory of plays based on the Greek story of Medea, William García cites four Spanish American modernizations prior to Manet's work. Although Manet's transformation of the classic myth is unique in a number of respects, it has some points in common with these precursor texts.

The action of *Ma'Déa* takes place in Haiti in 1946. Ma'Déa, a wealthy mulatto, has been happily married for fifteen years to Jérémie, a white American who came to Haiti as part of the marines' invasionary force.[12] Distraught by the knowledge that her husband plans to abandon her for his new love, the young Algerian Jasmine, Ma'Déa seeks the help of Ma'Bo. Through voodoo rituals, the two Haitians evoke the spirits of Ma'Déa's family. Despite her growing sense of identification with the younger woman, Ma'Déa stands aside while Ma'Bo proceeds to kill the pregnant Jasmine, as planned, with a poisoned gown. Gone from Manet's

---

12. The American occupation of Haiti lasted from 1915 to 1934.

Fig. 13 Fatima Soualhia Manet, actor Jean-Claude Fernandez, and Eduardo Manet, at Manet's apartment in Paris, 1996 (photo by P. Zatlin).

version is one of the key elements of the Greek myth: his Medea figure is sterile, and so the child she kills is Jérémie and Jasmine's unborn baby. Manet attributes the change to Barthélemy, who played the role of Ma'Déa; as a mother herself, she refused to kill her own children, even in the theater (interview, Temkine 39). No longer guilty of the most heinous crime and a reluctant participant in the murder of her rival, Ma'Déa becomes a more sympathetic character than the classic tragic heroine.

In the original myth, the sorceress Medea falls in love with a stranger, deceives her father and kills her brother to help him, then flees with him to his land, where she becomes the Other. Spanish American versions shift the action to the New World and raise the subject of racial identity. In the case of Peruvian and Mexican plays, Jason is equated with the white conquistador, Medea is representative of the indigenous people, and their children are among the first mestizos.[13] Reflective of their Cuban origins, Triana and Manet use Caribbean settings and focus on

---

13. García discusses Juan Rios's *La selva* (The jungle; Peru, 1950), Jesús Sotelo Inclán's *Malintzin, Medea americana* (Mexico, 1957), and Sergio Magaña's *Los argonautas* (Mexico, 1965), in addition to the Triana and Manet texts.

black, rather than Indian, culture; José Escarpanter points out that the theme of the mulatto woman betrayed by her white lover was a common one in Cuba's popular *teatro bufo* and *zarzuela* (light opera) in the 1930s (1991: 10). Through the process of white colonization, the Medea figure, whatever her racial background, becomes Other within her own land.

Triana's *Medea en el espejo* (Medea in the mirror) premiered in Havana in December 1960, at a time when Manet, too, was back in Cuba. Manet, who reviewed a production of Euripides's tragedy for *Pueblo* in 1948, told Temkine that he had been fascinated by the Medea myth since his youth; but he must also have had at least vague memories of the Triana production when he began his own writing.[14] According to Escarpanter, it is through the use of Afro-Cuban religious elements that *Medea en el espejo* succeeds in breaking with realism/naturalism to reach a poetic plane (1994: 34). Citing Fernando Ortiz, Escarpanter clarifies that the mirror of the title is used in religious ritual for locating an absent person; Triana's María also uses it to find herself, to verify her own identity (1994: 34). *Ma'Déa* likewise is a poetic, antirealistic drama that emphasizes Afro-Caribbean ritual and the symbolic value of mirrors. Both texts call for a background of bongo or voodoo drums.[15]

On the other hand, Manet's tragedy differs from Triana's in significant ways beyond the radical change to the source story. Pedro Manuel Barreda credits Triana's "restoration of the classic Greek chorus" with achieving a poetic, ritualistic effect (24). Manet's work has no chorus and is limited to a three-actress cast. *Ma'Déa* is an intensive poetic ritual, played without an intermission and running, in its premiere production, a scant hour and twenty minutes. Much of the text consists of ritual chants, of invocations and incantations; only intermittent passages approach more conventional dialogue or narration. In that many of the chants are given in patois, passages like the following will generally be incomprehensible to the French audience; they function primarily as rhythmic sound rather than verbal texts.

---

14. During his presentation to my theater seminar, García observed that the 1991 edition of *Medea en el espejo* incorporates changes with respect to Triana's original text that may, in turn, reflect the influence of *Ma'Déa*. In that Triana has lived in Paris since 1980 and he and Manet are friends, Triana doubtless saw Manet's play.

15. In the production he directed, Manet eliminated both the "forty sacred drums" and passages of taped voices. He explained to Temkine that the Poche-Montparnasse was simply too small for sound effects that require a large theater (interview, Temkine 39). In his analysis, García correctly notes that the taped passages intended to express the thoughts of the characters would function as a kind of stream of consciousness (57).

Zo li maché, li maché, li maché
Cowa li maché
La vi nou nan min bon dié. (211)

Erzulie ... eh! ... oh! ...
Erzulie ... eh! ... oh! ...
Nan lan mé
Kannot moin charivé
Erzulie ... eh! ... oh! ... (223)

Many passages in French likewise emphasize rhythm and sound over literal meaning. In the opening scene, for example, Ma'Déa's incantation is based on the repetitive lament "Mon homme m'a quittée! / Mon homme m'a quittée!" (My man has left me), followed by a series of short, disjointed sentences built on the same key verb (209–10).

The poetic effect of Manet's language is enhanced throughout by a musical sound track, in addition to the sometimes distant, sometimes thunderous, ritual drums. There is no special scenery and props are minimal. An area of the bare playing space is left in shadow to facilitate the frequent transformations of characters; roles within roles are visually marked by slight wardrobe changes. The courtyard of the *solar* (tenement house) in Triana's three-act tragedy might also be presented with minimal set, but the story line of *Medea en el espejo* is both longer and more complicated, the dialogue more natural, and the cast considerably larger: seven characters plus the chorus.

When Manet first conceived his Medea, he planned to write a monologue for Barthlémy, a singer and tragic actress who, like the character, is a Haitian mulatto. Then Manet met Soualhia, a French Algerian who bears a striking physical resemblance to Barthlémy. The play-in-progress shifted direction to develop the implicit sisterhood of two women of color who are misused by the handsome, blond American and, by extension, the symbolism of two nations victimized by white imperialism. Following the climactic mirror scene, Ma'Déa sees Jasmine as her double and proclaims: "We are both in love. We are both rendered powerless. We have both been betrayed. We are both dead. Two exploited lands. Two poor, bleeding lands. Two trampled cultures" (254). Identifying strongly with Jasmine and unable to proceed with her murderous plan, Ma'Déa relinquishes control to Ma'Bo.

The role of Ma'Bo—the nurse of the Greek tragedy—was played by Maïté Vauclin, a black actress from Martinique. It is Ma'Bo who advises against killing Jérémie and who proposes instead the particular form that Ma'Déa's revenge should take. When Ma'Déa loses her hatred for Jasmine and hesitates, it is the intransigent Ma'Bo who leads Jasmine away and dresses her in the poisoned gown. There is an implicit racial and class tension in the unforgiving resentment of the black Ma'Bo toward her mixed-race mistress who has, for fifteen years, sacrificed her Haitian identity and given herself and her wealth to the white enemy invader. Through her unbridled passion and submission to her husband, with her concomitant rejection of her people, her culture, and her gods, Ma'Déa has ceased to be Ma'Déa.

Manet often incorporates elements of Afro-Caribbean religions. In *La Mauresque* and *L'Ile du lézard vert*, his fictional autobiographies, he creates a Haitian nurse who introduces the narrator and his mother to the clandestine rituals.[16] The fascinated child describes what he sees as "theater." This theatrical aspect is exploited as well in some other plays, most notably *Eux ou La prise du pouvoir*. *Les Nonnes* is also set in Haiti against a background of voodoo drums. *Ma'Déa*, however, is the one work to date that places religious rites at its center. All of the action, from the invocation of spirits in the opening scenes to the death of Jasmine, is ritual; in its painful intensity, it has the force of psychodrama. When Temkine questioned the authenticity of Manet's portrayal of voodoo, he admitted taking some liberties precisely for the purpose of emphasizing this latter aspect (39).[17]

The ritual has already begun when the play begins. Ma'Déa sits on the floor, rocking back and forth, while chanting. Ma'Bo, the priestess, stands behind her in the shadows and plays the *açon*, a ritualistic instrument. Ma'Bo calls on the *loas*, or voodoo gods, and specifically on Legba, the gatekeeper for departed spirits. The spirits of Ma'Déa's mother, father, and brother answer, speaking through Ma'Déa and Ma'Bo. Because of its obvious intertextuality with the Greek myth and its concentration on ritual, *Ma'Déa* readily falls within the metatheatrical mode. The doubling of the two women in multiple roles moves the performance to a powerful, eerie level of metadrama. The central characters lose control of themselves as the voices of the invoked spirits take over. Ma'Déa

---

16. In his 1980 interview with Ezzedine Mestiri, Manet observes that Castro outlawed black congregations precisely because Afro-Caribbean religions by nature are clandestine (154). Such clandestine meetings obviously could be used as a cover for launching political movements.

17. In his insightful analysis of *Ma'Déa*, García has researched and clarified the various voodoo references.

alternately becomes her mother and herself at earlier ages. The mother, trying to guide her daughter, imitates the voice of Ma'Bo. The actress thus must be able to assume a role within a role within a role. For ensuing dialogues Ma'Bo first becomes Ma'Déa's father while Ma'Déa becomes her brother; then Ma'Bo shifts to the brother while Ma'Déa is herself. At the culminating point in the ceremony, Ma'Déa declares the voices of her loved ones to be the voice of all Haiti, accusing her of betraying her people because of a white stranger and demanding that she kill him in revenge (239–40).

The invocation of the spirits leads to an encapsulated narration of Ma'Déa's life, including her initiation both to Catholicism and to voodoo. In the scene of her first communion, played against appropriate church music, Ma'Bo as priest and Ma'Déa as her eleven-year-old self speak simultaneously, as if chanting a duet. The scene terminates with Ma'Déa's rejection of voodoo. In the corresponding voodoo initiation, the eighteen-year-old dedicates herself to Erzulie. As the goddess of love, Erzulie parallels the Greek Aphrodite whom Medea served, but García points out certain problematic differences. For practitioners of voodoo, Erzulie is a beautiful, sensuous mulatto who has prejudiced feelings based on color; Ma'Déa's identification with this particular goddess thus represents arrogant pride, her tragic flaw (García 197).

Ma'Déa continues to reject suitors for three more years, but from this point forward she is no longer in control of her actions. At her first sight of the American, she is blinded by passion; she becomes, in Ma'Bo's words, a "femme-volcan, femme-ouragan" (female volcano, female hurricane; 214). The encounter with Jérémie takes place at an elegant ball in the capital city on Midsummer Night. The dance music, of European origin, signals the outward acceptance by a sector of Haitian society of the imposed foreign influence. The summer solstice in many cultures is a magical evening; in Hispanic legend, it is a night when one may meet one's future mate. Jérémie's white radiance converts him in Ma'Déa's eyes to a sun-man, an angel. Stunned by the mere sight of him, she quickly yields to his dominance. Jasmine, who is free of such voodoo and magic spells, sees Jérémie far more clearly; she resists becoming his lover even when she realizes that she is in his power, and she eventually labels him a liar. Significantly, she meets the blond American on 21 March; the spring solstice is a sign of her fertility and the child she will bear.

Ma'Déa's life is told through the invocation of the spirits. Jasmine tells hers directly to Ma'Bo, who deceitfully seeks out Jérémie's young lover; that dialogue is recounted to Ma'Déa by Ma'Bo, whose narration is supplemented by expressionistic flashbacks. Reminiscent of *Mendoza, en Argentine* . . . in particular and of Greek tragedy in general, both women's stories center on family betrayals. Jasmine works as a chambermaid in her half brother's hotel in Marseille, where Jérémie, traveling alone, awaits a boat back to Haiti. The brother sells Jasmine to Jérémie, puts her on the boat, and tricks her into believing that he, too, is making the trip and the rest of the family will follow. The exchange of the woman as object in this case has clear racial connotations. Like Asuncion in the earlier play, the brother is only half white. By selling his sister to the white man, he bonds with the dominant class. Ma'Déa's older brother is a soldier who fights against the invading American forces. Taped voices accuse her of having betrayed her brother to the enemy marines because of her love for Jérémie. Although the rapid transition from mourning to wedding scenes hints at her guilt, Ma'Déa does not confess to having precipitated her brother's death. She does reveal a latent incestuous desire for an admired older brother who abandoned her to follow his militant cause.[18]

Other aspects of these characters and their personal relationships are repeated elsewhere in Manet's work. Ma'Déa, before surrendering to her passion for Jérémie, is an aggressive woman—a "garçon manqué" (tomboy) who rides her horse for hours at a time—not unlike Asuncion; in the absence of her brother, she assumes management of their land when the father's health begins to fail. The brother-sister relationship, explored here with respect to both Ma'Déa and Jasmine, will be developed at further length in the 1996 novel, *Rhapsodie cubaine*. Jasmine's situation is somewhat like that of La Mauresque: Jérémie, who takes her from Europe to the Caribbean, tells her of his love but fails to mention that he is already married. The absent father is a familiar motif in Manet's novels with male protagonists. In *Ma'Déa*, both the title character and Jasmine suffer because of separation from their mothers.

Ma'Déa, who is raised by Ma'Bo, often invoked her mother's spirit as she was growing up. Jasmine has a strong attachment to her mother, who is in Algeria when the half brother and Jérémie conspire to deceive and dishonor the young woman. In her loneliness, and as her pregnancy

---

18. In invoking her brother's spirit, Ma'Déa recalls how he introduced her to the joys of poetry. She recites a stanza by the nineteenth-century Cuban-French poet José Maria de Heredia (222). The source of the text might escape the audience but Manet is obviously paying tribute to a compatriot whose path he has followed.

advances, she yearns for the lost mother whom she may never see again. Perhaps because of the collaboration of the two actresses, *Ma'Déa* strikes a resonant chord in female experience, of a woman's desire for communication with her mother or her child. In their moment of sisterly solidarity, Jasmine asks if Ma'Déa thinks she's crazy to talk to her unborn baby; Ma'Déa responds that for years she constantly spoke to her dead mother, and assures her, "We are never alone, Jasmine" (256). Jasmine's initial fear of Ma'Déa is overcome by her deep need to confide in another woman, coupled with the effects of *mojito*, a potent rum-based Cuban drink that Ma'Déa has served without the Algerian's fully realizing what it contains.[19]

As the two women draw closer, the tragic irony of their situation increases. The audience, conscious always of the Medea myth, knows that Jasmine's trust is misplaced. Ma'Déa's empathy with the Algerian softens her resolve; Ma'Bo's inflexible hatred quickly destroys any hope of averting the inevitable end. As the younger women look together into the mirror, they see themselves reflected in each other: their images are interchangeable. Simultaneously, they also see the mask of death. Jasmine cries out in terror but is comforted by the presence of Ma'Déa, whom she calls "un ange" (255); the audience, of course, knows that if Ma'Déa is an angel, she is the angel of death. Delighted as a child at the beautiful wedding gown, the fulfillment of a dream, Jasmine expresses undying gratitude for the fatal gift; and then the poison begins to take hold.

Ironic, too, is Ma'Déa's comparison of Jasmine with the Hollywood film image of an Egyptian queen. Ma'Déa confides that she, a mulatto, would never be accepted by Jérémie's racist family in the United States. She therefore has never met her American in-laws. "But you're Arab, Jasmine. When they look at you, they'll think of Cleopatra" (253). The audience will think not of the physical appearance of Elizabeth Taylor in the 1963 movie but rather of the Shakespearean heroine's death from asp bites. Indeed, as the poison moves through Jasmine's body, she equates the effects to that of a venomous snake (257).

When Ma'Déa welcomes Jasmine into her home, she tells the frightened young woman that life is like the puppet shows her father took her

---

19. There are references within the text to Jasmine's religion. Both Jérémie and Ma'Déa coerce her into breaking her Moslem beliefs. As someone who abstains from drinking alcoholic beverages altogether, she would logically be affected quickly by the consumption of the rum. In *Habanera*, his Cuban friends warn Mario that tourists tend to misjudge the potency of the island's famous drinks.

to when she was a child. He assured her then that she should not be dismayed by the action she saw on the little stage because it was only theater; the curtain would fall and order would be restored. The note of assurance in that message was contradicted by another of his thoughts: we are only puppets, being pulled by invisible strings (246–47). The self-reference to the tragedy in progress is equally contradictory.

In some ways, when the curtain falls on her rival, order is restored to Ma'Déa's life: through her act of vengeance against Jérémie, she has recouped herself and her Haitian identity. She taunts Jérémie that he, who thought himself a conqueror, was incapable of saving Jasmine (257). In direct address to the audience, she accepts responsibility and invites accusations. Basing himself on Alfred Métraux's study of Haitian voodoo, García points out that Ma'Déa's deed will not result in punishment. Jasmine and Ma'Déa are *marassas*, or twins, and in voodoo the *marassa* has the force of a god; according to Métraux, if one twin causes the death of the other, "people will even take care not to show him the slightest resentment" (qtd. in García 201). On the other hand, although Jasmine is a sacrificial victim, Ma'Déa, too, is a mere puppet in someone else's text that she is powerless to change. Ma'Bo pulls the strings of hatred that prevent natural allies from banding together against exploitation. If we place the action in its sociohistorical context, viewing the women not within their personal drama but rather as symbols of their nations, those "two poor, bleeding lands," it is less clear that Ma'Déa's action signals a new independence for the colonized peoples they represent.

An Italian Trilogy

Manet's multicultural background includes a strong focus on Italian language and literature. In the 1950s, he lived for an extended period in Italy, where he studied at the University of Perugia. During his association with the mime troupe of Jacques Lecoq, he increased his knowledge of commedia dell'arte and toured in Italy. His Italian experiences have been happy ones and he has an abiding affection for the country. Thus it is not unexpected that Manet's plays and novels at times deal with Italian characters and settings or that his multilingual games comprise Italian expressions. The tendency first surfaces in fully developed form in *Les Gozzi*, subtitled "A commedia dell'arte in three rounds," and occurs with equal impact in *Le Primerissimo*. These two lighthearted and entertaining theatrical spectacles were staged in the 1980s and remain unpublished. A third Italian work, the grant-funded *Pour l'amour de Verdi*, has yet to be performed. The trilogy reveals various facets of Manet's theatrical interests: an emphasis on body movement—a subject that he has often taught—in *Les Gozzi*, the challenging opportunity for comic actors to play ever changing roles in *Le Primerissimo*, and, of course, a love of opera in the Verdi homage.

Les Gozzi, a fast-moving farce filled with moments of slapstick and dueling, was written and directed by Manet for the Nouveau Théâtre de Nice as a spectacle for young audiences. Starting in January 1981, it was available for staging in schools and, having the advantage of a small cast and readily portable single set, traveled throughout the country for months. It was also performed at Nice's Centre Dramatique National and, in May 1981, reached the Théâtre de l'Est Parisien. In his favorable review for a newspaper in Lyon, J. J. Lerrant notes that although Manet had directed productions elsewhere, this was his first in France. Unquestionably it was a successful debut. The lead paragraph in *Arts Magazine*, prefacing Manet's comments on commedia dell'arte and the martial arts, expressed envy for the adults lucky enough to accompany children to the Parisian performances.

The play title alludes to the Venetian playwright Carlo Gozzi (1720–1806), who rejected the theatrical reforms of Goldoni. In his opposition to emerging bourgeois realism, Gozzi "sought initially to restore to the stage the masks and improvisation of the traditional commedia dell'arte" (Richards 404). The commedia dell'arte, which emerged in the mid-sixteenth century, was "[a]n improvised masked comedy of traditional situation, social caricature, emblematic costume, and high visual impact, with no basis in a written script . . . in which action takes precedence over character, where physical skills are at least as important as verbal skills" (Green 222). Manet's *Les Gozzi* pays tribute to the eighteenth-century writer's admiration of this traditional form by introducing masks, constant physical action, and, to a certain extent, an improvisational style; in the unfolding of its story, it also coincides with Gozzi's later interest in Spanish drama. To these elements Manet characteristically adds cinematographic ones—background music incongruously drawn from Hollywood Westerns, body movements that imitate silent movies or slow motion—and aikido, a Japanese martial art. The actors received extensive training not only in aikido, but also in acrobatics and the gestural technique required by the use of masks, which preclude reliance on facial expression. The playing space was to be roped off, like a boxing ring, with the audience seated around it in a semicircle; a screen facilitated entrances, exits, and costume changes. As the author-director explains, the resulting spectacle relates as much "to the circus and choreography as to pure theater" (Manet, "Commedia dell'arte").

The improvisational nature of the "commedia dell'arte in three rounds" is belied by the existence of Manet's complete manuscript. The action in the script takes place in an unnamed Italian-speaking state where democracy has finally arrived after 1,349 years of authoritarian regimes. Each of the 125 candidates for governor must first build a tower from which to deliver a campaign speech. The Commendatore-Dottore, Giovanni dei Sancti-Spiriti Gozzi, is being helped in the election contest by his sometimes overbearing son Arnolde, designer of the tower and author of the parodic campaign speech, and his supposedly dimwitted, illegitimate nephew Bertolde. Their bungling work crew is infiltrated by two spies sent by rival candidates. Borrowing freely from Spanish Golden Age theater and novel—most specifically Cervantes's *La gitanilla* (*The Little Gypsy*)—the farce ends with a recognition scene in which one of the male spies, Fraschito, turns out to be the disguised half sister of Bertolde and the other, the Captain Carlos Emilio de la Concepción Fernández y Cuervo, is in fact Bertolde's long-lost Spanish father. The Gozzi clan is reunited, Arnolde and his cousin Mandarina become betrothed, and the Commendatore is the triumphant candidate as all the rival towers collapse, thanks to unexpected magic powers of Mandarina's fan.

The complete manuscript notwithstanding, the Nouveau Théâtre de Nice's playbill does suggest improvisation and moreover eliminates the deus ex machina ending. The traditional commedia dell'arte was based on a scenario: "a chronological plot-summary which was pinned up backstage" (Green 223). The playbill contains such a detailed plot summary, sequence by sequence. It also features a briefer description of twelve scenes: three in round 1, four in round 2, and five in round 3. Despite occasional slight differences in wording between the playbill descriptions of the first eleven sequences and the counterpart headings in Manet's manuscript, the action is basically the same up through the final moments of sequence 11, with which the manuscript concludes. In the staged version, Mandarina's magic power has disappeared and, in an added twelfth sequence, the infant democracy is abolished by a coup d'état. At Mandarina's suggestion, the newly reunited family sets off to find a free country where it will be possible to build the Gozzi tower.

Manet does not utilize such popular commedia dell'arte figures as the young lovers and the zealous old father or guardian, but his story line and five characters are drawn in part from the traditional, improvised farces. When Mandarina is still playing the role within the role of Fraschito, Arnolde is disconcerted that the young "man" is physically attracted to him. Cross-gender dressing causes similar confusion in the commedia dell'arte scenario that María de la Luz Uribe identifies as "Los siervos fingidos" (The false servants; Uribe 72); the basic situation later became a familiar one on the Golden Age and Elizabethan stages. Bertholde, as the exploited, poor relative who is never given enough to eat, bears some resemblance to the classic Arlecchino, who was often portrayed as dim-witted and famished. Phyllis Hartnoll reminds us that the braggart and cowardly Capitano, from his earliest appearance in Italy, in 1520, "seems to have been recognizably Spanish" (63); this particular captain's Spanish name, invented by Manet, certainly falls within the convention for a stock character associated with high-flown, sonorous appellations.

Les Gozzi is a challenging and creative vehicle for energetic actors with refined skills in body movement and mime. Similar to such equally demanding works as *Eux ou La prise du pouvoir* and *L'Autre Don Juan*, the performance text's appeal to actors lies in the opportunity it presents to showcase all of one's talents. In clownish mime routines, the characters rush around the ring at ever increasing speed, taking measurements with a huge tape, trampling on the tower plans, or assembling and disassembling the tower. There are stylized duels with unorthodox weapons, moments of singing and dance, and frequent changes of costume and character. Bertholde puts in an appearance disguised as a female belly dancer. The Capitano, in his capacity as spy, assumes the role of a Buddhist monk. The actress who creates Fraschito/Mandarina in her male role fights a duel using a nunchaku and does a comic drunk scene; in her female role she sings suggestive Spanish songs and plays coquettishly with her fan. In response to the arrival of the young woman, the men disappear only to return all decked out in fancy new clothes to impress her; the sudden change in their appearance recalls a similar comic moment in *Lady Strass*.

Les Gozzi goes beyond music and dance, rapid physical action, and role reversals to incorporate an array of comic devices and gags, both verbal and physical. Exaggerated Italian and Spanish names and numerous expressions in these foreign languages will doubtless make the audience laugh. Repeated blowing on a whistle will also evoke laughter, both from repetition and because the action is usually followed by the actors freezing in place, thus suddenly stopping the hectic, farcical pace. Bertholde at times pops up from behind the screen or pretends to faint from hunger. The Commendatore, ostensibly to watch the construction of rival towers, aims his telescope at the spectators, who will find it funny to become part of the action.

The audience is drawn into the action in other ways as well. The critic for *Nice-Matin* observes that the masked actors in performance deliberately turned their spectators into accomplices by looking at them as part of a theatrical game. "In this game, the actor's gaze executes a triangular movement intended to establish a double relationship between the audience, the partner, and the object. For example: the character is holding a stick. He looks at it, then looks at his partner, and one already guesses his intention of hitting. As the moments pass, the insistence of this gaze confirms the intention; then the actor turns to the audience that, by this means, is alerted implicitly of the action that will take place before their eyes" (C. S.). It is worth observing that although the triangular movement is not unlike that used by clowns, the masks necessitate a somewhat different strategy of communication.

Manet's written text, through the use of asides, provides the kind of comic irony that likewise pulls the audience into the action. For example, at the end of round 1, the Captain identifies himself and his function as spy directly to the spectators and announces that he will shortly return disguised as the monk Ying-Yang. In round 2, the audience will know what the other characters do not and will, of course, have the pleasure of seeing through the deceptions and misunderstandings. The audience is also in on the gag when the Captain/Monk persuades Bertholde to sabotage the Gozzi tower and the two of them take the structure apart as fast as the others can build it. Throughout most of the action, comic irony is in force, but the revelation that Mandarina is Faschito will come as a surprise unless the actress's appearance provides visual clues.

Les Gozzi is, in essence, a compendium of surefire strategies for amusing a youthful audience. These strategies function in a variety of ways, but unquestionably the outstanding ones are the most visual: games of slapstick and mime, rapid motion, and acrobatics.

All of Manet's stage plays are metatheatrical to some degree, and *Les*

Gozzi is certainly no exception. On occasion, however, Manet presents full-blown examples of theater within theater, of texts that deal with theatrical companies in the process of staging their performances. Such is the case of *Le Primerissimo*, the second among his works set in Italy. In this respect, it is related to *L'Autre Don Juan* and *Un Balcon sur les Andes*, but unlike the earlier plays, which focus on productions of a single text or play concept, *Le Primerissimo* involves ever-changing performance texts within a frame play that itself contains a complex bedroom farce, presented with melodramatic kitsch. The work's fragmented action and wide-ranging use of parody places it clearly within the postmodern mode.

The set of *Le Primerissimo* calls for steps leading down toward the audience and for two platforms: a large one, representing the backstage for a traveling theater company; and a small, raised platform, representing the stage within the play. The spatial arrangement facilitates movement and even simultaneity between the frame play and the interpolated texts while also foregrounding the farce's theatricalism. In Brechtian fashion, *Le Primerissimo* has an episodic structure and utilizes narrative strategies. The action, which consists of a prologue and forty-six scenes, spans four years. Posters, musical interludes, and direct address to the audience mark the major transitions.

Le Primerissimo was first staged at the Festival de Malaucène, 15–17 July 1988, under the direction of the author. Written at the request of Michel Galabru, described by Manet, in a personal interview, as "currently one of France's great actors," the farce was intended to be "a reflection on theater, on the actor's art. And a homage, of mad love for Italy."

Underlying the farcical action of *L'Autre Don Juan* are astute commentaries on such serious artistic concerns as antitheatrical prejudice and the tendency of a dominant culture (French, in this case) to cannibalize foreign (Spanish) texts. *Un Balcon sur les Andes*, also wildly comic on the surface level, satirically equates theater and Latin American politics, to the detriment of the latter. The outside world, represented most specifically by the absence of freedom of expression under a series of military regimes, repeatedly encroaches upon the daily existence of the itinerant actors, forcing them into exile and placing their lives in danger. *Le Primerissimo*, more lighthearted throughout, lacks a related textual or subtextual agenda; it is the characters' livelihood, not their lives, that is under threat, and even that threat functions comically in that they habitually demonstrate cartoonlike resilience to adversity. Nevertheless, the farce's setting in Italy from 1910 to August 1914, a time coinciding with the outbreak of World War I, along with its passing reference to Benito Mussolini, implies that the closed world of the theatrical troupe, in which actors need react only to audience satisfaction with their artistic work, is but an illusion. *Le Primerissimo* is not overtly political like the plays considered in the previous chapter, but it does deliberately call attention to its own escapism.

In *Un Balcon sur les Andes*, the play-within-the-play, performed with variations by the traveling company, is a classic bedroom farce about marital infidelity. In *Le Primerissimo*, the conventional scenario underpins a complex frame play. The theatrical troupe of the Italian farce consists of the star Arnoldo Pozzo-Mastrocinque, whose sonorous name repeats the time-honored comic element also found in *Les Gozzi*; his actress wife, Letizia—or, to be more precise, Letizia Rossi Malaparte, as she will assert in a moment of anger; their daughter and son, Fabiola and Gino; Arnoldo's half brother, the impresario and prompter Don Felice Martirio, whose "speaking name" effectively reveals that he will spiritedly—if not happily—play the martyr at each financial crisis; Arnoldo's illegitimate teenage daughters, Tina and Lina, and his somewhat older goddaughter, Mina; the stage manager and actor Michèle di Lucca, who is really a disguised Belgian and would-be playwright, Bruno Bonsang; and an actress, whose pretense at being the British Miss Fussy and then the German Marika Weber conceals her past as the Spanish prostitute Pepa la Candela.[20] Even disregarding the plays-within-the-play of *Le Primerissimo*, the web of relationships among the members of the company and the layered identities of two of them yield a dizzying array of role-playing within the roles.

Given the combination of this exuberant frame play and the several interpolated texts, the three-act farce results in a kaleidoscope of rapidly changing scenes and character relationships, along with ample opportunity for multilingual games and jokes based on ethnicity and names. Aside from an anticipated introduction of Italian expressions because of the setting, the chameleon-like nationality of "Miss Fussy" allows for fre-

---

20. The intention is not similarly comic, but Manet also plays with sonorous Italian names in the novel *Habanera*. One of Mario and Arsenio's surnames, like that of Letizia, is in fact Malaparte, which could be construed to mean "bad part," the antonym of the more famous Bonaparte. In his analysis of theater semiotics, Marvin Carlson defines four categories of "speaking names"; Felice Martirio, "Happy Martyr," is an example of character description, the one most associated with major characters. The other categories are animal names, names derived from objects used in the character's trade, and actions linked to the character's trade (Carlson 34–35).

quent use of English, German, and Spanish words, all to comic effect. (An "improvised" play-within-the-play will also throw in fake Russian.) For the French, the Belgian is a traditional butt of jokes; Michèle is thus the object of stereotypical ethnic slurs, and his "real" surname, Bonsang, additionally provides opportunities for punning on its idiomatic meaning: "Damn it!" The rhyming names of the three girls also are intended to evoke laughter, as will their functioning on occasion as a unit, with concomitant similarities in appearance and manner. As Bergson points out in his classic study of laughter, the reduction of human beings to mechanical repetition or duplication is funny; thus twins have been a stock comic device from the days of Plautus to the present. If two characters who look and act alike may make us laugh, then Manet's quasi triplets will surely do so.

Structurally, *Le Primerissimo* is a *mise-en-abîme* of levels of performance. The actors are each playing actor-characters who, because of various love intrigues and other veiled games, are engaged in constant role-playing within the role of the frame play while also assuming multiple acted roles, some ostensibly rehearsed and some improvised. The result, as we shall see from a synopsis of the first act, is a stimulating challenge for the cast. For the spectators, pleasure will be determined by the actors' skill at differentiating between their "real" identities, their efforts at deceiving the other members of the troupe, and their pretend, "fictional" roles. As was true in *L'Autre Don Juan*, the audience will have the chance to compare the difference between "theatricality" and "naturalness."

The flurried prologue of *Le Primerissimo* introduces conflicts between Letizia and both Miss Fussy and her daughter, Letizia's attraction to Michèle, her motherly hovering over Gino, Gino's arrogant attitude toward Michèle and the three girls, and Mina's attraction to Gino. In a tour de force of flicker acting, Letizia must switch instantaneously in tone and gesture from hostility and irritability towards the two women to charm aimed at Michèle; Gino similarly switches from being overbearing big brother to the girls one moment to being talked down to by his mother the next. And all this action precedes the conventional three knocks that presumably announce the play's opening scene.

Unexpectedly, scene 1 is merely a continuation, at slightly less frenetic pace, of the behind-the-scenes activity: of the crisis caused by the star's absence at curtain time and the related development of the bedroom farce. Snowballing complications in the frame play are interrupted in scene 6 when Gino, promising the desperate impresario that he can hold the audience's attention until the "real" play can begin, "improvises"—with the help of actresses using wigs, masks, and dance routines—a hilarious vaudeville rendition of the mythical origins of the food of the gods: tortellini. The drunken Arnoldo arrives at last, but his return does not yield the awaited play but rather a melodramatic confrontation between deceived husband and unfaithful wife. In scene 10, Felice as prompter announces to Arnoldo that the play is at last beginning, but the star's emotional distress leads him to yet another delay. The opening scene of the melodrama, in which Michèle as villain accosts Fabiola as ingenue, is juxtaposed with Felice's frantic efforts to get Arnoldo to perform. Finally, in scene 13, Arnoldo makes his grand theatrical entrance in the role of noble father—to the accompaniment of enthusiastic applause by Tina-Lina-Mina—only to reveal that he has forgotten his lines. His improvised reference to a Russian wife and his call for a samovar cause a comic scramble among the actor-characters backstage who must meet the demands of his new script, one that turns their usual melodramatic play-within-the-play into farce. The "improvised" acted roles are so badly done, in contrast with the actor-characters' "real" roles, that they are hysterically funny.

Although the total frame play comprises a series of shifting love triangles and melds into various subgenres, including touches of mystery farce and romantic comedy, the first act foregrounds only the melodramatic Arnoldo-Letizia-Michèle triangle. In a parody of classic love scenes, Letizia proclaims the passion she has felt for Michèle, ever since he joined the company "two years, six months, five days, twelve hours, thirty-seven minutes, and twenty seconds" earlier (13). Gradually we learn that the distraught Arnoldo has just found some, but not all, of the love letters she hid in a laundry basket. It is his exaggerated response to her infidelity—his washing of their dirty linen in public—that turns their much delayed performance into as great a comic shambles as the conclusion of *L'Autre Don Juan*.

According to Richard Hornby, in fully developed metadrama, the spectator "sees double" and hence experiences a kind of dislocation; the person before us on the stage may simultaneously appear as the real-life actor or actor-character and as the character being portrayed. In his typology of the play-within-the-play, Manfred Schmeling establishes that levels of "reality" and "fiction" may remain separate or may come to occupy the same theatrical space (Schmeling 11); in the latter case, the frame between the reality of the dramatic world and the fiction of the interpolated text is broken.

In the improvised play-within-the-play at the close of *Le Primerissimo*'s first act, the breaking frame leads both actor-characters and spectators to see double.

In the company's habitual melodrama, the father and daughter actor-characters play father and daughter, while Michèle is the villain: the deceitful friend who would seduce the innocent daughter. Arnoldo's entrance as noble father interrupts a scene of sexual harassment to which the young woman reluctantly acquiesces. She quickly alerts the villainous count: "let's pretend to act natural" (35) and improvises a "natural" dialogue to keep her father from realizing what has transpired. The count instantaneously adopts her proffered script, explaining that he has casually dropped by to see the father—and just happened to bring along a bouquet of flowers.

The role-playing required by the play-within-the-play immediately calls attention to the deliberate "naturalness" of theatricality itself. The daughter-character recommends acting—that is, deception—in order to protect her father from an unpleasant truth, and the lecherous count no doubt is accustomed to playing roles in order to conceal his villainy. The irony of the situation cannot escape either the actor-character Arnoldo or the spectators. Within the "real" world of the frame play, Michèle has been the villain: seducing—or being seduced by—Arnoldo's wife and feigning loyalty to the cuckolded husband. With respect to the two levels of reality, only the amorous partner has changed. The frame breaks as Arnoldo sees Michèle himself, not the fictional role he is creating; thus the indignant husband reinvents his role-playing in order to respond to his "real" situation. For Arnoldo the would-be seducer of his daughter within the fiction is simultaneously the real lover of his wife: the villain is the villain. Indeed, the disabused Arnoldo now sees not only double but quadruple, for Michèle has a double identity in each of the two levels of reality: the actor-character who plays a would-be seducer who in turn pretends to be the noble father's friend is Letizia's Belgian lover who pretends to be Arnoldo's Italian colleague. At the same time, to the extent that Arnoldo is played as drunk, his inebriated state will have a frame-breaking function for the real spectators and perhaps as well for the imaginary audience of the play-within-the-play; his drinking in the frame play will carry through directly in the acted performance. Retrospectively, the scene as a whole will take on greater comic irony when the spectators become aware of Fabiola's love for Michèle, whom she eventually wins away from her mother. The father-daughter-lover triangle of the interpolated text thus will mirror the counterpart roles in the frame play. (Bruno-Michèle eventually drops his role as Letizia's lover to become Fabiola's husband.)

Within the interpolated play of the first act, Arnoldo continues to see Michèle only in relationship to Letizia and hence calls for the entrance on stage of his wife, Elisabetta Fedorovna. The stunned actor-characters remind him that he is a widower, to which he responds that he has remarried. In Lionel Abel's terms, Arnoldo is now a would-be dramatist who imposes his script on the other players. Moreover, he rejects any efforts to amend his new text. When Gino tries to write himself in as their son, Piotr Pétrovitch Kornokoff, in order to be on stage with his mother and perhaps protect her, Arnoldo immediately changes Piotr into an adopted, epileptic foundling and almost strangles him. Gino goes down on all fours, begins to bark, and continues to play the dog for the remainder of the act.

Arnoldo writes the character Elisabetta into the fictional text for the purpose of humiliating the "real" actor-character Letizia. He describes her body to Michèle as the count and forces him to pat her buttocks. The imaginary audience for the play-within-the-play might be assumed to see only the interaction between the fictional characters of a pseudo-Russian farce, but the real spectators of *Le Primerissimo* will surely see the scene as the "real" Arnoldo's way of getting even with Letizia and Michèle. In his historical overview of metatheater, Schmeling reminds us that role- or game-playing within the role ("le jeu dans le jeu") is a strategy within the baroque play for revealing wrongs and taking revenge. In serious drama, the strategy will be subtle; in Manet's rollicking burlesque, it is a surface-level comic device. The madcap action and use of macaronic Russian assure that the scene will be greeted with laughter, and, in linguistic terms, the spectators will have the pleasure of seeing, or hearing, triple: French actors playing Italian actor-characters who in turn play Russian characters.

The remainder of the frame play continues to build on a series of love triangles, sometimes mingled with mystery farce. Obligatory scenes in the second act reveal that both Miss Fussy and Fabiola also found love letters in the dirty laundry. In the case of the former, Letizia has done her own sleuthing and is now prepared to blackmail the blackmailer. The dejected Arnoldo discovers—or remembers—the charms of Miss Fussy/Pepa la Candela and takes further revenge on the unfaithful Letizia by casting her in secondary roles while giving his new lover the female leads. Letizia's sad plight is mitigated by Felice Martirio, who has been secretly in love with her for twenty years. Meanwhile, in a scenario verging on romantic comedy, Mina pursues Gino.

Juxtaposed with this chain of love intrigues on one level are the ever changing plays-within-the-plays on the other. Responding to the company's repeated, and hence comic, financial crises, the constant revision of repertoire leads to pastiches of various genres: from melodrama, farce, and Shakespearean tragedy, to silent and then talking movies. The wild improvisation at the end of act 1 is so well received by the imaginary audience that it inspires the replacement of the company's habitual tearjerkers by laugh-provoking farces. When light comedy ceases to attract fickle spectators, Arnoldo proposes the switch to serious drama, namely *Hamlet*: the story of "a guy who kills his mother, his uncle, his fiancée's brother and father, three soldiers, and fifteen guards in order to defend the memory of his cuckolded father" (69). His approach to casting, however, readily turns tragedy into farce. Arnoldo will portray the title character; his son will be his father's ghost, his wife will be his mother, Michèle will be Polonius.

The role reversals created by incongruously assigning younger actor-characters to the older parts and vice-versa are predictably funny. On the other hand, the casting of Felice as Claudius opens up a somewhat more subtle comic irony. Felice exits in dismay after asking if that is how Arnoldo sees him, as a man who "deceives and kills his brother . . . murders people right and left . . . tries to assassinate his nephew" (71). Felice is not a murderer, but we will soon learn that he has long coveted his half brother's wife.

Manet may have intended *Le Primerissimo* as a homage to Italy, but the third act proves to be more of a homage to another of the author's loves: cinema. Stage directions throughout the play have made use of Manet's characteristic reliance on filmic techniques: fade-outs, slow motion, and freeze-frames. The simultaneous backstage and onstage action might be viewed as equivalent to split-screen montage. But as the theatrical company converts to the seventh art, intertextual references to film proliferate and moviemaking becomes the farce's central theme, pushing aside the romantic entanglements. Arnoldo, who has seen but one film in his life—and that one in 1902—initially greets Felice's proposal with derision. Cinema, he says is but a "piece of dirty cloth one puts against a wall to see ridiculous, heavily made-up characters grimace and throw cream pies in people's faces" (97). In keeping with the farcical tone and rhythm, he does a rapid about-face, not only agreeing to the new project but demanding total artistic control, as actor, author, and director; after all, "it's just one step from cooking macaroni to producing a movie" (98). Predictably, their first movie is a spaghetti Western.

The concluding two scenes contain nonstop and sometimes simultaneous parodic simulations of film sequences, complete with musical sound tracks; these are variously inspired by *Johnny Guitar* (renamed *Marika Mandoline*), melodramatic silent movies, and American musicals. In their presentations, they might be considered analogous to the category of theatrical tableaux that Marvin Carlson has defined as pictorial or emblematic (105). Carlson observes that in the nineteenth century there was a vogue for creating plays around moments in which the actors could simultaneously "freeze" in order to visually represent a famous painting or sculptural group. Martin Meisel further clarifies the difference between the dramatic tableau and the *tableau vivant*: "Both present a readable, picturesque, frozen arrangement of living figures; but the dramatic tableau arrested motion, while the *tableau vivant* brought stillness to life" (45). The latter artifice was capable of turning a still image into a "moving picture" (51). In *Le Primerissimo*, because the image the actors wish to create is not static but rather a moving picture, the action does not freeze. Audience pleasure at recognizing the filmic source of such moving tableaux should be similar to the impact of the convention of bringing famous paintings to life. That Manet has theatrical tableaux in mind becomes readily apparent at two particular moments. Stage directions specifically place the actors in position for a family portrait, a "*[b]elle photo de famille*" (108). Under special lighting effects, the actor-characters are to take on robotic stances in homage to Gordon Craig as Mina, Lina, and Tina hold up signs announcing the end (112).

During the series of pseudofilm sequences, the taped voice of Felice Martirio provides a running narration of both the kaleidoscopic action and the company's accomplishments. Turning the question of influence upside down, he credits their actors with providing models for such Hollywood stars as Lillian Gish, Lon Chaney, and Kay Francis. A transformed Arnoldo enters, dressed flamboyantly like a movie idol and flanked by bodyguards wearing T-shirts with his image. Even Letizia recoups center stage, appearing in an impression of Sarah Bernhardt playing the male lead of *L'Aiglon*; she is so taken by the lines of Edmond Rostand's play that she rebels against silent films and pushes the group into the era of the talkies. The lighthearted tone is momentarily broken in the final minutes as a depressed Arnoldo recounts the outbreak of the Great War. With customary resiliency, the troupe is soon enthusiastic about a new stage project: a production of a play by Michèle, set in Argentina, that has a perfect role for each of them. Like the actor-characters in *Un Balcon sur les Andes*, they will abandon the Old World to seek their fortune in South America.

The action of the unstaged and unpublished *Pour l'amour de Verdi* moves back in time, to the nineteenth century. The general tone, despite a number of comic moments, is much more serious than in the other two Italian plays; the series of intertexts, taken from Verdi's operas, are treated respectfully, not parodically. The political context—the fight of Italian patriots for independence from Austria—links the work to the comparable revolutionary struggle in *Mendoza, en Argentine*...; Manet foregrounds historical connections between Europe and the Western Hemisphere by pointing out that Garibaldi, whose wife was South American, fought for South American independence before returning to his native land to join the battle there. Not coincidentally, *Pour l'amour de Verdi* shares with Manet's earlier Latin American works a cinematographic structure that more closely resembles a movie script than a traditional play.

In early 1991, Manet became aware of a special grant, available through the Beaumarchais Foundation, that would fund the writing of "an ambitious spectacle." Taking advantage of an idea he had had in mind for a long time about Verdi and the Risorgimento (the Italian struggle for independence and unification), he applied for and received the grant, which allowed him to do research in Italy. In his proposal, Manet clarified that in presenting Verdi and revolutionary leader Garibaldi, he would follow the Brechtian principle of seeing historical events through the eyes of common people. Thus he created the saga of three generations of a family with close connections to the artistic and military worlds.[21] The play was to be structured "musically," not only by Manet's incorporating Verdi's operas into the background but also by his envisioning the fictional characters' spoken dialogues as parts of an operatic score. The strategy of writing individual and ensemble lines in counterpoint with other voices within the text shifts to the verbal plane Manet's longstanding interartistic approach to movement: the creation of sequences that are choreographed like dance.

---

21. Even though the unfinished novel is set in a later period, the play structurally recalls *Nunzietta*, a roman-fleuve that similarly presents the life of an Italian family over a half-century period.

The finished script adheres closely to the ideas presented in the proposal's detailed synopsis, except in one respect: Manet simplified the play by substituting linear time for temporal fluidity. Even so, the script is long and complex. Its three acts are divided into eight tableaux, most of which include episodes over an extended period: 1842–43, 1845–48, 1859–63, 1864–67, 1867–70, 1871–75, 1882–89, 1894. Much of the action takes place in Milan, but some scenes are set not only elsewhere in Italy but also in France, England, Cairo and New York. At times, action is simultaneous. In the opening scenes, Gino, a factory worker, and Anna, a seamstress who works in her Uncle Carlo's shop, are getting dressed for their opera date that evening; they are at their places of employment, where they are being respectively teased or helped by their fellow workers. Throughout the preparations for going to La Scala, the music of Verdi's *Nabucco* (Nebuchadnezzar) is heard in the background; then the music rises and a third area of the stage becomes the site for performance of a scene from that opera. Now Gino and Anna, in the upper gallery, and Carlo, in an expensive seat, become spectators for the opera-within-the-play. Gino, who has already allied himself with the independence movement, subsequently explains the political subtext to Anna so that she—and the audience of the frame play—will understand the subversive message that Verdi conveyed in the 1840s to the historical audiences of his operas.

With variations, the method of incorporating *Nabucco* is repeated with fragments of twelve other operas, chosen from among master and minor works: *I Lombardi, Giovanna di Arco, Macbeth, Luisa Miller, Un Ballo in Maschera, La Forza del Destino, La Traviata, Don Carlos, Il Trovatore, Aïda, Othello,* and *Rigoletto*. The earliest operas are melded with Gino's involvement in the Italian political struggle. For *Un Ballo in Maschera*, the corresponding action in the frame play mirrors the opera as several characters make preparations for attending a masquerade ball. In the case of the romantic *La Forza del Destino*, the power of destiny reverberates ironically on the other level: Gino is away in battle and Anna is desperate because both of their sons, Beppo and Antonio, have been arrested—for writing "Viva Verde!" on a wall. Over time members of Anna's family enter the opera world as designers or singers, and the play's metatheatricalism is further developed. The scene from *Don Carlo* is viewed from backstage, where Carlo is working as a designer; Carlo and Beppo, who sings in the chorus, are present, behind the scenes, at the Cairo premiere of *Aïda*. Verdi's Manzoni Requiem Mass is also featured; Anna is taken ill while attending its first performance and the scene leads into her subsequent death.

Much like the Cuban novels, which weave together three narrative strands, *Pour l'amour de Verdi* intertwines the composer's career, the Italian independence movement, and the conflicts that arise within Gino and Anna's personal lives. For years Gino is away fighting, in Italy and in France, while Anna supports the family; like the narrator of the fictional autobiographies, Gino and Anna's boys are raised in a female-dominated household with an absent father. Unlike Lorna in *Mendoza, en Argentine* . . . , who enters wholeheartedly into the guerrilla movement, Anna at times resents Gino's commitment and the sacrifice it represents for her and her children. At opposite poles are Gino, who dedicates himself solely to Garibaldi's cause, and Carlo, who places aesthetic values far ahead of political ones and prefers to ignore the subtext of Verdi's operas. When he takes three-year-old Beppo (played by a mannequin) to the Joan of Arc opera (performed by marionettes), he carefully explains to the little child that Verdi's musical creation will transcend its historical context. In a later scene, Carlo is dismayed to receive a personal letter from Verdi in which the great composer speaks only of politics and not at all of music.

The split between Anna's husband and her uncle is widened by Gino's intolerance of Carlo's homosexuality. The conflict later extends to Beppo, who is also gay. Beppo and his soldier brother Antonio eventually make peace, but for years Gino totally disowns Beppo; the young man moves with his Egyptian lover to New York, where their backstage work in the opera world emulates that of Carlo in Italy. The eventual reconciliation of father and son comes only at the play's end when Gino goes to New York to hear his granddaughter Anna-Vittoria sing. Anna-Vittoria's triumph—performing Verdi arias—coincides with the grandfather's death; while applause for her rings out, the lights dim on the dying old man, who is surrounded by the ghosts of his departed loved ones: his wife, his other son, his daughter-in-law, and even Uncle Carlo.

Manet somewhat reduces the costs of a potential production through the doubling of actors in multiple roles. For example, the same actress will play Anna and her granddaughter, and Gino's fellow factory workers will later portray policemen. Repeating the strategy of *Un Balcon sur les Andes*, some of the characters may be represented by mannequins. Manet's stage directions indicate that the opera choruses could be taped. Sets are minimal and particular locations may be suggested impressionistically: two simple chairs for the young people in the gallery at the opera in contrast with a velvet armchair for the uncle's expensive seat. As in *Mendoza, en Argentine* . . . , some backgrounds can be established through projections or other simple means: a blue cyclorama can be used to suggest a ship at sea. Nonetheless, *Pour l'amour de Verdi*, as stipulated by the Beaumarchais grant, is an ambitious spectacle. It requires a large, well-equipped stage with sophisticated lighting and sound support, an experienced technical crew, a large wardrobe, and at least five singers of operatic caliber. Moreover, the principal actors must be able to convey the aging process over an extended period of years. By 1993 the author anticipated the text's publication and had someone interested in staging it; these production plans have not yet materialized.

Pour l'amour de Verdi reflects a number of Manet's favorite theatrical strategies. Stage directions once again call for such cinematographic effects as slow motion and freeze-frames. Two sequences in particular are strongly reminiscent of *Mendoza, en Argentine* . . . : *Pour l'amour de Verdi* calls for a "dissolve" to merge Gino and Anna's marriage celebration into a scene of political unrest; when Gino, in prison, reads aloud a letter received from Anna, a split-screen effect allows us to see his wife at work in Carlo's prosperous new boutique. While Gino reads, Anna simultaneously asks an influential friend to intervene and secure Gino's release. Branching out to other visual effects, Manet introduces another family photo and a *tableau vivant*, similar to the one in *Le Primerissimo*. Gino, Anna, and their fellow patriots work frantically in a wordless scene of ever increasing rhythm. Finally the women unfurl their freedom flag and the men, who have been distributing and loading guns, stand with their weapons drawn. Manet says that his "freeze-frames" are generally inspired by cinema, yet this particular scene for some viewers may well evoke a familiar nineteenth-century image, in the style of Romantic painter Eugène Delacroix (1798–1863). (I am thinking specifically of *La Liberté guidant le peuple*, 1830.)

The two principal historical figures, Verdi and Garibaldi, do not directly intervene in the action. Verdi's personal contact with the characters of the frame play is revealed most closely through the letter that Carlo reads aloud; Garibaldi is represented by a mannequin, asleep on a chaise, when Gino and Anna are traveling with him by boat. On the other hand, French novelist Alexandre Dumas does appear in three scenes. As a war correspondent, Dumas interviews Gino at the front. Gino's response belongs to a series of historical narrations that provide a running account of political events throughout the play. In this scene, Gino's narration is illustrated by imaginatively painted canvases that are raised and lowered "as if by magic." During their first encounter, there is also a comic touch as the admiring but nervous Gino attributes to the famous author not only Dumas's *The Three Musketeers* but also Victor Hugo's *The Hunchback of Notre Dame*.

This first dialogue between Gino and Alexandre Dumas highlights an important concern in the contemporary debate about history and fiction. Hayden White points out that those who favor a scientific approach to history reject the narrative mode, whereas others affirm that "what distinguishes 'historical' from 'fictional' stories is first and foremost their content, rather than their form. The content of historical stories is real events, events that really happened, rather than imaginary events, events invented by the narrator" (27). Such a position of course ignores the writer's subjective stance. In Manet's play, Dumas clearly intends to base his articles on real events; he has traveled to the front lines to get eyewitness accounts. But when Gino asks the writer how he will use the facts, Dumas answers: "The way I always do with everything that touches sad, sordid reality: I'll embellish a bit, I'll spice up the concrete facts with a dash of art and imagination. I know that my readers need dreams, beautiful adventures, heroic figures, like you and General Garibaldi" (49). In Manet's fictional world, the historical Dumas obviously fictionalizes history to make it more palatable to his readers. Manet himself is more likely to add a dash of the grotesque to his treatment of the facts. When Gino and two of his fellow patriots reunite years later, Gino has lost an arm, one companion has a missing leg, and the other has a missing eye.

In the third scene featuring Dumas, Manet returns to the kind of commercialization that he had previously satirized in *Histoire de Maheu le boucher*. It is March 1864 and Garibaldi is in London. Carlo and Dumas, champagne glasses in hand, move about as if in a ballet; they narrate aspects of the hero's reception in England, including a West End musical production based on his military exploits. Simultaneously, three women are hawking Garibaldi souvenirs: postcards, medals, photos, "I love Garibaldi" stickers, and shirts bearing his picture. The deliberate anachronisms are comic but also serve to further underscore the inevitable fictionalization of historical figures.

In its focus on political history and its panoramic structure, *Pour l'amour de Verdi* is closely related to the plays we have examined under the category of historiographic metatheater. The nucleus of the work, however, as indicated by the title, is Verdi, not Garibaldi. Whereas Carlo's opinion is treated within the text with comic irony, he is no doubt correct that Verdi's music transcends its historical context. When Gino's struggle for freedom is over, Anna-Vittoria's operatic career, specializing in Verdi, is only beginning. Potential audiences for Manet's ambitious spectacle are more likely to be drawn to the theater by their love of opera than by their knowledge of nineteenth-century history. The saga of Gino and Anna's family in the frame play is entertaining theater, but in *Pour l'amour de Verdi*, the creative use of the operas-within-the-play will no doubt prove the main attraction.

Not limiting himself either to his native Cuban heritage or to his adopted French one, Manet has an abiding love for a wide range of literature and culture. In the plays examined here as examples of multicultural metatheatricalism, he weaves into his texts such diversified sources as a Mexican-Spanish Golden Age comedy, two nineteenth-century English novels, a Greek tragedy, commedia dell'arte characters and plots, and a dozen Italian operas. To these he adds frequent dashes of Hollywood movies. The result is a brilliant array of intertextual and interartistic games.

7

Continued Experimentation

In the past decade, Eduardo Manet has maintained both his high level of productivity and his willingness to experiment with theatrical themes and approaches. Despite his continued use of multilingualism and filmic images, most of his work from the late 1980s and early 1990s falls outside the categories analyzed in the previous chapters. Some of these new plays remain unstaged and will be mentioned only briefly here, but it is important to remember that Manet's manuscripts on occasion have been successfully produced years after he completed the original version.

In *Deux siècles d'amour* (Two centuries of love, 1992), Manet repeats the whimsical approach to time that he previously used in *Un Balcon sur les Andes* and *Pierre, Esmeralda y Quasimodo*; his characters can live for hundreds of years without aging. In other recent texts, Manet also introduces fanciful settings. *Les Chiennes* (The female dogs, written 1987) and *Mare Nostrum* (written 1994) are fables that take place after cataclysmic disasters. Although the second act deals realistically with the contemporary drug scene, the first act of *Les Anges déçus* (Deluded angels, written 1989) is set in paradise, before the fall.[1] Realistic throughout is *Monsieur Lovestar et son voisin de palier* (Mr. Lovestar and the man on his floor, written 1987), an intense two-character drama that differs in structure and tone from the metatheatrical, small-cast tours de force of Manet's earlier period. In one respect, it serves as a prelude to *Les Poupées en noir* (*The Black Dolls*, 1990), a play also focusing on the relationship of two men who live in the same building; the later text is a kind of memory play whose central theme is the Holocaust. Distinct from all of these is *Les Couples et les paravents* (The couples and the screens, 1992), a playful farce written for a festival of "apartment theater."

Of the unstaged plays mentioned in this chapter, *Anges déçus* has received the least attention to date and appears not to be among projects that Manet is currently pushing forward. The idyllic, if boring, blue paradise of the first act and the urban setting and theme of the second act set it apart from Manet's theater in general. Nevertheless, one can draw a certain parallel between this play's Black Angel and the Mad Spirit of the youthful *Presagio*, both of whom lure the virtuous away from their stagnated existences. *Presagio* does not tell what happens afterwards; *Anges déçus* reveals a tragic denouement. In paradise, the third angel tries to resist, but at the act's end, all three succumb to the Black Angel's influence; the background music shifts to rock. In the second act, we discover that the three angels (now respectively named King-Kong, Star Wars, and Jeff) are tattered, dirty, blue-jeans-clad junkies who live in an abandoned warehouse and deal drugs for Dario (formerly the Black Angel). Dario wears Italian shoes and expensive suits but is only the pawn of a more powerful drug lord. Jeff, who has vague memories of happier days, finally pulls a knife and kills Dario. The abandoned-warehouse setting, the manipulation and fighting among characters previously identified as angels, and the absence of real control by the equivalent to the Mother Superior (Dario) bear some similarities to *Les Nonnes*.

Two Futuristic Fables

Les Chiennes was aired on France-Culture in 1988 and received a staged reading in Paris in May 1992. The fable begins in a barren, war-devastated area where there are only three survivors: Petrus, a male chauvinist, and

---

1. Manet's title *Anges déçus* is a play on the expression "anges déchus," fallen angels. A possible translation to retain the pun might be "Fall guy angels."

two women he quite literally treats as dogs, keeping them leashed and even calling them Dog 1 and Dog 2. In narrative fashion, Petrus tape records his day by day impressions; he hallucinates about his lost mother and believes that he hears the song she used to sing—in Spanish. The unliberated Dog 2 dreams that a man will come to their rescue; she is so desirous of becoming an attractive female that she trades precious food for makeup. After braving an enchanted forest, Petrus discovers an earthly paradise, which he hopes to claim. But the garden of earthly delights belongs to La Proprio, a gun-toting, horseback-riding, forceful woman who immediately takes command of the group, turns Petrus into an apron-wearing cook, and gives the "dogs" back their real names (Alma and Rita) and their human identities.[2] Rita accepts La Proprio as the lover she had longed for, and Petrus discovers that La Proprio was, in fact, the singer he thought he had heard only in his imagination. The comic action builds on a series of thwarted rebellions and a La Proprio-Petrus-Rita love triangle. In the end, Alma goes off on her own to conquer the world while the other two women, both visibly pregnant, remain in paradise with Petrus.

Mare Nostrum elaborates upon the underlying structure of *Les Chiennes*. In a similar vein, the action takes place in the fifth decade of the twenty-first century, after "the disaster." Unspecified at first, the disaster in this case is the death from pollution of the Mediterranean Sea (the Mare Nostrum of the title). Invited to prepare the script for a "big spectacle" by the Ministry of Culture and a director in Toulouse, Manet began work early in 1993 on a text that would allow him "the pleasure of using French, Arabic, Spanish, and maybe Italian and Portuguese as well, that to be decided along the way" (letter, 22 April 1993). The idea was to create a brash comedy that could be performed under a circus tent before audiences in France, Spain, Morocco and Tunisia (letter, 30 May 1994). The finished manuscript, although incorporating Manet's typical multilingual games, is primarily in French, focuses only on France and North Africa, and contains no Arabic. Its style, somewhat reminiscent of *Histoire de Maheu le boucher*, is in the cartoon mode. Not yet staged, it was aired on France-Culture on 23 March 1996.

A Master of Ceremonies, whose costume is a cross between thirteenth-century samurai and Mad Max, manipulates a triangle of monarchs through their respective advisers. The Master of Ceremonies is a magician who can change his voice and his appearance; his voices as royal advisers are

---

2. La Proprio (short for "Proprietor") recalls other forceful women characters in Manet's work. Like the gun-toting Lady Strass, she turns the tables on the would-be invaders of her property; she controls the land and her workers, like Asunción in *Mendoza, en Argentine* . . .

recorded on a sound track. The separate realms are represented by well-defined areas of the playing area, set at different levels. The stage directions do not so specify, but perhaps we should think of them as the constituent parts of a three-ring circus.

Farius IV, queen of what used to be the Mediterranean, is advised by her fantastical bird, Hyspride. Beltrane, queen of what once was France, listens to a talking orchid. Amar, king of the realm of North Africa, is guided by Cormoran, the only adviser role played by an actor. Cormoran is a kind of idiot savant who tinkers with the technological gadgets left from a forgotten age. In the end, thanks to his electronic skills, he appears to triumph over the Master of Ceremonies, whose place he will assume as grand manipulator.

Mare Nostrum incorporates many of Manet's favorite tricks, including linguistic games, filmic images and references, and multicultural intertexts. Expressions from various languages are used for comic effect. Beltrane's French is corrupted by dreadful English obscenities. Farius repeatedly invents new words, or mispronounces old ones. The stage directions call for the projection of old maps and comic drawings. Amar appears dressed like Rudolph Valentino and begins to dance the tango. A recording of Frank Sinatra's "My Way" is followed by Amar's proof that the song is stolen from Claude François's "Comme d'habitude"; it is one of the strategies Amar uses in convincing Beltrane to fight colonization by American language and culture. Farius's incomprehensible prayer, handed down by oral tradition from generation to generation, is none other than Federico García Lorca's "Romance sonámbulo": "Verde que te quiero verde. / Verde viento. Verdes ramas . . ." (Green, I love you green. / Green wind. Green branches . . . ; 25).

Repeating the love triangle of *Les Chiennes*, Amar eventually becomes the husband of both queens, as permitted by his religion. Along the way to that resolution, there is the marriage of Amar and Beltrane, Farius's efforts to break them up by seducing first one and then the other, and lots of playfully ribald humor.

A Portuguese Love Letter

Manet originally wrote *Monsieur Lovestar et son voisin de palier* with Jean-Claude Fernandez, a French actor of Spanish-Moroccan origin, in mind for the role of the Portuguese neighbor. Fernandez had recently performed as Jehan in *Histoire de Maheu le boucher* and has since appeared in a half dozen Manet texts. *Monsieur Lovestar*, however, was set aside for several years before its initial staging. Part of the script was presented in a staged reading, arranged by Micheline and Lucien Attoun of Théâtre Ouvert, at the Centre Georges Pompidou in Paris in December 1993. The play premiered in March 1995 at the Centre Culturel du Languedoc-Théâtre Lakanal in Montpellier at the initiative of Fernandez and fellow actor Alain Trétout, under the direction of Patrick Haggiag. In March 1996 it received its first production abroad when the original cast was invited to perform the play at the Comédie de Genève in Geneva, Switzerland. The text has already been translated into English and German.

Monsieur Lovestar, a famous literary translator, receives an unexpected evening visit from his unknown neighbor, a Portuguese laborer. Still deeply in love with the wife who has left him, Ramon Salcedo has written a fifty-two-page love letter that he wants Lovestar to translate. He is ready to pay a small fortune to ensure a poetic French version. Lovestar's initial refusal, laden with intellectual snobbery as well as latent classism and racism, leads to a verbal sparring match, a threat of violence,

Fig. 14. Eduardo Manet with Jean-Claude Fernandez and Alain Trétout, actors from original cast of *Mr. Lovestar et son voisin de palier*. Paris, 1996 (photo by P. Zatlin).

and the consumption of a considerable quantity of good wine. By evening's end, the men have found a basis for friendly collaboration, and the translation work begins.

Although Manet has created several small-cast plays, including the two-character *Eux ou La prise du pouvoir* and *Sur la piste*, the early works tend to be metatheatrical texts involving extensive role-playing within the role. *Monsieur Lovestar et son voisin de palier*, with its intense and realistic confrontation between two characters, is an exception in his oeuvre. It belongs to a familiar current on the contemporary stage in France and elsewhere. A play with two actors and one set obviously costs less than a big-cast production and travels with relative ease; if the actors are popular and the text interesting, it can stay on the road for years. If only for economic reasons, two-actor plays, like monodramas and other one-person performances, are now pervasive in many countries.

There are a number of possible variations on the two-actor play. The list includes texts in which two actors double in multiple roles or act out a series of skits, metaplays that present a series of situations and performances within the text in episodic fashion, absurdist/Artaudian tours de force of role-playing within the role, more realistic cat-and-mouse games or other power struggles (between strangers or casual acquaintances), a television-inspired "intimate theater" (between close family members or friends),[3] far more static—and poetic—duets, and quasi-documentary interviews. *Eux ou La prise du pouvoir* belongs to the category of absurdist role-playing within the role; action dominates over dialogue or character development. *Monsieur Lovestar et son voisin de palier* falls into my "cat and mouse" grouping but, because of the consciousness-raising it evokes, edges close to intimate theater; there is a concentration on dialogue and character revelation over action. Spanish author Jaime Salom has an explanation for the audience appeal of "intimate" plays, akin to that of soap operas: at their best, they provide the illusion of eavesdropping on an intense, personal conversation. Two-actor plays may be chosen for production because they are relatively inexpensive to stage, but

---

3. I attribute the label "intimate theater" to Spanish playwright Jaime Salom (personal interview 1990). Salom's own entry in the field, *Una hora sin televisión* (An hour without television, 1987) toured in Spain for four years with the original cast. Intimate theater presents realistically a moment of crisis or consciousness-raising in the lives of two people who have been very close: mother and daughter, sisters, husband and wife, best friends. Typically the pair has become estranged, and there is a past or projected separation that provokes reminiscences, confessions, and perhaps recriminations.

they fill theaters because spectators enjoy their glimpse of the human drama of everyday life.

In interviews that appeared in the playbill accompanying the Geneva production, actors Fernandez and Trétout highlight the richness of the drama that unfolds between the two characters. Fernandez points out that the dialogue of an intellectual with a laborer is quite uncommon in the theater; the emphasis here, however, is not on social or political aspects but on daily life and the emotional depth of the two men. Trétout similarly notes that Monsieur Lovestar and the Portuguese on the surface have nothing in common, socially or culturally, that they do not even see each other despite living side by side. But that, according to Trétout, is part of a message that resists the destructive isolation of contemporary society. The laborer's deep feelings break down the intellectual's prejudice and disdain, leading him to reveal his inner suffering.

As *Monsieur Lovestar et son voisin de palier* begins, the distinguished translator is dining in his book-lined study while listening to a tape of his own public lecture about T. S. Eliot. To his satisfaction, the speech is punctuated by laughter and applause. The strategy quickly establishes the character's scholarly importance, intellectual pretensions, and egotistical self-involvement. To the audience in the background of this tape, he makes fun of the ignorance of a previous audience; the current listeners chuckle appreciatively but are themselves the target of Lovestar's patronizing tone. In emphasizing the difficulty of translation, he quotes the same Italian expression, *traduttore, traditore*, that Manet introduced in *L'Autre Don Juan*. Reminiscent of a scene of interpolated English poetry in *Lady Strass*, Lovestar recites one of Eliot's poems: "Let us go then, you and I, / When the evening is spread out against the sky" (*Lovestar* 9).

Engrossed in his food and his own voice, Lovestar is oblivious to the entrance of Salcedo through the open apartment door. Only when the tape stops does the visitor cough to announce his presence; in the interlude, there is increasing audience expectation of the inevitable encounter between the two. The physical contrast between the men is marked. A trim Salcedo is dressed in a warm-up suit and running shoes, with an athletic bag swung across his chest. Lovestar is a sedentary man who eats and drinks too well. Once the dialogue begins, differences in personality also are readily apparent. Salcedo can recall the exact date and time when he once spoke to his neighbor and can even describe in detail what both of them were wearing, but Lovestar, wrapped up in himself, says he's never seen the Portuguese before and claims not to know that anyone lived behind the closed door across the hall. When Lovestar finally invites Salcedo to sit down, their difference in status is visually signaled by the same props used in *Le Jour où Mary Shelley rencontra Charlotte Brontë*: Lovestar has a comfortable armchair while Salcedo sits at the edge of a straight chair.

Manet once again fully exploits multilingual/multicultural games. André Guillaume Lovestar, son of a French mother and British father, realistically code-switches between French and English. He is also a polyglot whose speech is sprinkled with expressions from several languages. Both he and Salcedo interject occasional words of Portuguese. The Spanish origins of their building super, Maria Pepa Pérez, justifies the use of some Spanish. *Monsieur Lovestar et son voisin de palier* is the point of departure for *Les Poupées en noir* thematically with respect to the relationship between two men who are neighbors; in the later play, Manet will emphasize even more the image of a city apartment building as melting pot. The physical closeness of neighbors is emphasized throughout *Monsieur Lovestar* by the sound of piano music from next door: music of Chopin and Schumann chosen, of course, to underscore the subjects of conversation.

The verbal duel begins with the deliberate, and increasingly comic, mispronunciation of each others' names. Lovestar, who knows Portuguese well, arrogantly changes Salcedo's name to make it sound French. Salcedo, who eventually proves that he can pronounce "Lovestar" correctly when he wants to, retaliates with variable manglings of the translator's name, the most outrageous of which is "Lobster." The battle of the names runs in counterpoint to Lovestar's disparaging comments on Salcedo's precious letter and Salcedo's declaration that he has bought all of Lovestar's works and has read the introductions with care. Salcedo offers Lovestar his text, for him to publish in his own name; he quotes a Harvard professor who says that Lovestar is a magician "who can change a minor work into a masterpiece" (25). Lovestar recommends that Salcedo tear up his own writing and instead plagiarize a real work of literature, *Les Lettres d'une religieuse portugaise* (Letters from a Portuguese nun). Salcedo puts a wad of money on the table, to show his willingness to pay; Lovestar is unimpressed by the money and indifferent to Salcedo's love letter and feelings. The duel reaches its climax when Salcedo pulls out a gun, shoots a glass statuette—"in cold blood," according to a horrified Lovestar (27)—and then holds the gun up to Lovestar's head. The threat of violence and the gunshot will doubtless have the same comic shock effect as similar moments in *Lady Strass*.

Lovestar, the gourmet/gourmand, declares a truce and brings out food and more wine. Salcedo, who initially refused alcohol but has been drinking all along, by now is somewhat intoxicated. While Lovestar is gone to the kitchen, he accuses the translator of living off borrowed texts and of taking refuge in absence. The later confidences of Lovestar, inspired by Salcedo's intimate confession of lost love and *saudade* (nostalgia), suggest that the Portuguese has hit the mark. Like Manet and the narrator of his fictionalized autobiography, a youthful Lovestar had published a small, private edition of poetry. At one time, before immersing himself in others' books, he was capable of feeling. Indirectly acknowledging his homosexuality and his cowardice, he talks of the slow death of his lover and of how he had stopped visiting the dying man. In his moving, poetic confession, Lovestar switches from "he" to "you" as his tone becomes more emotional. By reliving his own past happiness and pain, he begins to feel solidarity with Salcedo. His earlier disdain is replaced by envy. The privileged man is not the wealthy prodigy but the humble laborer who can live in the hope of regaining his lost love and can react to his sorrow by writing from the heart.

Remembering the Holocaust

In the final scene of the fictional autobiography *La Mauresque*, Manet's narrator discovers that his mother is neither Moorish nor Gypsy, as she has often claimed, but rather a Sephardic Jew. In the sequel novel, *L'Ile du lézard vert*, the adolescent narrator wrestles with a variety of identity crises, including the issue of his own Jewish heritage and that of several friends. In recent years, as Manet has become increasingly interested in his Spanish Sephardic roots, the Jewish theme also appears in his theater. It can serve as an element of farce: a stereotypical Jewish mother, whose speech is sprinkled with insults in Yiddish, is among the characters in *Histoire de Maheu le boucher*. As the author has also become increasingly concerned about anti-Semitism, he has approached the subject from a serious perspective. In this respect, the treatment of the Holocaust found in his *Les Poupées en noir* is a timely response to neo-Nazism. It continues in the vein of French movies, such as *Le Dernier métro* (1980, dir. François

Truffaut) and *Au revoir les enfants* (1987, dir. Louis Malle) that similarly draw attention to the atrocities of the past.

Les Poupées en noir was produced as a radio play by France-Culture on 10 November 1990, under the direction of Catherine Lemire and with an outstanding cast headed by the well-known actor Daniel Mesguich. Critical and audience reaction was extremely positive and Manet's drama immediately began to attract international attention. The rights were purchased for Germany, and discussion was initiated on a possible German-French film version. In response to more than a thousand letters from listeners, the play was rebroadcast on France-Culture the following spring. In 1991 *The Black Dolls* (translation by David Mairowitz) was aired on the BBC. By September 1992, the Israel Broadcasting Authority also had sought permission to produce the radio drama (letter, Kimkhi). Some of Manet's stage plays have been given initial radio readings, but *Les Poupées en noir* is undoubtedly the most successful of his works written expressly for broadcast.

The immediate proposal for a film version was inspired not only by the current, international wave of Holocaust movies—culminating perhaps in the 1991 German-Russian *Europa, Europa* and the 1994 American *Schindler's List*—but also specifically by Manet's script. The text incorporates narrative strategies that lend themselves well to cinema and reflect Manet's own extensive background in film. There is considerable spatial and temporal fluidity: the action shifts between the 1950s and 1960s in New York and the 1930s and 1940s in Berlin. The entire play is screened through the memory of a narrator; within his recounting is imbedded the story of Jacob Zacharias Steiger, narrated in turn with a series of interpolated flashbacks. Within each time and locale, there is movement from animated street scenes to interiors as well as movement and change within the interiors. The story centers on only two figures: Jacob and the narrator; but the cast includes nine other speaking roles, and both dialogue and sound track allude to many other characters. Thus Manet's script, as written, includes all of the elements necessary for opening the text up to cinematographic space, action, and characterization.

It should not be forgotten that Manet was also an avid radio fan as a child and therefore knows well how to evoke the listener's imagination. His script calls for extensive musical background and other use of sound track. He was fortunate in having the full cooperation of the French national radio in producing his text as he intended: not only was his play given the best director and lead actor available, but excellent technical support allowed for exterior recording of outside sequences. The result, when coupled with Manet's descriptive dialogue, is the creation of realistic characters and scenes that may have an indelible, visual impact on the audience.

The frame for Manet's play consists of the narrator's memories, from the vantage point of ten years later, of two hot summer months he spent in New York City in the early 1950s, when he was eighteen. A friend had lent him a two-room, seventh-floor, walk-up flat in Soho, which was then a rundown immigrant neighborhood. The unnamed narrator is only somewhat younger than Manet was in 1951 when he visited New York himself in late summer on his way to study in Paris. Some of the authenticity of setting and of the young intellectual's response to the city thus may draw upon the author's remembered experiences. (Manet's personal knowledge of the American city at the required time may also explain his character Jacob's decision after the war to go to his uncle in New York rather than to relatives in Argentina. With respect to this kind of personal identification between author and his fictional characters, it is worth noting that Jacob's birthday, 19 June, coincides with Manet's.)

Although Manet's script begins with a violin rendition of Ravel's "Mélodie hébraïque"—the leitmotif identified with Jacob Zacharias Steiger—and an immediate reference to this central figure, the introduction of Jacob and his story is deliberately delayed. The narrator first introduces the audience to the apartment building and the tenants on each floor: a reclusive madwoman, an Italian family, a cabinetmaker, an amorous middle-aged woman who attempts to pursue the young man, a couple who are Cuban political refugees. Some of these characters are strongly linked to Manet's other work: the madwoman, who recalls the title character of *Lady Strass*; the Italian husband and wife, whose shouted insults allow Manet his typical multilingual word games; the Cuban exiles, whose silent, fearful presence comments on political unrest in Batista's Cuba.

At the outset, the quarreling of the Italian couple and the teenager's haste when escaping from the amorous woman provide a somewhat comic note; later in the narrative, all of these secondary figures underscore the passage of time when the young man receives letters from Jacob recounting the changes in their lives. More important, the several anecdotes with their accompanying background noises allow for the creation of realistic space: the listener can envision the old apartment building as a whole while the narrator, in the sweltering August heat, laboriously climbs the stairs—picking up the pace only when entering the "danger zone" of the amorous lady. Thus the arrival at the partially burned-out top floor, shared by the unseen violinist in an apartment at the landing and by the narrator in the little flat along a back corridor, takes on vivid meaning.

The inevitable telling of Jacob's story is further delayed by the gradual development of the friendship between the curious narrator and the somber, violin-playing occupant of the other seventh-floor apartment. The two speak to each other only after the young man spots his neighbor in a used-book store. Jacob, who inherited the store from his uncle, has the appearance of a rabbi and looks far older than his actual years. The two men's love of books leads to shared meals and finally to Jacob's revelation, which shifts between a narrated past and the greater immediacy and pathos of dialogues presented as flashbacks.

Although Jacob's nightmare experiences are not repeated in other works by Manet, there are points in common with wealthy and cultured Jewish friends of the narrator in *L'Ile du lézard vert*. Like Hanna, he is a gifted musician. Like Lohengrin, as a child Jacob had a privileged life in Germany. Lohengrin's family in the novel escaped and took up residence in Cuba; Jacob's father elects not to flee. From the street, where a crowd gathers, the twelve-year-old witnessed his parents and grandmother being dragged from their affluent home. The boy is saved by his grandmother's friend Helga, who convinces her husband, a doll maker, to hide the boy in a basement storage area in spite of the great risk to themselves. Thus Jacob spent years, shut away with his books, his violin, and a collection of dolls that over time changed from regional folkloric figures to different regiments of Nazi soldiers and SS officers. The boy adjusts to his confinement with passive resignation until one violent moment, after Helga has died and Ludwig has disappeared, when he savagely assaults the black-clad dolls.

Manet develops interest in his melancholy and mysterious protagonist through a variety of means that go beyond the delay in satisfying the narrator's curiosity. Jacob, who is initially known to the narrator and audience only by the sound of his violin, is an accomplished musician. (Later we learn that his mother was a celebrated singer.) He is a bibliophile whose profound love of literature transcends any desire to make a profit from the books he sells. His indifference to money is coupled with generosity—traits introduced perhaps to subvert traditional anti-Semitic stereotypes. To his new friend he gives a priceless possession: a small calendar that his father had made for him to mark, day by day, the tragedies of the Jewish people over the centuries as well as their notable contributions to humanity. Jacob's ascetic life in the partially burned-out top floor mirrors his teenage years of enclosure. When the narrator finally makes his promised return trip to New York long after his correspondence with Jacob has ceased, he can find no trace of the prematurely aged and sensitive aesthete. The open ending to Jacob's story enhances the pathos surrounding a privileged and talented boy who had lost his family, his freedom, his youth, his happiness, and his dreams.

Given that his stage plays are characterized by a cinematic use of sound track, it is not surprising that Manet has made extensive use of auditory signs in the development of his radio narrative. As previously observed, different noises or music identify the inhabitants on each floor of the narrator's building and create the impression of realistic space. The same strategy is used for evoking other locales: for example, traffic sounds establish New York street scenes and remain in the background when the narrator visits Jacob's bookstore; the fall of Berlin at the end of the war is signaled through the sound of sirens, airplanes, and bombing. During Jacob's narration of his past, the grandmother is introduced solely through the sound of a voice praying in Yiddish; later the distant chant of Jewish prayers underscores Jacob's narration of the horrifying events. Ravel's haunting "Mélodies hébraïques," which serve initially as an index of Jacob and then of his mother, gradually assume a symbolic level.

The musical motifs are, in fact, the most significant aspect of the sound track. The description of Ludwig's folkloric dolls is accompanied by player piano; their replacement by Nazi soldiers is predictably marked by military marches. (In the radio performance, these are sprightly marches, sung by children as a referent to the Nazi youth movement.) Less predictably, the growing violence against the Jewish citizens of Berlin is underscored by an ironic use of carousel music. At first the light-hearted music connotes the child's happy visits to the park; then it goes off track, suggesting the tragedy to come. Played against the yelling crowd in the street, the carousel music becomes distorted as the sound track shifts from reality to nightmare and the music melds into a chilling scream. When the horrified Helga sees her friend's grandchild in the crowd and places her hand over his mouth, the musical background changes to an angry version of Ravel.

In *Les Poupées en noir*, Manet has brought the horror of the Holocaust down to an individual level, where the listener can fully comprehend the lasting suffering of the survivors. Fully utilizing the resources of dialogue, verbal narration, sound track, and audience imagination, Manet successfully creates the images of Jacob Zacharias Steiger's life experiences, thereby converting them into a poignant and powerful statement against anti-Semitism.

In France, *Les Poupées en noir* has had an unprecedented third airing on national radio; the play has yet to reach German airwaves. The project to broadcast it there fell through when Manet denied a request, apparently prompted by neo-Nazis, to reduce the references to Jacob's experiences in Berlin and accordingly shift most of the action to New York (letter, 30 May 1994).

It's All Done with Screens

Over the years, Manet's work has been characterized by constant experimentation. In the early 1990s he embarked on yet another new project: a play written expressly for "a very special Festival: apartment theater!" (letter, 30 December 1991). As part of the unusual festival, Manet's text, *Les Couples et les paravents*, would be given twenty performances in private homes before becoming available for regular theater stagings. The author was excited by the challenge of this extended "tryout" of a play that he considered different from anything he had previously written and an important, if modest, manifestation of a "modern theater" he was developing in response to theoretical discussions with actor-director Daniel Mesguich (letter, 17 January 1992). The play met with unexpected success; unfortunately the acting company, which included Manet's wife, Fatima, had other commitments that precluded their accepting the invitations they received "from everywhere" for additional stagings immediately following the festival (letter, 25 February 1992).

The concept of "apartment theater" may initially seem novel, but in some ways it is a continuation of an established tradition in France, Spain, and elsewhere of private theatrical readings and stagings. One recalls, for example, that Pablo Picasso's *Le Désire attrapé par la queue* in 1944 received its first public reading in a private home, under the direction of Albert Camus and with a celebrity cast including Simone de Beauvoir, Jean-Paul Sartre, and Raymond Queneau. In Manet's own *Lady Strass*, the action takes place in an old home that had been equipped with a stage for amateur theatrical performances. *Les Couples et les paravents* is notable, however, for its intentional adaptability to living-room stagings. The cast is logically small: two men and two women. Screens provide a portable set suitable for creating an acting area out of limited, nontraditional space. Given the particular requirements of apartment theater, the mode of representation is openly theatricalist: spectators must imagine that an aisle between their chairs is a street and that characters make entrances through an invisible door; the actors make noises to simulate knocking or ringing the doorbell; some costume changes take place in full audience view; actors mouth words and laughter soundlessly to allow another character's "thoughts" to be heard. At times one of the women characters becomes a narrator who addresses the audience directly to relate how she met her husband and how their relationship deteriorated.

Despite justification for the author's claim that *Les Couples et les paravents* represents a new phase in his theater, there is also much in the play that is typical of his work, dating back at least to *Eux ou La prise du pouvoir*. *Les Couples et les paravents* is lighter in tone, more erotic in its humor, and freer of political interpretations than that 1971 metaplay, but in some ways it is a doubling of the earlier pas de deux: two couples, rather than one, play out their interpersonal conflicts, recall their pasts, engage in dancing and ritualistic celebrations.

The recent play, like much of Manet's oeuvre, is permeated with filmic conventions, including the previously mentioned "voice-overs" to convey characters' thoughts. The music for the several dance scenes functions like a sound track to set shifting moods. The narrator figure, who establishes that some scenes are flashbacks, declares that she has just seen her life go by like a film in slow motion (19). Stage directions call for action that imitates camera/editing effects, from fast forward to freeze-frames. "Stop motion" is typically used to separate levels of reality; "slow motion," which occurs frequently in dance sequences, may signal a filmic dissolve from one scene to the next. There is even a "split screen" function to represent simultaneous action of the two couples in their respective homes; one character watching another watching him might also be considered equivalent to a shot/reverse-shot strategy. Also in cinematographic fashion, the text is divided, not into acts and scenes, but into twenty-one sequences.

Facilitated by the appropriate placement of the screens, the acting area represents two apartments with facing windows. When the amorous Couple B (Bettina and Benito) move in across the street from by now bored Couple A (Anioushka and Adrien), they are dismayed to find that their neighbor is spying on them through his binoculars. After Bettina takes the initiative of meeting the nosy neighbors, the two couples swap partners. A final sequence, in which the characters revert to their original costumes, suggests that they may also return to their original mates. Rapid farcical action highlights the changing patterns in the young couple's relationships, and the role reversals themselves are stock comic techniques.

Given Manet's propensity for metatheatrical games and farce, the play is characterized throughout by role-playing within the roles and by lively, colloquial dialogue, including frequent use of foreign expressions—another classic comic device. Code switching in several languages serves not only for humorous effect but also to emphasize the growing presence in France of diverse ethnic groups. As Benito points out, only Adrien is "100 percent French" (38), and even he uses some Spanish. Anioushka is half Russian and half French. Bettina, rejecting her mother's Cuban heritage, identifies only with her Italian half. Benito, however, frequently lapses into his native Spanish while singing, expressing terms of endearment—or swearing. Bettina labels him "the neighborhood Berlitz of obscenity" (17).

Beyond their multilingualism and multiculturalism, the characters tend to hybrid identities. In the first sequence, Couple A enter dressed as young professionals but quickly switch costumes to transform themselves into hippies: their escapist Friday night entertainment consists of dancing to the music of the 1970s. Both men have avocations with which they are obsessed: Adrien works furiously at developing a miracle beauty cream, and Benito spends hours training as a bicyclist.[4] Anioushka meanwhile takes refuge in her personal diary and account books; through the latter she uncovers the evidence of Adrien's role-playing within the role: an affair that he has carried out behind his wife's back.

While metatheater has the subversive potential of mirroring the games that people in the audience may also be playing, the predominant effect of *Les Couples et les paravents* is more comic than serious. Spectators might be able to relate to the communication problems of Anioushka and Adrien, who no longer listen to each other, or Bettina's annoyance at Benito's constant cycling, but they are more likely to laugh at the antics and derive pleasure from the dance sequences and theatricalist use of

---

4. In *Mare Nostrum*, Amar is forced to ride an exercise bike as a form of torture. In both plays, the references to the bike are comic.

filmic strategies. For the acting company, the play—typical of Manet's theater—offers a rich vehicle for showcasing a full range of their performance talents.

A Never-Ending Love Story

Continuing in the light, nonideological vein of *Les Couples et les paravents*, *Deux siècles d'amour* is written in a spirit of fun that provides ample opportunity for the three on-stage actors to display their talents in ever changing roles. In his enthusiastic review of the Paris première, André Camp described the play as a "delirious sequence of adventures in which poetry and humor join hands" and labeled the production, "two hours of happiness." That happiness is doubtless enhanced by multiple costume changes, a rich musical background, and frequent dance sequences. Although in some ways the text is unique in the trajectory of Manet's theater, it bears certain reminiscences of other plays of various tendencies, most notably *Scherzo*, *Lady Strass*, and *Un Balcon sur les Andes*.

Deux siècles d'amour was performed in December 1992–January 1993 at the Roseau Theater in Paris by Petit Bouffon, under the direction of Didier Vieville. The troupe, which was formed a decade earlier, specializes in new works by contemporary authors. The company had commissioned the play, which Manet obligingly wrote "as a 'wink' at Marivaux and Musset."

Like *Un Balcon sur les Andes*, the action of *Deux siècles d'amour* begins in the mid-nineteenth century and, without regard to normal longevity, continues on and on with the same, seemingly ageless characters. The first act takes place in 1850, the second in 1927–29, and the third in 1995. An epilogue, identified as New Year's Eve, 1999, closes the century but provides an open ending to the play itself.

To achieve his desired farcical tone, Manet borrows from classical comedy the use of identical twins. Laurent and Sébastien are both hopelessly in love with their childhood friend, the capricious Camille. Recalling a similar rivalry in the equally fanciful and stylized *Scherzo*, the two men, like knights of old, seek to prove their relative merit so that their lady may choose between them. The fact that the brothers are as alike as "two drops of water" makes Camille's task difficult, but so does her yearning for an "absolute, mad, wild love that defies . . . Death!"

The stage is set for a series of comic reversals as the twins return over time, transformed into such divergent figures as a stockbroker—immensely rich in 1927 and suddenly impoverished in 1929—or a seductive Rudolph Valentino–style gigolo who later becomes a Buddhist monk, dedicated solely to the search for spiritual values. The juxtaposed images of the twins will provoke laughter both when they are presented as so identical that Camille cannot tell them apart and when they are presented in comic contrast. Camille, too, is subject to radical change. In act 2, recently returned from Latin America, she downs glass after glass of tequila; by act 3, she has become health conscious and switches to carrot juice.

As the characters undergo transformations, each new entrance delights the audience with visual surprises, but their seesawing attitudes will also have a comic effect. Camille prefers first one, then the other of the twins. In the final act, when the brothers seem far removed from each other in lifestyle and appearance, Laurent incongruously expounds the theory that they, like all identical twins, are, in fact, just one person. His pseudoscientific explanation is built on "zygotes," a correct but low-frequency biological term that not only sounds funny to the layperson but is deliberately repeated three times for a predictably humorous effect: "Il s'agit de gênes, d'ovules, de spermatozoïdes, de zygotes . . . de facteurs d'hérédité . . . selon que nous soyons jumeaux monozygotes ou dizygotes." (It's a question of genes, of ova, of spermatozoids, of zygotes . . . of hereditary factors . . . depending upon whether as twins we're monozygotes or dizygotes.)

Word play in general and multilingual games in particular are favorite strategies throughout Manet's theater. In the third act, Laurent is the source not only of continuing gobbledygook about monozygotes but also of an incredible catalog of adjectives, defining his virtues, which he incongruously recites while Sébastien and Camille carry on their own conversation, ignoring him. He begins predictably ("gentil, fidèle, charmant" [nice, loyal, charming]) but as he runs out of appropriate descriptors, he resorts to Italian musical terms ("moderato-cantabile," "allegro," "ma non troppo"), Spanish ("Chihuahua-chihuahua-chihua-ha . . . ayayayayayaya"), and finally, in desperation, calls on the Virgin Mary ("madonne-pitié . . . pour-les-pleurs-de-la-Vierge-pitié" [Holy Mary, have mercy. By the tears of the Virgin, have mercy]).

In the 1920s act, Camille throws in some newly learned English, but Spanish language and culture emerge at various points throughout the play. The romantic love that Camille seeks is inspired by the story of a man who killed himself for love of her grandmother. Both the grandmother's long name and that of her would-be lover would doubtless strike French spectators as funny: María Eugenia Montalvo Carrillo de la Parca, Don Francisco Rosales Quintana de las Armerías. Here, as in *L'Autre Don Juan*, there is a parody of *espagnolade* (the French stereotyping of Spanish traits). Camille describes Don Francisco as "Violent. Ardent. Jealous. Passionate. In a word, magnificent!" Alas, María Eugenia preferred a bullfighter.

Grandmother's thronelike chair and mantilla are key props for the play's most elaborate role-playing within the role scenes. Camille uses them as she becomes the judge for entertainment that the twins improvise to cure her of her "spleen." As in *The Gong Show*, she can cut the performers off whenever she is dissatisfied, but her signal is a more discreet black handkerchief. She rapidly rejects the "fictional" scenes they act out but approves and even enters into the reenactment of her own life. The strategy recalls the "autobiographical" plays-within-the-play of *Madras, la nuit où* . . . and *Lady Strass* but, lighter in tone, features the added comic device of having the adult actors re-create their voices as children.

Role-playing and role reversals are typical of Manet's metatheatrical farces, but in *Deux siècles d'amour* he introduces a level of fantasy not found in his previous work. Borrowing a concept from animated cartoons, he gives life to Camille's favorite objects: a mirror, a music box, and a clock.[5] Offstage voices and sound effects provide the desired animation for these unusual characters, whose dialogue frames the action of the first and second acts. Initially their rivalry for Camille's attention leads to scenes rich in comic name-calling; later their humor becomes more ribald as they spy on and describe amorous activities out of the audience's sight. In the third act, a fourth offstage voice joins the cast to portray a "speakerine": a kind of robot who gives quasi radio newscasts of what is happening in a fanciful, futuristic world in which the names of familiar places around Paris have been changed to honor the cultural icons of our own time. Manet elaborates on this satire by having the music box switch from a Weber waltz to a Madonna song and by having a white glove, à la Michael Jackson, emerge from the mirror.

From the beginning, these whimsical objects, with their intertextual references to Disney cartoons, set a parodic tone for the farce. Even more

---

5. The device here is related to the talking bird and orchid in *Mare Nostrum*.

so than *Le Jour où Mary Shelley rencontra Charlotte Brontë*, the first act of *Deux siècles d'amour* is a playful pastiche of nineteenth-century literary conventions and the Hollywood films they have inspired. Camille attributes her peevishness to "spleen," and the name Camille itself evokes the famous romantic heroine created by Dumas *fils* and immortalized by Greta Garbo. Laurent, in the midst of game-playing, recites a poem by Musset, and the brothers start a scene from *Lorenzaccio*. The sound of the opening dialogue of the human characters might be taken for nineteenth-century verse drama, except that the potential poetic effect is deliberately subverted by having the twins constantly finish each other's sentences.

In the second act, the Roaring Twenties are evoked through filmic images and music, with emphasis always on comic effect. Even the stock market crash is treated humorously as Laurent is transformed from his dapper image of success (white pants and shoes, sailor hat, and blazer—"like Bing Crosby in *Road to Morocco*") to a down-and-out carrying a cardboard suitcase. Laurent's clean-cut Bing Crosby image is contrasted with Sébastien's wicked Rudolph Valentino mold. The straitlaced Bing Crosby figure has not yet learned to do the Charleston; recalling a dance sequence in *Lady Strass*, Camille teaches him. She also teaches him to mix his own margaritas; in a snowball effect, the pace of fixing drinks becomes faster and faster as the characters become drunker and drunker. The sexy Valentino twin, on the other hand, displays proficiency at doing the tango and drinking, without any lessons from Camille.

The brothers' rivalry reaches its climax in act 3; in the closing scene, there is a stylized fight in which we might presume that they kill one another. For Camp, this was the logical point to end the play, with the reciprocal and simultaneous death of Sébastien and Laurent: "Pour des jumeaux naître et mourir les mêmes jours c'est plus qu'un comble, c'est un summum!" (To have twins be born on the same day and die on the same day is not just a high point but the absolute highest.) Manet's brief epilogue first shows us a lonely, aged Camille—no longer preserved by love—and then allows a return to her youth when the twins magically reappear, looking just as they did at the beginning. Camille's initial image here is that of *Whistler's Mother*; with the twins' help, and out of open view of the audience, she removes the bonnet and long robe to emerge as the young woman. Announcing that they have experienced two centuries of a love that overcomes death, the trio dances once again to the music from the play's opening scene. The twins' double death might have made a more dramatic, closed ending, but the play's circular structure no doubt leaves the audience happier. The magical, playful tone of *Deux siècles d'amour* remains intact along with the characters' youth and love.

Conclusion

The present study is only an introduction to the multifaceted work of Eduardo Manet. That is true not only because this is the first book to examine Manet's novels and plays, but also because he is a dynamic author and man of the theater who continues his creative activity at an intense pace. Even as I write these lines, he is completing a new novel of Cuban theme, titled *D'Amour et d'exil* (Of love and exile), that will be published before this book is in print. Some of the texts I have identified here as unstaged will have reached audiences by then, and new projects, not even mentioned, will have emerged.

In the late 1940s, while still a university student in Havana, Eduardo Manet rose to a position of prominence in the cultural community of his native country. These poetic, yet irreverent, and ironic plays form part of Cuban theater history; they are remembered by Cuban playwrights and critics of Manet's generation and the one that followed as prompting a renaissance of the Cuban stage and are so cited in studies of the period. By the 1950s, the volume of his published plays, in Spanish, was already being used as a text in graduate programs in Latin American literature at Yale University and elsewhere.

Manet's decade of study and performance in France and Italy—a period of voluntary exile during the Batista years—did not erase his memory in Cuba; he was invited home when Castro took power. In the early years of the Cuban Revolution, Manet once again rose to a prominent position in the cultural life of Havana. His work in the 1960s as theater and film director was instrumental in bringing Cuba into contact with European artists and theorists.

During his second exile, beginning in 1968, Manet has achieved fame in France as both playwright and novelist—writing in French.

Osvaldo Obregón has characterized Manet's integration into the French theater world as virtually unique for an author of Latin American origins. His novels, particularly the series dealing with the Cuban experience (*La Mauresque, L'Ile du lézard vert, La Habanera, Rhapsodie cubaine*) have been released by the most prestigious publishing companies in France, have been nominated for the Prix Goncourt, have won other important prizes, and have been translated into several European languages. Two of them have become best-sellers.

Manet's political stance on Cuba resists stereotypical definition. He is anti-Castro but takes a liberal, indeed leftist, stance in his criticism of political and economic injustice. Much to the dismay of some of his fellow exiles, he favors lifting the U.S. embargo of Cuba. Similarly, his writings are so varied that it is difficult to pinpoint their appeal. He habitually explores different genres and subgenres.

As I review Manet's work to date, I find great diversity and yet a certain cohesiveness. Underpinning both novel and theater, structurally and intertextually, is his lifelong love of cinema. The persistent metatheatricalism of the plays has a certain parallel in the narrative works; characters within the novels also become involved in role-playing of one sort or another, along with an associated quest for self-identity. And certainly both genres over the years have reflected his own bilingual-bicultural background as a Cuban-French writer as well as his depth and breadth of interest in other languages and cultures. His love of Italy and of British literature and his knowledge of Afro-Caribbean rituals surface frequently; increasingly he has also been inspired by the Jewish heritage on his mother's side.

Although Manet writes in French, most, if not all, of his novels and at least some of his plays reflect his experience as an exile and his love-hate relationship with Cuba. The autobiographical novels evoke his childhood and youth directly; if at times romanticized and nostalgic, they simultaneously provide a critical view of modern Cuban history. Some of the plays also allude directly to Latin American political reality, but even when the references are not overt, plays of entrapment and enclosure (*Les Nonnes, Le Borgne, Madras, la nuit où* . . . , *Lady Strass*) may be read as clear examples of the Latin American theater of crisis.

Some of the novels, particularly the fictionalized autobiographies, are marked by their humor, as are many of Manet's plays. He has written a number of farces and grotesque tragicomedies that in performance require training in commedia dell'arte or a high level of gymnastics or other physical skills; they call attention to the author's background in mime and his career teaching body movement to acting students. In the rapid pace of his farces, characters, like those of *Les Gozzi*, may function as clowns. At times the comic aspects are enhanced by kaleidoscopic role-playing within the role, sometimes complicated by cross-gender acting: for example, *L'Autre Don Juan*.

Manet is an actors' author: among his most frequently staged plays, starting with *Eux ou La prise du pouvoir*, are several that serve as true showcases for each individual performer's range of abilities. In this respect, his plays, especially those with small casts, are often written for ensemble acting: their several roles are of equal importance. *Lady Strass* is specifically structured on a series of pas de deux, thus spotlighting Manet's interest in dance. Cast members in this and other plays have ample opportunity to tango and Charleston.

Manet's best-known plays tend toward the comic or the tragicomic, but he has also written more serious, even tragic works, such as his Haitian modernization of Medea. I have emphasized original stage plays that have already been produced or published. In order to reveal the broad scope of his theater, I included the acclaimed radio play *Les Poupées en noir* and the as yet unperformed *Pour l'amour de Verdi*. These two scripts not only help to uncover Manet's more serious side but also provide further evidence of his multicultural focus and his love of music.

Unlike his novels, Manet's theater is far removed from conventional realism. He is the author of whimsical farces and madcap satires. In his dramatic world, it is natural for men to be nuns (*Les Nonnes*), for fictional characters to assault their authors (*Le Jour où Mary Shelley rencontra Charlotte Brontë*), for the passage of time to have no effect on the aging process (*Un Balcon sur les Andes, Deux siècles d'amour*), or for amputations to heal immediately (*Histoire de Maheu le boucher*). Nevertheless, as *Monsieur Lovestar et son voisin de palier* abundantly demonstrates, Manet is capable of developing realistic theatrical dialogue and interaction between characters.

In her groundbreaking study on *Holocaustum ou le Borgne*, Judith Suther astutely observed that the underlying subject of Manet's absurdist farce is not so much the human condition in an existentialist sense as the ambiguities of human nature. Critics, particularly those approaching his theater from a French perspective, have found several of Manet's plays to be anti-Catholic and anti-Christian. Suther looks beyond such questions. In my own reading and rereading of Manet's novels and plays,

I find little emphasis on doctrine per se or, except for the description of Afro-Caribbean rituals, on religious beliefs. Manet's characters are faced with monumental problems, whether of a farcical or serious nature, but these dilemmas have little to do with the existence or non-existence of God, the divinity of Christ, or with being and nothingness. There is a touch of existential anguish in the youthful *Diálogos* and in the adolescent protagonist of the autobiographical novels. The theme resurfaces in *Le Jour où Mary Shelley rencontra Charlotte Brontë*, where it might be taken seriously, but Sartrean anguish is in fact parodied in *Histoire de Maheu le boucher*. Far more frequent in Manet's works, as Suther suggests, are the conflicts and pitfalls caused in large part by the eternal human failings: greed, gluttony, lust, jealousy, hypocrisy, the desire for power. And individual flaws in turn inform the political turmoil that further entraps the characters in situations from which there is no obvious escape. Nuns and priests are exploitative not so much because of their church affiliation as because of their own human weaknesses. It is the virtue of Manet's theater that he unmasks nuns, one-eyed men, and Latin American generals so that we may discover their frailties and thereby perhaps discover our own shortcomings that help to perpetuate the status quo.

Selected Bibliography

Works by Eduardo Manet

Original Stage Plays
(In order of performance. Editions of plays in Spanish, French, or both are listed chronologically following data on stage première. For unpublished plays, I have indicated those for which a typescript is available in the author's files.)

Scherzo. Havana, 1948.
La Infanta que no quiso tener ojos verdes. Havana, 1950.
Presagio. Havana, 1950.
Scherzo, Presagio, La Infanta que no quiso tener ojos verdes, Diálogos. Havana: Ediciones Prometeo, 1949.
La santa. Paris, 1951; Musical version, Havana, 1964. Unpublished.
Helen viendra nous voir de Hollywood et nous lui ferons la plus belle des parties. Montreal, 1968. Unpublished.
Les Nonnes. Paris, 1969. In *L'Avant-Scène Théâtre* 431 (15 August 1969): 8–22, 27; Paris: Gallimard, Collection Le Manteau d'Arlequin, 1969. *Las monjas*. In *Teatro: 5 autores cubanos*. Selection, prologue, and edited by Rine Leal. Jackson Heights, N.Y.: OLLANTAY Press, 1995. 61–107.
Eux ou La prise du pouvoir. Paris, 1972. Paris: Gallimard, Collection Le Manteau d'Arlequin, 1971.
Sur la piste. Paris, 1972. Unpublished.
Holocaustum ou le Borgne. Brussels, 1972. Paris: Gallimard, Collection Le Manteau d'Arlequin, 1972.
L'Autre Don Juan. Montreal, 1974. Paris: Gallimard, Collection Le Manteau d'Arlequin, 1973.
Madras, la nuit où . . . Avignon, 1974. Paris: Gallimard, Collection Le Manteau d'Arlequin, 1975.
Les Ménines de la mer Morte. Geneva, 1977. Unpublished.
Lady Strass. Paris, 1977. In *L'Avant-Scène Théâtre* 613 (1 July 1977): 5–31.

Le Jour où Mary Shelley rencontra Charlotte Brontë. Paris, 1979. In *L'Avant-Scène Théâtre* 654 (15 July 1979): 3–19; Lézignan-Corbières: Théâtre Avant-Quart, 1993.
Un Balcon sur les Andes. Nice, 1979. Paris: Recherche-Action Théâtre Ouvert, Tapuscrit 4, 1978; Paris: Stock, 1979; with *Mendoza, en Argentine . . . , Ma'Déa*, Paris: Gallimard, 1985.
Les Gozzi. Nice, 1981. Unpublished typescript.
Sacrilèges. Paris, 1981. Unpublished typescript.
Mendoza, en Argentine . . . Champagne, 1984. Paris: Recherche-Action Théâtre Ouvert, Tapuscrit 33, 1983; with *Un Balcon sur les Andes, Ma'Déa*. Paris: Gallimard, 1985.
Ma'Déa. Paris, 1986. With *Un Balcon sur les Andes, Mendoza, en Argentine . . .* Paris: Gallimard, 1985.
Histoire de Maheu le boucher. Avignon, 1986. Paris: Gallimard, Collection Papiers, 1986.
Les Chiennes. Festival International de Théâtre, Parma, Italy, 1985. Paris: Recherche-Action Théâtre Ouvert, Tapuscrit 47, 1987.
Le Primerissimo. Malaucène, 1988. Unpublished typescript.
Les Couples et les paravents. Melun-Sénart, 1992. Unpublished typescript.
Deux siècles d'amour. Paris, 1992. Unpublished typescript.
With Gilles Herzog. *Poupée Fidel, Papa Marx, Buffalo Bill et la femme à barbe.* In *La Règle du Jeu* 4, no. 10 (May 1993): 97–135. Spanish version (by Manet): *Papa Fidel, Papa Marx, Buffalo Bill y Taïna, la mujer barbuda.* Staged reading, Madrid, 1992. Unpublished typescript.
Monsieur Lovestar et son voisin de palier. Montpellier, 1995. Paris: Actes Sud-Papiers, 1995.
L'Ame artiste. In *Brèves d'ailleurs (théâtre).* Paris: Actes Sud-Papiers, 1997. 95–104.

Published English Translations of Stage Plays

The Nuns, trans. Robert Baldick. Playscript 43. London: Calder and Boyars, 1970.
Lady Strass, trans. Phyllis Zatlin. In *Modern International Drama* 28, no. 1 (1992): 5–35. Revised version in *Playwrights of Exile: An International Anthology.* New York: Ubu Repertory Theater Publications, 1997. 1–80.

Novels

Spirale. Paris: René Julliard, 1956?
Les Etrangers dan la ville. Paris: René Julliard, 1960.
Un Cri sur le rivage. Paris: René Julliard, 1963.
La Mauresque. Paris: Gallimard, 1982.
Zone interdite. Paris: Gallimard, 1984.
L'Ile du lézard vert. Paris: Flammarion, 1992; Paris: France Loisirs, 1993; Paris: Flammarion, Collection Points, 1994.
Habanera. Paris: Flammarion, 1994; Versailles: Editions Feryane, 1995.
Rhapsodie cubaine. Paris: Grasset, 1996; [Paris: Grasset, Le Livre de Poche, 1996] Paris: Grand Livre du Mois, 1997; Paris: Corps 16, 1997.
D'Amour et d'exil. Paris: Grasset, 1999.

English Translation of Novel

Green Lizard Island (excerpt), trans. Laura Golden Mansfield. *Sites: The Journal of 20th-century/contemporary French Studies* (Storrs, Conn.) 2.2 (1998): 273–77.

Essays and Miscellaneous Creative Works Cited in Text

"La clase." *Carteles*, 20 November 1946, 6.
Pequeños poemas y nocturnos. Havana: Valcayo, 1947.
"Pequeños poemas." Individual poems in *Pueblo*, 14 and 22 August, 13 and 19 September 1947. Found in Manet's files.
Review of *Medea* by Euripides. Dir. Antonio Vázquez Gallo. Teatro Universitario, Havana. *Pueblo*, 8 November 1948, n.p.
"Portocarrero." *Cine Cubano* 4, no. 17 (1963?): 5–11.
"Où en est le théâtre cubain?" *Les Lettres Nouvelles* (December 1967–January 1968): 286–91.
Mirage dans un miroir sans reflets. Unpublished typescript. 12 March 1974. France-Culture. R-20914.
Cahiers intimes. Unpublished typescript. 1980.
"Commedia dell'arte et arts martiaux." Comments reported by G. C. *Arts Magazine* (Paris), 30 April 1981, 12.
Pierre, Esmeralda et Quasimodo. Unpublished typescript. 1986.
Juan y Teresa en busca de Dios. Unpublished typescript. 1987.
Les Anges deçus. Unpublished typescript. 1989.
Les Poupées en noir. Unpublished typescript. 4 September 1990. France-Culture. R-27263. Tape recording of broadcast. 10 November 1990.
Projet pour une demande de Bourse à la Fondation Beaumarchais. *Viva Verdi!* (Théâtre) (Grant application). Paris, 1991.
Pour l'amour de Verdi. Paris, 1991–92.
Mare Nostrum, 1994.
Series of personal letters. 3 November 1987–1 November 1998.
Viva Verdi suivi de *Mare Nostrum*. Paris: Actes Sud-Papiers, 1998.

Interviews Cited in Text

(In chronological order. Interviews available in press-clipping books at the Bibliothèque de l'Arsénal in Paris are indicated by the notation BA. Other interviews without page numbers or exact dates were located in Eduardo Manet's personal files. Interviews cited in the text only by date were personal interviews with the present author.)

With Omar Vázquez. "Eduardo Manet habla de una nueva película: Alicia." *Granma* 7 (July 1967): n.p.
With Simone Benmussa and Roger Blin. *L'Action Théâtrale* (2ᵉ trimestre 1969): 9–16. Extracts reprinted in *L'Avant-Scène Théâtre* 431 (15 August 1969): 6–7.
With Françoise Varenne. *Le Figaro*, 28 March 1974. BA.
With Nathalie Godard. *Combat*, 10 April 1974. BA.
With Lawrence Sabbath. *Montreal Star*, 27 April 1976, C-10.

With Christiane Salducci. *Nice-Matin*, 23 October 1979, n.p.
With Ezzedine Mestiri. In *Les Cubains et l'Afrique*. Paris: Editions KARTHALA, 1980. 149–61.
With Fernando Villaverde. *Miami Mensual*, 1981 (n.d.), 78–79.
With Amei Wallach. *Newsday*, April 1982 (n.d.), pt. 2, 37.
With Jean Mambrino. *Revue Etudes*, March 1985, 359–74.
With Raymonde Temkine. *Théâtre Acteurs*, 36 (May 1986): 38–39.
In playbill for *Lady Strass*. Théâtre Royal du Parc, Brussels, 25 October–24 November 1990.
With Jean-Rémi Barland. *Le Provençal*, 16 October 1994, n.p.
With Phyllis Zatlin. Series of personal interviews, 19 October 1987–1 June 1998.
With Nathalie Goulet. *El Diario Vasco*, 10 December 1996, n.p.
With Emmanuelle Leroyer. *Livresse* (Angers) 9 (April–May 1997): 10–13.
With Jason Weiss. Conducted October 1996. Excerpted in *Sites: The Journal of 20th-century/contemporary French Studies* (Storrs, Conn.) 2.2 (1998): 261–67.

Works About Eduardo Manet

Articles and Sections of Books

Alea, T. G. "Tránsito." *Cine Cubano* (n.d.) 64–69.
Baralt, Luis A. Prologue to *Scherzo*, by Eduardo Manet. Havana: Ediciones Prometeo, 1949. 7–12.
Beltrán, Fabiola. "Amlatina-Libros: Eduardo Manet, el otro cubano de los franceses." Ansa news release from Paris. 4 November 1994.
Blin, Roger. *Souvenirs et propos*. Edited by Lynda Bellity Peskine. Paris: Gallimard, 1986. 239–44.
Bradby, David. *Modern French Drama (1940–1980)*. 2d edition. New York: Cambridge University Press, 1991. 236–39.
García, William. "Capítulo 3: Medea." In "Subversión y relaboración de mitos trágicos en el teatro latinamericano contemporáneo." Doctoral dissertation. Rutgers, The State University, 1995. 142–214.
González Freire, Natividad. *Teatro cubano (1927–1961)*. Havana: Ministerio de Relaciones Exteriores, 1961. 83, 126–28.
Larraburu, Colette. "Il était une fois, Cuba." *La Semaine du Pays Basque* 110 (13–19 October 1995): Culture section, 3.
Leal, Rine. "Ausencia no quiere decir olvido." In his *Teatro: 5 autores cubanos*. Jackson Heights, N.Y.: OLLANTAY Press, 1995. ix–xxxiii.
Obregón, Osvaldo. "Eduardo Manet." In *Dictionnaire encyclopédique du théâtre*, ed. Michel Corvin. Paris: Bordas, 1991. 525.
Riding, Alan. "Neocolonialists Seize French Language. An Invading Legion of Foreign Writers Is Snapping Up the Medals." *New York Times*, 8 October 1997, Arts section, 1, 8.

Suther, Judith D. "*Godot* Surpassed—Eduardo Manet's *Holocaustum ou le Borgne.*" *Research Studies* 43 (March 1975): 45–51.

Valette, Christine. "Eduardo Manet: Monsieur Lovestar et son voisin de palier ou Quête du paradis perdu." Memoire de Maîtrise. Université Paul Valéry (France), 1998.

Zatlin, Phyllis. "Politics as Metatheatre: A Cuban-French View of Latin America." *Latin American Theatre Review* 23, no. 2 (1990): 13–19.

———. "Cinematic Devices in the Cuban-French Theatre of Eduardo Manet." *Studies in Modern and Classical Languages and Literatures* 3, ed. Richard A. Lima. (1990): 37–43.

———. "Eduardo Manet, Hispanic Playwright in French Clothing?" *Modern Language Studies* 22, no. 1 (1992): 80–87.

———. "Interlingual Metatheatricalism: Manet's *L'Autre Don Juan*." *Symposium* 45, no. 4 (1992): 303–15.

———. "Nuns in Drag? Eduardo Manet's Cross-Gender Casting of *Les Nonnes.*" *TDR The Drama Review* 36, no. 4 (1992): 106–20.

———. "The Play-in-the-Novel: *The Nuns* in *Opening Nights*. *Modern Language Studies* 23, no. 2 (1993): 37–47.

———. "Play or Movie Script? Eduardo Manet's Latin American Theatre." *Gestos* 16 (November 1993): 25–34.

———. "Eduardo Manet." In *Contemporary World Authors*, ed. Tracy Chevalier. Chicago: St James Press, 1993. 342–44.

———. "Vindicating Ruiz de Alarcón: *L'Autre Don Juan*." In my *Cross-Cultural Approaches to Theatre: The Spanish-French Connection*. Metuchen, N.J.: Scarecrow Press, 1994. 163–78. (Revision of article previously published in *Symposium* 1992.)

———. "Metatheatrical Games as Political Metaphor: A Triptych by Eduardo Manet." *Symposium* 48, no. 3 (1994): 239–46.

———. "The Day Eduardo Manet Introduced Us to Mary Shelley and Charlotte Brontë." *Anales Literarios/Dramaturgos* 1, no. 1 (1995): 63–73.

———. "A Postmodern Subversion of Chivalry: Manet's Cartoon Approach to the Medieval Battlefield." *Ollantay* 3, no. 1 (1995): 92–102.

———. "The Cuban-French Novels of Eduardo Manet." *Revista/Review Interamericana* 23, no. 3–4 (1993; released 1996): 75–91.

Cited Reviews of Individual Works

(Reviews available in press-clipping books at the Bibliothèque de l'Arsénal in Paris are indicated by the notation BA. Other reviews without page numbers were located in Eduardo Manet's personal files.)

A. B. V. Review of *La Mauresque*. *Figaro Magazine*, 26 June 1982, n.p.

Alter, André. Review of *Le Borgne*. *Témoignage Chrétien*, 15 November 1973. BA.

Alzola, Conchita. Review of *Pequeños poemas y nocturnos*. *El Sol*, 11 November 1947.

Barthoneuf, José. Review of *Un Balcon sur les Andes*. *Miroir de Paris*, 1 February 1980. BA.

Bruckner, D. J. R. Review of *Lady Strass*. *New York Times*, 14 October 1996, C16.
Camp, André. Review of *Deux siècles d'amour*. *L'Avant-Scène Théâtre* 222 (January 1993): 45.
Canby, Vincent. "Screen: Alonso Shines on Film." *New York Times*, 28 October 1977, C13.
Cartier, Jacqueline. Review of *Sur la piste*. *France-Soir*, 13 April 1974, BA.
Cerf, Jean-François. Review of *Habanera*. *Cooperation* 42 (20 October 1994): 45, 47.
Croce, Arlene. "Dancing. The Godmother." *New Yorker* 53 (21 November 1977): 183–87.
C. S. Preview of *Les Gozzi*. *Nice-Matin*, 21 December 1980, n. p.
Deslandes, Jacques. Review of *Un Balcon sur les Andes*. *Le Fígaro*, 18 October 1979. BA.
Dumur, Guy. Review of *Les Nonnes*. *Le Nouvel Observateur*, 12 May 1969, 48.
Galey, Matthieu. Review of *Le Borgne*. *Combat*, 19 October 1973. BA.
———. Review of *Sur la piste*. *Le Quotidien de Paris*, 15 April 1974. BA.
Gautier, Jean-Jacques. Review of *Le Borgne*. *Le Figaro*, 19 October 1973. BA.
Gazier, Michèle. Review of *La Mauresque*. *Télérama*, 8 September 1982.
Gousseland, Jack. Review of *Eux ou La prise du pouvoir*. *Combat*, 7 March 1972. BA.
Jamet, Dominique. Review of *Sur la piste*. *L'Aurore*, 15 April 1974. BA.
Josselin, Jean-François. Review of *Habanera*. *Le Nouvel Observateur*, 27 October 1994, n.p.
J. S. Review of *Les Nonnes* at the Théâtre de Quat'Sous. *La Libre Belgique*, 21 October 1970. BA.
Kanters, Robert. Review of *Le Borgne*. *L'Express*, 29 October 1973. BA.
———. Review of *Le Jour où Mary Shelley rencontra Charlotte Brontë*. *L'Express Magazine*, 20–26 January, 1979, 22.
Lamont, Rosette. Review of *Lady Strass*. *Theater Week*, 2–8 December 1996, 53–54.
Leblanc, Alain. Review of *Lady Strass* for *Nouvelles Littéraires*. Excerpted in *L'Avant-Scène Théâtre* 613 (1 July 1977): 30.
Lerrant, J. J. Review of *Les Gozzi*. *Gros Plan* (Lyon), October 1981, n.p.
Marcabru, Pierre. Review of *Les Nonnes*. Reprinted in press kit, Théâtre de Feu, 1986.
Mueller, John. "Films: Alonso in Cinemascope." *Dance Magazine* 52 (June 1978): 16–17.
Nores, Dominique. Review of *Sur la piste*. *Combat*, 15 April 1974. BA.
Oramas, Ana. Review of *La Santa*. *Mujeres* 4 (March 1964): 74.
Ortiz, Pedro. "'El huésped' en Gibara." *Granma*, 13 April 1966, 8.
Pancrazi, Jean-Noël. Review of *L'Ile du lézard vert*. *Le Monde*, 18 September 1992, n.p.
———. Review of *Rhapsodie cubaine*. *Le Monde*, 18 October 1996, n.p.
Petit, Véronique. Review of *Rhapsodie cubaine*. *France Today* (San Francisco), June 1997, 20.
Puga, Ana. Preview of *Lady Strass*. *Village Voice*, 8 October 1996, 82.
Roussel, Jean-Paul. Review of *Les Nonnes*. *L'Humanité*, 21 March 1974. BA.
Saint Vincent, Bertrand de. Review of *Rhapsodie cubaine*. *Le Figaro Littéraire*, 23 October 1996, n.p.

Sandier, Giles. Review of *Un Balcon sur les Andes*. *Le Matin*, 6 February 1980. BA.
Sauvage, Christian. Review of *Rhapsodie cubaine*. *Le Journal du Dimanche*, 20 October 1996, n.p.
Sebbar, Leila. Review of *Habanera*. *Magazine Littéraire* 325 (October 1994): n.p.
Servat, Henry-Jean. Review of *Histoire de Maheu, le Boucher. Libération*, 28 July 1986, n.p.
Temkine, Raymonde. Review of *Le Jour où Mary Shelley rencontra Charlotte Brontë. Europe*, May 1979, quoted in *L'Avant-Scène Théâtre* 654 (15 July 1979): 19.
Verdot, Guy. Review of *Un Balcon sur les Andes*. *La Nouvelle République*. BA.
Vigneron, Jean. Review of *Le Borgne*. *La Croix*, 4 November 1973. BA.
Villaverde, Fernando. Review of *Zone interdite*. *El Miami Herald*, 14 April 1985, 13.

Oral Interviews, Personal Letters, Program Notes, and Performances

Burroway, Janet. Letter to Manet. 21 July 1984.
Day Mary Shelley Met Charlotte Brontë, The. By Eduardo Manet. Dir. Jay Kogan. Society Hill Playhouse, Philadephia. 11 April 1992.
día en el solar, Un. ICAIC trilingual (Spanish, English, French) program to accompany film.
Eux ou La prise du pouvoir. Program for production, Théâtre du Peuplier Noir, Festival D'Avignon. 9 July–2 August, 1991. Studio Saint-Thomas.
Fantasia, Louis. Telephone interview. 14 March 1992.
García, William. Presentation to theater seminar. Rutgers, The State University. 27 November 1995.
Gozzi, Les. Playbill for production, Nouveau Théâtre de Nice, 1981.
Hunt, William E. Personal interview. New York. 11 March 1990.
Kimkhi, Nissim. Letter from Israel Broadcasting Authority to Manet. 15 September 1992.
Kogan, Deen. Telephone interview. 9 March 1992.
Lady Strass. By Eduardo Manet. Dir. Aurelio Roberto Adelfio. Théâtre Marie Stuart, Paris. 13 October 1987.
Lady Strass. Program for production, Théâtre Royal du Parc, Brussels. 25 October–24 November 1990.
Lady Strass. By Eduardo Manet. Dir. André Ernotte. Ubu Repertory Theater, New York. 1 October 1996.
Madras, la nuit où . . . Program for production, Compagnie "Le Pantographe," Festival d'Avignon. 9 July–2 August, 1991. Ile Piot sous chapiteau.
Monsieur Lovestar et son voisin de palier. Playbill for production, Comédie de Genève, Geneva, 5–9 March 1996.
Nuns, The. By Eduardo Manet. Dir. William E. Hunt. The 45th Street Theater, New York. 6 January 1990.
Realengo 18. ICAIC trilingual (Spanish, English, French) program to accompany film.
Santa, La. Playbill for production, Consejo Nacional de Cultura, Havana, 1964.
Schull, Rebecca. Program note for *The Nuns*. Fows Theatre, Dublin. 1971?

Suárez Radillo, Carlos Miguel. Personal interview. 19 April 1991.
Triana, José. Telephone interview. 9 June 1991.
Voutsinos, Andréas. Interview with Nathalie Godard. *Combat*, 10 April 1974. BA.

Other Works Cited in Text

Abel, Lionel. *Metatheatre: A New View of Dramatic Form*. New York: Hill and Wang, 1963.
Albuquerque, Severino João. *Violent Acts: A Study of Contemporary Latin American Theatre*. Detroit: Wayne State University Press, 1991.
Almendros, Néstor, et al. "Cuban Talent Amends List of Cuban Pictures." *Variety* 323 (7 May 1986): 8, 509.
Austin, Gayle. *Feminist Theories for Dramatic Criticism*. Ann Arbor: University of Michigan Press, 1990.
Bakhtin, Mikhail. *The Dialogic Imagination*. Trans. Caryl Emerson and Michael Holquist. Edited by Michael Holquist. Austin: Texas University Press, 1986.
Barish, Jonas. *The Anti-theatrical Prejudice*. Berkeley and Los Angeles: University of California Press, 1981.
Barreda, Pedro Manuel. "*Medea en el espejo*: Coralidad y poesía." In *Palabras más que comunes: Ensayos sobre el teatro de José Triana*, ed. Kirsten F. Nigro. Boulder, Colo.: Society of Spanish and Spanish-American Studies, 1994. 23–31.
Bergson, Henri. "Le rire." In *Oeuvres*. Paris: Presses Universitaires de France, 1959.
Birringer, Johannes. *Theatre, Theory, Postmodernism*. Bloomington: Indiana University Press, 1993.
Bruce-Novoa, Juan. "From Paragonia to Parador: Hollywood's Strategy for Saving Latin America." *Gestos* 6, no. 11 (1991): 175–85.
Burroway, Janet. *Opening Nights*. New York: Atheneum; London: Victor Gollancz, 1985.
Burunat, Silvia, and Ofelia García, eds. *Veinte años de literatura cubanoamericana: Antología 1962–1982*. Tempe, Ariz.: Bilingual Press/Editorial Bilingüe, 1988.
Busquets, Loreto. "Borges y el barroco." *Cuadernos Hispanoamericanos* 505–7 (July–September 1992): 299–319.
Carlson, Marvin. *Theatre Semiotics: Signs of Life*. Bloomington: Indiana University Press, 1990.
Case, Sue-Ellen. "Gender as Play: Simone Benmussa's *The Singular Life of Albert Nobbs*." *Women and Performance* 1, no. 2 (1984): 21–24.
———. *Feminism and Theatre*. New York: Methuen, 1988.
Coe, Richard N. *When the Grass Was Taller: Autobiography and the Experience of Childhood*. New Haven: Yale University Press, 1984.
Copi. *Eva Perón*. In *Théâtre*. Vol. 1. Paris: Christian Bourgois Editeur, 1986. 89–135.
Corvin, Michel. *Le Théâtre nouveau en France*. 5th ed. Que sais-je? Paris: Presses Universitaires de France, 1980.

Desuché, Jacques. *La técnica teatral de Bertolt Brecht.* Trans. Ricard Salvat. Barcelona: Ediciones Oikos-Tau, 1966.
Díaz, Jorge. *El cepillo de dientes.* In 9 *dramaturgos hispanoamericanos.* Vol. 3 of *Antología del teatro hispanoamericano del siglo XX,* ed. Frank Dauster, Leon Lyday, and George Woodyard. 2d ed. Ottawa, Girol Books, 1983. 63–120.
Dolan, Jill. "Gender Impersonation Onstage: Destroying or Maintaining the Mirror of Gender Roles?" *Women and Performance* 2, no. 2 (1985): 5–11.
Eder, Richard. "The Return of Fernando Arrabal." *New York Times,* 28 March 1982, Arts and Leisure section, 3.
Escarpanter, José A. Introduction to *Medea en el espejo. La noche de los asesinos. Palabras comunes.* By José Triana. Madrid: Editorial Verbum, 1991. 9–12.
———. "Elementos de la cultura afrocubana en el teatro de José Triana." In *Palabras más que comunes: Ensayos sobre el teatro de José Triana,* ed. Kirsten F. Nigro. Boulder, Colo.: Society of Spanish and Spanish-American Studies, 1994. 33–40.
Esslin, Martin. *The Field of Drama: How the Signs of Drama Create Meaning on Stage and Screen.* London: Methuen, 1987.
———. "Actors Acting Actors." *Modern Drama* 30, no. 1 (1987): 71–79.
Garber, Marjorie. *Vested Interests: Cross-Dressing and Cultural Anxiety.* New York: Routledge, 1992.
Gilbert, Sandra M., and Susan Gubar, *The Madwoman in the Attic: The Woman Writer and the Nineteenth-Century Literary Imagination.* New Haven: Yale University Press, 1979.
Gilman, Sander L. *Jewish Self-Hatred.* Baltimore: John Hopkins University Press, 1986.
González-Cruz, Luis F., and Francesca M. Colecchia, eds. and trans. *Cuban Theater in the United States: A Critical Anthology.* Tempe, Ariz.: Bilingual Press/Editorial Bilingüe, 1992.
González Freire, Natividad. *Teatro cubano* (1927–1961). Havana: Ministerio de Relaciones Exteriores, 1961.
Green, A. E. "Commedia dell'arte." *The Cambridge Guide to World Theatre,* ed. Martin Banham. Cambridge: Cambridge University Press, 1988. 222–24.
Guérin, Jeanyves. "Is There Something Rotten in the State of French Theater?" In *Myths and Realities of Contemporary French Theater: Comparative Views,* ed. Patricia M. Hopkins and Wendell M. Aycock. Lubbock: Texas Tech Press, 1985.
Hartnoll, Phyllis. *A Concise History of the Theatre.* New York: Charles Scribner's Sons, n.d.
Havana. Dir. Sidney Pollack. U.S.A., 1980.
Henderson, Mae, ed. *Borders, Boundaries, and Frames: Cultural Criticism and Cultural Studies.* New York: Routledge, 1995.
Hornby, Richard. *Drama, Metadrama, and Perception.* Lewisburg, Pa.: Bucknell University Press; London: Associated University Presses, 1986.
Hutcheon, Linda. *A Poetics of Postmodernism: History, Theory, Fiction.* New York: Routledge, 1988.
———. *Irony's Edge: The Theory and Politics of Irony.* New York: Routledge, 1994.

Jackson, Rosemary. *Fantasy: The Literature of Subversion.* New York: Methuen, 1981.
Jump, John D. *Burlesque.* The Critical Idiom, no. 22. London: Methuen, 1972.
Kubiak, Anthony. *Stages of Terror: Terrorism, Ideology, and Coercion as Theatre History.* Bloomington: Indiana University Press, 1991.
Leacock, Stephen. *Humour: Its Theory and Technique.* London: John Lane The Bodley Head, 1935.
———. *Humor and Humanity: An Introduction to the Study of Humor.* New York: Henry Holt, 1938.
Leal, Rine. *Breve historia del teatro cubano.* Havana: Editorial Letras Cubanas, 1980.
Lewis, Ward B. "Exile Drama: The Example of Argentina." *Latin America and the Literature of Exile.* Ed. Hans-Bernhard Moeller. Heidelberg: Carl Winter Universitätsverlag, 1983.
Lima, Robert. *Dark Prisms: Occultism in Hispanic Drama.* Lexington: University Press of Kentucky, 1995.
Londré, Felicia Hardison. "Lorca Production in France: Abstraction or 'Espagnolade'?" MLA Convention. New Orleans, 29 December 1988.
———. *The History of World Theater: From the English Restoration to the Present.* New York: Continuum, 1991.
Lyday, Leon. "Jorge Díaz." In *9 dramaturgos hispanoamericanos.* Vol. 3 of *Antología del teatro hispanoamericano del siglo XX*, ed. Frank Dauster, Leon Lyday and George Woodyard. 2d ed. Ottawa: Girol Books, 1983. 59–62.
Macintyre, Margaret, and David Buchbinder. "Having It Both Ways: Cross-Dressing in Orton's *What the Butler Saw* and Churchill's *Cloud Nine.*" *Journal of Dramatic Theory and Criticism* 2, no. 1 (1987): 23–39.
Mandel, Barrett J. "Full of Life Now." In *Autobiography: Essays Theoretical and Critical.* Ed. James Olney. Princeton: Princeton University Press, 1980. 49–72.
Márquez Rodríguez, Alexis. "Alejo Carpentier: Teorías del barroco y de lo real maravilloso." *Nuevo Texto Crítico* 3, no. 1 (1990): 95–121.
Meisel, Martin. *Realizations: Narrative, Pictorial, and Theatrical Arts in Nineteenth-Century England.* Princeton: Princeton University Press, 1983.
Molinero, Rita Virginia. *José Lezama Lima o el hechizo de la búsqueda.* Madrid: Playor, 1989.
Montes Huidobro, Matías. *Persona, vida y máscara en el teatro cubano.* Prologue by Julio Matas. Miami: Ediciones Universal, 1973.
Moon over Parador. Dir. Paul Mazursky. U.S.A., 1988.
Nieva, Francisco. "Esencia teatral del relato de Genet." *Pipirijaina* 7 (June 1978): 38–41.
———. "El espectáculo como técnica de persuasión en Brecht." *Primer Acto* 184 (1980): 29–37.
Nigro, Kirsten F. "*El cepillo de dientes.*" In *International Dictionary of Theatre.* Vol. 1: *Plays.* Ed. Mark Hawkins-Dady. Chicago and London: St. James Press, 1992. 114–15.
Obregón, Osvaldo. "Apuntes sobre el teatro latinoamericano en Francia." *Cahiers du Monde Hispanique et Luso-Brésilien* 40 (1983): 17–45.

Ortega, Julio. "De Lezama Lima a Severo Sarduy: El barroco latinoamericano." In *Identità e metamorfosi del barroco ispanico*, ed. Giovanna Calabrò. Naples: Guida, 1987. 199–212.

Poesse, Walter. *Juan Ruiz de Alarcón*. Twayne World Authors Series, no. 231. New York: Twayne, 1972.

Puig, Manuel. A Dialogue with Manuel Puig and Literary Critics. Barnard College. New York, 9 April 1987.

Purdie, Susan. *Comedy: The Mastery of Discourse*. Toronto: University of Toronto Press, 1993.

Red Madonna, The. By Fernando Arrabal. Dir. Fernando Arrabal. INTAR, New York. 16 November 1986.

Renza, Louis A. "The Veto of the Imagination: A Theory of Autobiography." In *Autobiography: Essays Theoretical and Critical*, ed. James Olney. Princeton: Princeton University Press, 1980. 268–95.

Richards, Kenneth. "Carlo Gozzi." In *The Cambridge Guide to World Theatre*, ed. Martin Banham. Cambridge: Cambridge University Press, 1988. 404–5.

Roblès, Emmanuel. *Montserrat*. [1948.] In *Théâtre: Montserrat. La Vérité est morte. Mer libre. Un Château en novembre*. Paris: Grasset, 1985.

Ruiz de Alarcón, Juan. *Las paredes oyen*. In *Teatro*, ed. Alfonso Reyes. Clásicos Castellanos. Madrid: Espasa-Calpe, 1961.

Sagredo, José, ed. and trans. *Diccionarios Rioduero. Literatura I*. Madrid: Rioduero, 1977. (Based on *Herder Lexikon, Literatur*, by Udo Müller.)

Salom, Jaime. Personal interview. 25 May 1990.

Sarduy, Severo. *Ensayos generales sobre el barroco*. México City and Buenos Aires: Fondo de Cultura Económica, 1987.

Schmeling, Manfred. *Métathéâtre et intertexte: Aspects du théâtre dans le théâtre*. Paris: Lettres Modernes, 1982.

Semprun Maura, Carlos. "Carta de París: Vino nuevo y viejos premios." *ABC Cultural* 57 (4 December 1992): 23.

Showalter, Elaine. *A Literature of Their Own: British Women Novelists from Brontë to Lessing*. Princeton: Princeton University Press, 1977.

Sontag, Susan. "Film and Theatre." In *Film Theory and Criticism*, ed. Gerald Mast and Marshall Cohen. 3d ed. New York: Oxford University Press, 1985. 340–55.

Stearns, David Patrick. "Bending Genders." *USA Today*, 14 August 1991, D1–2.

Styan, J. L. *Modern Drama in Theory and Practice*. Vol 2: *Symbolism, Surrealism and the Absurd*. New York: Cambridge University Press, 1981.

Suárez Radillo, Carlos Miguel. "Apuntes incompletos para una historia del Teatro en Cuba en el siglo XX." *Guadalupe* (Revista del Colegio Mayor Hispano Americano Ntra. Sra. de Guadalupe de Madrid) (December 1958): 3–7.

Szanto, George. *Theater and Propaganda*. Austin: University of Texas Press, 1978.

Taylor, Diana. *Theatre of Crisis: Drama and Politics in Latin America*. Lexington: University Press of Kentucky, 1991.

Thomas, Hugh. *Cuba: The Pursuit of Freedom*. New York: Harper and Row, 1971.

Torres Monreal, Francisco. *El teatro español en Francia (1935–1973): Análisis de la penetración y de sus mediaciones*. Madrid: Fundación Juan March, 1976.

Triana, José. *Medea en el espejo. La noche de los asesinos. Palabras comunes.* Madrid: Editorial Verbum, 1991.
Uribe, María de la Luz. *La comedia del arte.* Destinolibro 209. Barcelona: Ediciones Destino, 1983.
Valle-Inclán, Ramón del. *Divinas palabras.* 1920. Madrid: Espasa-Calpe, 1970.
Versényi, Adam. *Theatre in Latin America: Religion, Politics, and Culture from Cortés to the 1980s.* New York: Cambridge University Press, 1993.
Watson-Espener, Maida. "Ethnicity and the Hispanic American Stage: The Cuban Experience." In *Hispanic Theatre in the United States*, ed. Nicolás Kanellos. Houston: Arte Público Press, 1984.
White, Hayden. *The Content of the Form: Narrative Discourse and Historical Representation.* Baltimore: Johns Hopkins University Press, 1987.
Willey, Mireille. *"Théâtres populaires" d'aujourd'hui en France et en Angleterre (1960–1975): Etude comparative.* Paris: Didier-Erudition, 1979.
Woodyard, George. "Myths and Realities in Latin American Theater: The French Connection." In *Myths and Realities of Contemporary French Theater: Comparative Views*, ed. Patricia M. Hopkins and Wendell M. Aycock. Lubbock: Texas Tech Press, 1985.
Zaslow, Jeffrey. "Straight Talk: Andy García." *USA Weekend*, 22–24 August 1997, 19.

Index

Abbot, H. Porter, 130
Abel, Lionel, 104, 155, 187
absurd. *See* theater of the absurd
Adamov, Arthur, 85 n. 7
Afro-Caribbean ritual, 51 n. 3, 79, 80, 96, 171, 173, 220, 222
   santería, 48, 50–51, 71
   voodoo, 80, 88, 105, 107, 148, 169, 171, 173–74, 177
Alarcón. *See* Ruiz de Alarcón
Albuquerque, Severino João, 86 n. 8, 129
Alea, T. G., 14
Alejandro, Ramón, 143 n. 9
Almendros, Nestor, xiii, 14, 16, 143 n. 9
Almodóvar, Pedro, 61
Alonso, Alberto, 13, 15, 17
Alonso, Alicia, 14, 16–17, 58
Alter, André, 98
Alvarez Rios, María: *Funeral*, 8
Alzola, Conchita, 2, 3, 4
Andrade, Béatrix, 83
Aristotelian mode, 128
Arocha, Juan, 143 n. 9
Arrabal, Fernando, 29, 30, 83, 84, 129 n. 5
   Bella Ciao, 92
   Et ils passèrent des menottes aux fleurs (*And They Put Handcuffs on the Flowers*), 128
   Extravagant Triumph of Jesus Christ, Karl Marx and William Shakespeare, The, 143
   Red Madonna, The, 93 n. 12
Artaud, Antonin, 83 n. 4, 84, 86 n. 9, 120, 128
   Artaudian, 201
   Les Cenci, 120
Astaire, Fred, 52, 110

Attoun, Lucien, 104, 201
Attoun, Micheline, 201
Au revoir les enfants (dir. Louis Malle), 206
Audoit, Jacques, 126 n. 3
Austin, Gayle, 132 n. 7
autobiography, as genre, 44, 45, 47
Avignon Festival, xiv, 90 n. 11, 95, 99 n. 15, 104, 105, 107–8, 111, 134

Badia, Nora: *Mañana es una palabra*, 8
Bakhtin, Mikhail, 84
   Bakhtinian, 134
Baldick, Robert, 18, 20 n. 6
Baliteau, Alain, 125
Ball, Lucille, 52, 61
Baralt, Luis A., 8–10
Barba, Eugenio, xiii
Barish, Jonas, 26
Barland, Jean-Rémi, 57, 58, 61
Barnum, P. T., 144
baroque, 29, 58, 82–85, 104, 110, 155, 187
Barrault, Jean-Louis, xii, 120
Barreda, Pedro Manuel, 171
Barthélemy, Michèle Armand, 169, 170, 172
Barthoneuf, José, 127
Batista, Fulgencio, xii, 12, 36, 37, 39, 48, 59 n. 6, 60 n. 8, 63, 64, 207, 219
Beaumarchais Foundation, xvi, 190, 193
Beauvoir, Simone de, 210
Beckett, Samuel, 18, 99, 130
   Waiting for Godot, x, 99, 103
Beltrán, Fabiola, xiv
Benda, David, 90 n. 11

Benmussa, Simone, 22, 30
  The Singular Life of Albert Nobbs, 22 n. 7
Bergman, Ingrid, 66
Bergson, Henri, 136, 184
Berliner Ensemble, xiii
Bernhardt, Sarah, 189
biculturalism, 65, 149, 160, 220
Bierry, Etienne, 27, 28
bilingualism, 37–38, 77, 81–82, 117, 158, 159, 160, 220
Birringer, Johannes, 116, 142
Bizet, Georges: *Carmen*, 157
Blin, Roger, ix, xiii, xiv, 18, 19, 21, 24, 25, 27, 75, 83, 84, 107, 120
Blow-Up, 40
Boal, Augusto, 129 n. 5
Bolívar, Simón, 116, 129, 130–31
Borges, Fermín: *Una vieja postal*, 8
Borges, Jorge Luis, 84
Bradby, David, 29, 75, 85 n. 7, 90, 98, 116, 117, 165
Braga, Sonia, 124 n. 1
Brecht, Bertolt, 72, 126, 128
  Brechtian, xiii, 116, 118, 120, 126, 146, 150, 153, 182, 190
  Mother Courage, 118
Broche, Jean-Claude, 134
Brontë, Charlotte, 148, 161, 165, 168, 169
  Jane Eyre, 160, 161, 164, 167, 168
Brontë, Emily, 165
  Wuthering Heights, 165
Bruce-Novoa, Juan, 124 n. 1
Bruckner, D. J. R., 111 n. 20
Buch, René, 7–8: *Nosotros los muertos*, 7
Buchbinder, David, 26, 27
Buenaventura, Enrique, 87
Buero-Vallejo, Antonio, 129 n. 5
Buffalo Bill (William Frederick Cody), 144–46
Buñuel, Luis, 31
Burroway, Janet, xvii, 25, 29–30, 32
  Opening Nights, 18, 25, 29
Burunat, Silvia, 76
Busquets, Loreto, 84
Byland, Pierre, 27
Byron, George Gordon, Lord, 163 n. 7, 165

Cage aux Folles, La, 28
Calderón de la Barca, Pedro, 149, 155
  gran teatro del mundo, El (*The Great Theater of the World*), 97
  príncipe constante, El (*The Constant Prince*), 151 n. 4
  vida es sueño, La (*Life Is a Dream*), 155, 159
Calero, Sonia, 13
Camp, André, xvii, 213, 216
Camus, Albert, 86 n. 9, 87, 210
  The Myth of Sisyphus, 6
Canby, Vincent, 17
Carballido, Emilio, 87
Carlson, Marvin, 183 n. 20, 189
Caroline of Monaco, Princess, 149
Carpentier, Alejo, 58, 84, 85
  El reino de este mundo, 80, 84
Carr, Hasol, 97 n. 14
Cartier, Jacqueline, 97
cartoon, as theatrical technique, 125, 133, 135, 136, 156, 182, 199, 215
Casaus, Victor, 17
Case, Sue-Ellen, 22 n. 7, 24
Casona, Alejandro (Alejandro Rodríguez Alvarez), 7
  árboles mueren de pie, Los, 78
  Otra vez el diablo, 9
Castro, Fidel, xiii, xiv, 12, 16, 22, 29, 30, 38–39, 40, 54 n. 5, 58, 64, 68 n. 12, 69, 71, 72, 73, 77, 78, 80, 89 n. 10, 90, 100, 112, 122, 142–46, 219, 220
Castro, Guillem de, 150, 155
Castro, Raúl, xiii, 145
Catholic reaction to plays, 22–25, 98–99
Cauchetier, Patrice, 125
Cela, Camilo José: *La colmena* (*The Hive*), 35, 36
Celestina, La, 152
Cerf, Jean-François, 58
Cervantes Saavedra, Miguel de, 96, 139
  Don Quixote, 139–40, 165
  gitanilla, La (*The Little Gypsy*), 180
Chaney, Lon, 189
Chanson de Roland (*The Song of Roland*), 137, 140–41
Chaplin, Charlie, 80, 96
Charles d'Orléans, 139
Chéreau, Patrice, 83
Chibás, Eddy, 54 n. 5, 63
Chocano, José Santos, 2
Chopin, Frédéric François, 96, 204
choteo (verbal humor), 79, 80, 81
Cid Campeador, 137
cinematic devices

in novels, 34–40, 48, 49–50, 51, 52, 57, 59–61, 63, 66, 67, 220
in radio plays, 206, 209
in theater, 76, 80, 85, 86, 91, 92–93, 104, 110, 111 n. 21, 116, 123–28, 148, 150, 155–56, 178, 188–89, 190, 193, 197, 200, 209, 211, 213, 216, 220
clowns, 97, 99, 110, 135, 180, 181, 221
Coe, Richard N., 44, 47
Colas, Jean-Pierre, 96 n. 13
Cole, Nat King, 68
Colecchia, Francesca, 76, 77
Comédie-Française, xiv, 85, 90, 160
comic devices, defined, 136–39, 145, 153, 158, 164, 180–81, 184, 187, 213–14, 215
commedia dell'arte, 11, 99, 177, 178–80, 195, 220
  Harlequin, 10
Compton-Burnett, Ivy, 35
Cooper, Gary, 52
Copi, 117
  Eva Perón, 117
Corneille, Pierre, 150
  Cid, Le, 150, 155
  Menteur, Le (*The Liar*), 157
Cortázar, Julio, 40
Corvin, Michel, 83 n. 4
Cox, Vivian, 160
Craig, Gordon, 189
Croce, Arlene, 17
Crosby, Bing, 216
cross-gender acting, 20–32, 85, 119, 153, 154–55, 180, 221
Cuban theater, defined:
  in exile, 76, 78, 79
  general characteristics, 78, 79, 86
  in revolutionary Cuba, 78, 79

Darío, Rubén, 2
Delacroix, Eugène, 193
Dernier métro, Le (dir. François Truffaut), 205–6
desaparecido (victim of political repression), 129
Descartes, René, 159
Desuché, Jacques, 126
Díaz, Jorge: *El cepillo de dientes*, 91–92, 97, 98
Dolan, Jill, 28
Dorfman, Ariel, 129 n. 5
Dos Passos, John, 35

Manhattan Transfer, 35
Dreyfuss, Richard, 124 n. 1
Dubois, Guy, 19
Dumas, Alexandre, *fils*, 216
Dumas, Alexandre, *père*, 193–94
  The Three Musketeers, 194
Dumur, Guy, 29
Duque, Manuel, 149 n. 2

Eder, Richard, 143
Eliot, T. S., 203
enclosure, as theatrical theme, 86, 88–89, 91, 92, 105, 107, 113–14, 115, 148, 164, 168, 220
Ernotte, André, 82 n. 3, 111 n. 20
Escarpanter, José, 171
espagnolade, 8, 20, 156–57, 215
esperpento (grotesque tragicomedy). *See* Valle-Inclán
Esslin, Martin, 122, 123–24, 125, 153
Euripides: *Medea*, 171
Europa, Europa, 206
exile, x, xiv, 43, 47, 55, 58, 64–66, 69, 75, 76, 77, 83 n. 5, 112, 113, 168, 182, 207, 219, 220
exile drama, 77–78, 87–88, 90, 92, 114, 143–44
exile literature, 44
  See also Cuban theater: in exile
existentialism, 79, 139, 221
  existential, 5, 32, 87, 130, 161, 222
Eysselinck, Walter, 25

Fagadau, Michel, 99
Falla, Manuel de, 157
Fantasia, Louis, 160
Fernandez, Jean-Claude, 170, 200–201, 203
Ferra, Max, 143, 149
Ferrer, Rolando, 7–8
  Cita en el espejo, 7
filmic devices. *See* cinematic devices
Fontaine, Joan, 163
Forest, Pierre, 126 n. 3
Fornes, Maria Irene, 77, 78
  Conduct of Life, The, 129 n. 5
  Fefu and Her Friends, 129 n. 5
Francis, Kay, 189
Franco, Francisco, 30, 36, 63, 77, 78, 96, 143
François, Claude, 200
Freny, Evelyne, 127 n. 4

Index

Galabru, Michel, xv, 182
Galey, Matthieu, 97, 99
Gambarro, Griselda, 84, 87, 129, 130
game-playing. *See* metatheatricalism
Garber, Marjorie, 27
Garbo, Greta, 11, 80, 93, 216
García, Andy, 60 n. 8
García Espinosa, Julio, 16
García Lorca, Federico, 3, 7, 82, 83, 156
  Bodas de sangre (*Blood Wedding*), 10
  casa de Bernarda Alba, La (*The House of Bernarda Alba*), 5
  romancero gitano, El, 3, 200
García Márquez, Gabriel, 145
  El otoño del patriarca (*The Autumn of the Patriarch*), 117–18
García, Ofelia, 76
García, Víctor, 83
García, William, 169, 171 n. 14–15, 173 n. 17, 174, 177
Gardel, Carlos, 145
Gardner, Ava, 93
Garibaldi, Giuseppe, 190, 193, 194, 195
Gasc, Yves, 160
Gaskell, Mrs. (Elizabeth Cleghorn Stevenson Gaskell), 168
Gautier, Jean-Jacques, 98
Gazier, Michèle, 46, 62–63
Genet, Jean, 18, 29, 30, 84, 86 n. 9
  Les Bonnes (*The Maids*), 29 n. 8
Gilbert, Sandra, 166, 168
Gilman, Sander, 132
Gish, Lillian, 189
Goggin, Dan: *Nunsense*, 20
Goldoni, Carlo, 150, 178
Gong Show, The, 215
González, Maydee, 143 n. 9
González-Cruz, Luis, 76, 77
González de Cascorro, Raúl: *Parque Bar*, 8
González Freire, Natividad, 7, 8
Gothic, 163, 164, 169
Goulet, Nathalie, xi n. 1, 68
Gousseland, Jack, 85, 96
Goya y Lucientes, Francisco José de, 120
Gozzi, Carlo, 178
Graham-Young, David, 127 n. 4
Grau San Martín, Ramón, 48
Green, A. E., 178, 179
Greek tragedy, 128, 129, 148, 169, 172, 173, 174, 175, 195
Grotowski, Jerzy, xiii, 151–52 n. 4, 158

Gubar, Susan, 166, 168
Guérin, Jeanyves, 83
Guevara, Alfredo, 13
Guevara, Ernesto ("Che"), 66, 80
Guillén, Nicolás, 2

Haggiag, Patrick, 201
Hartnoll, Phyllis, 18
Havana (dir. Sidney Pollack), 60
Hayworth, Rita, 61
Hegel, Georg Wilhelm Friedrich, 96
Henderson, Mae, 44
Heredia, José María de, 175 n. 18
Hernández, Felix, 143 n. 9
Hernández, Gilda, 12
Hertzog, Gilles, 143–46
Hitler, Adolf, 49, 63, 112
Hollywood movies, as explicit intertext, 50–51, 55–56, 66, 80, 92–93, 108, 145–56 n. 10, 156, 160, 163, 176, 178, 195, 216
  Affair in Trinidad, 61
  Barefoot Contessa, The, 93
  Casablanca, 37, 60 n. 8
  For Whom the Bell Tolls, 52, 66
  Frankenstein, 163
  Jane Eyre, 163
  Johnny Guitar, 189
  Road to Morocco, 216
  Sign of the Cross, The, 51
  Snow White, 52
  Strange Love of Martha Ivers, The, 52
  Third Man, The, 61
  Wuthering Heights, 163, 165
Hornby, Richard, 26, 61 n. 10, 117, 150–51, 153, 154, 155, 185
Hugo, Victor: *The Hunchback of Notre Dame*, 148, 194
Hunt, William E., 26–27
Hutcheon, Linda, 112, 116, 134, 142
Huxley, Aldous: *Point Counter Point*, 35

Igonet, Alain, 90 n. 11
imperialism, 105, 107, 111 n. 21, 112, 119, 126, 172
INTAR (New York theater), xv, 93 n. 12, 143, 149
interlingual. *See* bilingual
Ionesco, Eugène, xiv, 85 n. 7
irony, 2, 41, 49, 54–55, 56–57, 58, 66, 97, 112, 154, 160, 164, 181, 188, 191, 209, 219

Jackson, Michael, 215
Jackson, Rosemary, 166
Jamet, Dominique, 97
Jarry, Alfred: *Ubu roi*, 119
   ubuesque, 116
Jimenez, Robert, 82 n. 3
Joan of Arc, Saint, 72, 135, 141–42
John of the Cross, Saint, 69, 148
Jordana, Lászaro, 143 n. 9
Josselin, Jean-François, 58
Jouvet, Louis, 85 n. 6
Julia, Raúl, 124 n. 1
Julien, André, 27
Jump, John D., 139

Kant, Immanuel, 96, 137
Kanters, Robert, 99, 168
Karloff, Boris, 163
Keats, John, 111
Kerbrat, Patrice, 163
Kogan, Deen, 161 n. 6
Kogan, Jay, 161
Kourilsky, Françoise, xvii, 82 n. 3, 110 n. 19
Kubiak, Anthony, 128–29

Laborti, Maria, 97 n. 14
Lamont, Rosette, 108
Larraburu, Colette, 64
Lavelli, Jorge, 80, 83, 92
Leacock, Stephen, 137
Leal, Rine, ix, 6, 78, 79, 86
Leblanc, Alain, 113–14
Lecoq, Jacques, xii, 177
Lemire, Catherine, 206
Lenin, Vladimir Ilyich, 144
Leroyer, Emmanuelle, 34, 67, 87
Lerrant, J. J., 178
Lettres d'une religieuse portugaise, Les, 204
Lewis, Jerry, 93
Lewis, Ward B., 77
Lezama Lima, José, 83 n. 5, 84
Lima, Robert, 51 n. 3
Lizarraga, Andrés: *Santa Juana de América*, xiii
Llorca, Denis, 150, 155
Londré, Felicia Hardison, 87, 156
Lorca. *See* Federico García Lorca
Lyday, Leon, 91
Lynn, Jonathan: *Nuns on the Run*, 20

Machado y Morales, Gerardo, xii, 48, 52
Machover, Jacobo, 143 n. 9

Macintyre, Margaret, 26, 27
Madonna, 215
Magaña, Sergio: *Los argonautas*, 170 n. 13
Mairowitz, David, 206
Malraux, André, xi n. 1
Mambrino, Jean, xii, xiii, 22, 75, 77, 80, 93, 99, 151–52 n. 4
Mandel, Barrett J., 47
Manet, Eduardo
   autobiographical elements in work, xi–xii, 3, 4, 44–45, 58, 62, 67, 68, 70–71, 114, 207, 220
   biography, general, xi–xvi
   co-editing of *Cine Cubano*, xiii, 13
   collaboration with *Pueblo* (Havana newspaper), xii, 3, 6, 171
   Cuba Démocratique (Paris), xiii, 143
   direction of Conjunto Dramático Nacional (Havana), xiii, 12
   early years in Cuba, 1–12, 87, 219
   father, xi–xii
   film direction, 12–17, 39 n. 4, 206, 219
   French citizenship, 114 n. 22
   Groupe d'Expression Libre, xv, 96 n. 13
   Havana theater in 1940s, 6–12, 219
   Instituto Cubano del Arte e Industria Cinematográficos (ICAIC, Havana), xiii, 12–13, 14, 15, 17
   Jewish identity, 205, 220
   mother, xi–xii
   poetry, xii, 2, 3–6, 205
   prizes, x–xi, 13, 18, 47, 53, 134, 220
   publishers, x, xii, xiv, xvi, 31, 220
   return to France, 75–76
   in revolutionary Cuba, 1, 12–17, 21–22, 151–52 n. 4, 219
   study in Cuba, xii, 219
   study in France, xii, 1, 219
   study in Italy, xii, 77, 177, 219
   teaching activities, xiv, 93, 178, 221
   visits to Miami, 68 n. 12
   WORKS: *Alicia*, 13, 16–17; *Anges deçus, Les*, 197–98; *Autre Don Juan, L'*, viii, xvi, 26, 80, 81, 115, 116, 135, 136, 147, 148, 149–59, 160, 180, 182, 184, 185, 203, 221; *babosas, Las*, 1 n. 1; *Balcon sur les Andes, Un*, 81–82, 86, 116–23, 124–27, 133, 134, 143, 144, 147, 148, 158, 160, 182, 183, 190, 192, 197, 213, 221; *Black Dolls, The*. See *Poupées en noires, Les*; *Bolivar et le Congrès de Panama*, 116;

Borgne, Le. See *Holocaustum ou le Borgne*; *Born = Cubano*, xvi; *Cahiers intimes*, 93 n. 12; *Cecilia Valdés*, 149; *Chemins et les nuits, Les*. See *Juan y Teresa en busca de Dios*; *Chiennes, Les*, xv, 114 n. 22, 197, 198–99, 200; "clase, La," 2–3, 4; *conquistadores, Los*, 1 n. 1; *Couples et les paravents, Les*, 198, 210–13; *Cri sur le rivage, Un*, xiii, 14, 34, 36–39, 40, 52, 62, 71, 100, 124, 127; *D'Amour et d'exil*, 219; *Day Mary Shelley Met Charlotte Brontë, The*. See *Le Jour où Mary Shelley rencontra Charlotte Brontë*; *Deux siècles d'amour*, xvi, 10, 114 n. 22, 197, 213–17, 221; *día en el solar, Un*, 15; "Diálogos." *See* "Laberinto"; *Eloïse, 2C27*, 34; *En el Club*, 13; *Etrangers dans la ville, Les*, xii, 33–34, 35–36, 52, 54, 57, 58, 60; *Eux ou La prise du pouvoir*, xiv, 50, 85, 90–96, 97, 98, 104, 108, 112, 173, 180, 202, 211, 221; *Gozzi, Les*, 147, 177–82, 221; *Habanera*, x–xi, 43, 57–64, 66, 67, 69, 70, 71, 73, 76, 77, 163 n. 7, 176 n. 19, 220; *Helen viendra nous voir de Hollywood et nous lui ferons la plus belle des parties*, 75; *Histoire de Maheu le boucher*, 125, 133–42, 194, 199, 201, 205, 221, 222; *Holocaustum ou le Borgne*, x, 32, 87, 91, 98–103, 104, 105, 108, 113, 164 n. 9, 168, 220; *huésped, El*, 15; *Ile du lézard vert, L'*, x, xi, xvi, 4, 36, 40, 41, 43, 44, 45, 50, 51–57, 58, 62, 67, 69, 76, 173, 192, 205, 208, 220, 222; *Infanta que no quiso tener ojos verdes, La*, 6, 8, 11–12, 17; *Jour où Mary Shelley rencontra Charlotte Brontë, Le*, x, 148, 160–69, 204, 216, 221, 222; *Juan y Teresa en busca de Dios*, 148–49; "Laberinto," 4–6, 222; *Lady Strass*, x, xiv, 10, 24, 70 n. 13, 80, 81, 82 n. 3, 83, 88, 90, 91, 92, 96, 104, 107–14, 116, 144, 164 n. 9, 180, 199 n. 2, 203, 205, 207, 210, 213, 215, 216, 220, 221; *Ma'Dea*, 50, 80, 93 n. 12, 148, 169–77; *Madras, la nuit où . . .*, xiv, 50, 80, 87, 90, 91, 92, 96, 104–7, 108, 112, 113, 164 n. 9, 215, 220; *Mare Nostrum*, 114 n. 22, 197, 199–200, 212 n. 4, 215 n. 5; *Mauresque, La*, x, xi, 34, 40, 41, 43, 44, 45, 46–51, 52, 54, 57, 58, 59, 62–63, 66, 67, 69, 70, 71, 76, 173, 175, 192, 205, 220, 222; *Mendoza, en Argentine. . .*, 70 n. 14, 80, 81, 86, 113, 124–25, 127–33, 157, 169, 175, 190, 192, 193, 199 n. 2; *Ménines de la mer Morte, Les*, 96 n. 13; *Mirage dans un miroir sans reflets*, 96 n. 13; *monjas, Las*. See *Les Nonnes*; *Monsieur Lovestar et son voisin de palier*, 198, 200–205, 221; *Napoleón gratis*, 13; *negro, El*, 13, 14; *Nonnes, Les*, ix, x, xiii, xiv, 1–2, 10, 14, 17–32, 50, 51, 75, 78, 79, 80, 84, 85–86, 87, 88, 89–90, 98, 99, 100, 101, 104, 105, 113, 144, 155, 160, 164 n. 9, 168, 169, 173, 198, 220, 221; *Nuit de la Terreur, La*, 34; *Nuns, The*. See *Les Nonnes*; *Nunziatta*, 34, 66, 190 n. 21; *Papa Fidel, Papa Marx, Buffalo Bill y Taïna, la mujer barbuda*. See *Poupée Fidel. . .*; *Pequeños poemas y nocturnos*, 2; *Pierre, Esmeralda et Quasimodo*, 148–49, 159, 197; *Portocarrero*, 13; *Poupée Fidel, Papa Marx, Buffalo Bill et la femme à barbe*, xvi, 143–46; *Poupées en noir, Les*, xvi, 33, 198, 204, 205, 206–10, 221; *Pour l'amour de Verdi*, xvi, 147, 148, 178, 190–95, 221; *Presagio*, 6, 8, 10–11, 12, 17, 198; *primera noche, La*, 8 n. 1; *Primerissimo, Le*, xv, 147, 178, 182–90, 193; *Realengo 18*, 14; *Rhapsodie cubaine*, x, xi, xiii n. 3, 43, 64–73, 76, 175, 220; *Sacrilèges*, 114 n. 22; *Salinas*, 13; *santa, La*, 1, 12, 17; *Scherzo*, 2, 6, 7, 8–10, 11, 12, 17, 62, 213; *Show*, 13; *Spirale*, xii, 33; *Sur la piste*, 90, 96–98, 202; *Topologie d'une cité fantôme*, 148 n. 1; *Tránsito*, 14–15, 39; *Vroum vroum*, xv; *Zarah*, 34; *Zone interdite*, 34, 39–41

Manet, Fatima Soualhia, xv, 148, 169, 172, 210

Marcabru, Pierre, 25, 85

Marivaux, Pierre Carlet de Chamblain de, 213

Márquez Rodríguez, Alexis, 85

Martínez Allende, Mario, 7

Marx Brothers, 51, 80

Marx, Karl, 144–46

   Marxist ideology, 13, 29, 51, 103, 116, 146 n. 10

Mas Martin, Luis, 54 n. 5

Meisel, Martin, 189

Mérimée, Prosper, 157
Mesguich, Daniel, 83, 206, 210
Mestiri, Ezzedine, 15, 30, 173 n. 16
metafiction, 61, 116, 220
metatheatricalism, 26, 30–32, 79–80, 84, 85–86, 89, 91, 92, 93, 96, 98, 104–5, 108, 112, 146, 147–95, 202, 211–12, 215–16, 220, 221
  historiographic metatheater, 115, 134, 141–42, 147, 194
  political metatheater, 117–23, 191
Métraux, Alfred, 177
Milland, Ray, 51
Miller, Arthur: *The Crucible*, 12
mime, xii, 20, 27, 77, 99, 157, 177, 180, 181, 221
Mnouchkine, Ariane, 83
  Méphisto, 116, 117
Molière (Jean Baptiste Poquelin), xv
  Les Précieuses ridicules (*The Affected Ladies*), xv
Molinero, Rita Virginia, 84
Mollien, Roger, 97 n. 14
Montes Huidobro, Matías, xviii, 79, 80, 86
Monty Python, 134
Moon over Parador (dir. Paul Mazursky), 124
Moreau, Jean-Jacques, 126 n. 3
Mueller, John, 17
Muller, Jean-Pierre, 90 n. 11, 95
multiculturalism, 65, 115, 147–95, 200, 204, 212, 221
multilingualism, 76, 82, 117, 124 n. 1, 137–38, 177, 183, 197, 199, 200, 204, 207, 212, 214
Murillo, Bartolomé Esteban, 49
Musset, Alfred de, 213, 216
  Lorenzaccio, 216
Mussolini, Benito, 59, 63, 183

neobaroque. *See* baroque
neoclassicism, in French theater, 82, 134, 152
Neruda, Pablo, 2, 116
Nerzer, Jonathan, 97 n. 14
Newton, Sir Isaac, 96
Nieva, Francisco, 84, 126, 128
Nigro, Kirsten, 91
Nores, Dominique, 97

Obregón, Osvaldo, 75–76, 78, 220
Odéon, L' (national theater, Paris), xiv, 84, 126

Petit Odéon, 85, 90, 160
Olivier, Laurence, 165
Oramas, Ana, 12
Ortega, Julio, 84
Ortiz, Fernando, 171
Ortiz, Pedro, 16
Orwellian, 34

Pancrazi, Jean-Noël, 54, 55, 56, 65, 83 n. 4
pantomime. *See* mime
parody, 79, 85, 96, 99, 102, 105, 116, 134, 137, 139–40, 142, 150, 156, 157, 164, 182, 215, 222
Pavlosky, Eduardo, 129 n. 5
Péron, Evita, 117
Péron, Juan, 129
Petit, Véronique, xiii n. 3, xiv–xv, 65, 96 n. 13
Petrarca, Francesco, 96
Peyrou, Georges, 126 n. 3
Picasso, Pablo: *Le Désir attrapé par la queue*, 210
Pinochet, Augusto, 116, 129
Pirandello, Luigi, 165 n. 10
  Pirandellian, 151, 165
play-within-the-play. *See* metatheatricalism
Poche-Montparnasse Theater (Paris), 18, 24, 27, 28, 78, 107, 169, 171 n. 15
Poesse, Walter, 152 n. 5, 159
Portocarrero, René, 13
postmodernism, 116, 124, 134, 142, 146, 182
  postmodern performance art, 128
propaganda in theater, defined, 119, 121
psychodrama, 91, 93, 107, 111, 173
Puga, Ana, 110 n. 19
Puig, Manuel, 80
Purdie, Susan, 136

Queneau, Raymond, 210

Racine, Jean Baptiste, 139
  Racinian, 158
  Phèdre, 139
radio, xvi, 33, 48, 50, 206–10, 221
  France-Culture, xiv, 96 n. 13, 126 n. 3, 127 n. 4, 148 n. 1, 198, 199, 206
Raft, George, 51, 66
Ravel, Maurice, 207, 209
Reagan, Ronald, 145
real maravilloso, 84–85
Redford, Robert, 60 n. 8
Renza, Louis A., 47

Rey, Antonia, 58
Richards, Kenneth, 178
Riding, Alan, xvi
Rios, Juan: *selva, La*, 170 n. 13
Robbe-Grillet, Alain, 67
　Topologie d'une cité fantôme, 148 n. 1
Roblès, Emmanuel, 131 n. 6
　Montserrat, 128, 130–31
Rodríguez, Carlos Rafael, 54 n. 5
role-playing. *See* metatheatricalism
Rollin-Weisz, Jeanne, 148 n. 1
roman à clef, 54, 58
Rostand, Edmond: *L'Aiglon*, 189
Roussel, Jean-Paul, 23
Rubens, Peter Paul, 96
Rubia Barcia, José, 7
Ruiz de Alarcón, Juan, 115, 148, 150, 152, 157, 158–59
　Las paredes oyen (*Les Murs ont des oreilles*), 80, 115, 149–59
Ruiz de Zarate, Guy, 143 n. 9

Sabbath, Lawrence, 22
Sagaert, M. F., 23
Sagredo, José, 83
Saint Vincent, Bertrand de, 67
Salducci, Christiane, 125
Salom, Jaime, 202
　Una hora sin televisión, 202 n. 3
Sánchez, Gustavo, 143 n. 9
Sandier, Giles, 127
Sarduy, Severo, 80, 83 n. 5, 84, 85
　Colibrí, 84
Sarraute, Natalie, 67
Sartre, Jean-Paul, 68, 86 n. 9, 87, 210
　Huis clos (*No Exit*), 139
Sartrean, 139, 222
Saura, Carlos, 157
Sauvage, Christian, 66
Savary, Jérôme, 80, 83
Schajowicz, Ludwig, 7
Schindler's List, 206
Schmeling, Manfred, 185, 187
Schnitzler, Arthur: *Frage nach dem Schicksal, Die*, 8
Schopenhauer, Arthur, 137
Schull, Rebecca, 23
Schumann, Robert, 204
Scott, Sir Walter, 165
Sebbar, Leila, 58
Sedgwick, Eve Kosofky, 132 n. 7

Semana de Teatro Cubano (Madrid), 8
Semprun Maura, Carlos, 53
Servat, Henry-Jean, 134, 139
Shakespeare, William
　Antony and Cleopatra, 176
　Hamlet, 105, 111, 159, 165, 188
Shelley, Mary, 148, 163 n. 7, 165, 166, 167 n. 11, 168, 169
　Frankenstein, 160, 161, 163 n. 7, 164, 165, 166
Shelley, Percy, 163 n. 7, 165
Showalter, Elaine, 167
Simon, Neil, 67 n. 11
Sinatra, Frank, 200
Sojcher, Frédéric, xv
Sontag, Susan, 123
Sotelo Inclán, Jesús: *Malintzin, Medea americana*, 170 n. 13
Soualhia, Fatima. *See* Fatima Soualhia Manet
Stanislavsky, Konstantin, 156
Stanwyck, Barbara, 52, 61, 66
Stevenson, Robert, 163
Styan, J. L., 99, 120
Suárez, Ramón F., 14, 15
Suárez Radillo, Carlos Miguel, xviii, 7, 8, 16
Suther, Judith D., x, 32, 99, 103, 221, 222
Swanson, Gloria, 51, 93
Synge, John Millington: *Riders to the Sea*, 8, 10
Szanto, George, 119

tableau
　theatrical, 189
　vivant, 189, 193
Taño, Tony, 15
Taylor, Diana, 30, 86–89, 91, 99, 104, 129, 131
Taylor, Elizabeth, 176
Taylor, Robert, 51, 61
Temkine, Raymonde, 11, 12, 21, 165, 170, 171, 173
Temple, Shirley, 51
Teresa of Avila, Saint, xv, 69, 73, 148–49
Thamin, Jean-Louis, 126 n. 3, 127
theater and terror. *See* torture
theater of crisis, 86–88, 90, 98, 99, 103, 104, 129, 220
theater of the absurd, 79, 86–87, 90–92, 99, 202, 221
Thomas, Hugh, 54 n. 5

Torch Song Trilogy, 28
Torres, Oscar, 14
Torres Monreal, Francisco, 157
torture, 86, 102, 128–33
traffic (exchange) in women, 132, 175
transvestism. *See* cross-gender acting
Trétout, Alain, 201, 203
Triana, José, ix, xiii, xviii, 7–8, 84, 87, 143 n. 9, 170–71
   Medea en el espejo, 171–72
   noche de los asesinos, La (*The Night of the Assassins*), 18, 30, 78 n. 1, 87, 88, 89
two-actor play, as concept, 202–3
Turner, Lana, 66

Unamuno, Miguel de, 6, 165 n. 10
   Niebla, 165 n. 10

Valentino, Rudolph, 110, 111 n. 21, 200, 214, 216
Valle-Inclán, Ramón del, 7, 31, 83, 85, 120, 156
   Divinas palabras (*Divine Words*), 84, 85, 157
Varenne, Françoise, 97
Vauclin, Maïté, 172
Vázquez, Omar, 16
Vega y Carpio, Lope de, 149
Velázquez, Rodríguez de Silva, Diego, 96 n. 13
Verdi, Giuseppe, 148, 178, 190, 193, 195
   Aïda, 191
   Ballo in Maschera, Un, 191
   Don Carlo, 191
   Forza del Destino, La, 191
   Giovanna di Arco, 191, 192
   Lombardi, I, 191
   Luisa Miller, 191
   Macbeth, 191
   Nabuco, 191
   Othello, 191
   Rigoletto, 191

Traviata, La, 191
Trovatore, Il, 191
Verdot, Guy, 126–27
Veríssimo, Erico: *Caminhos cruzados* (*Crossroads*), 35
Versényi, Adam, 78
Vieville, Didier, 213
Vigneron, Jean, 98–99
Villaverde, Fernando, 2, 40
violence, 86, 89, 90, 91, 92, 98, 101, 102, 103, 129, 131, 135, 137, 140, 160, 166, 205, 209
Voutsinos, Andréas, 97

Wagner, Richard, 112
   Tristan and Isolde, 110
Walcott, Derek, xv
Wallach, Amei, 143
Watson-Espener, Maida, 76, 79
Weber, Karl Maria von, 215
Weiss, Jason, xi n. 2, xviii, 35 n. 2, 43, 44, 59 n. 6–7, 67 n. 11, 68 n. 12, 73
Welles, Orson, 61
West, Mae, 80
Whale, James, 163, 164
Whistler's Mother, 216
White, Hayden, 194
Whitman, Walt, 2
Willems, Tony, 23, 90
Willey, Mireille, 92, 150
Winters, Jonathan, 124 n. 1
Wolff, Egon, 87
Wollstonecraft, Mary, 167 n. 11
Woodyard, George, 79–80 n. 2, 86 n. 9, 117
Wyer, William, 163

Xirgu, Margarita, 7

Yordanoff, Wladimir, 126 n. 3

Zayas, Alfredo, xii